# COMMON CORE

## ELA EXEMPLAR RESOURCE

## Instruction with Performance Assessment

## Grades K–1



Printed in the U.S.A.

ISBN 978-0-544-02515-8

10 0928 21 20 19 18 17 16

4500592570 A B C D E F G

# Table of Contents

## About the Common Core ELA Exemplar Resource



## K-1 TEXT EXEMPLARS

### Stories



### Poetry

## Poetry *(continued)*



## Read-Aloud Stories



## Read-Aloud Poetry

# Overview

**The *Common Core ELA Exemplar Resource* was developed to provide instruction for the Grades K–1 text exemplars listed in Appendix B of the *Common Core State Standards for English Language Arts*.**

**Use this guide to complement the reading instruction of exemplars within your main reading program, or use it separately to provide children with questions and activities that deepen their comprehension of text exemplars selected for independent reading or group discussion.**

## Text Exemplars

The list of text exemplars provided in Appendix B of the *Common Core State Standards for English Language Arts* was compiled based on the texts' quantitative and qualitative complexity, quality, and range.

The text exemplars are presented in bands of two grade levels each (K–1, 2–3, and 4–5) and are meant to suggest "the breadth of texts that students should encounter in the text types required by the Standards." The works listed were never intended to serve as a partial or complete reading list but rather as a guide to the types of reading materials that will help children successfully meet the Standards.

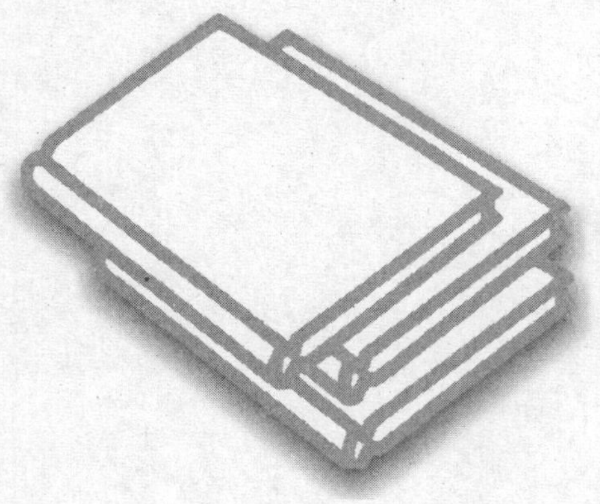

## Organization of This Guide

This guide is organized into three parts.

**CONTENTS WITH SUGGESTED PACING** The table of contents lists all the exemplars in the order given in Appendix B, along with the page references for where to find each exemplar in this resource. You will need to select and obtain the texts separately. This section also includes suggested pacing for reading each exemplar and teaching its lesson.

**EXEMPLAR LESSONS** Most lessons for stories and informational texts are four pages, while most lessons for poetry are two pages. See **Lesson Setup** on p. vii for more information.

**ENDMATTER RESOURCES**

- **Copying Masters** In the back of this guide, you will find copying masters for several public-domain text exemplars, provided for your convenience.
- **Student Performance Checklists** Aside from checklists for writing and speaking and listening, at Grades K-1, there is an additional performance-task copying master for every lesson in the guide.

- **Academic Vocabulary** This compilation lists all the academic vocabulary, or Tier 2 words, introduced and defined in each lesson.
- **Bibliography and Exemplar Websites** These sections include the bibliographic information for each exemplar included in this guide, as well as a list of useful websites that offer additional information for teaching the exemplars and implementing the Standards.

## Lesson Setup

Here is the basic setup of a four-page lesson.

**PAGE 1** The first part of each lesson provides background information about the text and guidance for introducing the lesson to the class. The following features are included:

- Objectives
- Suggested Instructional Segments
- Options for Reading
- Summary
- About the Author
- Discuss Genre and Set Purpose
- Text Complexity Rubric
- Common Core State Standards met

**PAGES 2–4** Each lesson includes two sets of questions that correspond to a "First Read" and a "Second Read" of the text.

- **First-Read Questions** Use these questions during and after an initial reading of the text to help children think through the text and learn to cite text evidence in their responses.
- **Second-Read Questions** Use these questions to guide children through a deeper analysis of the text. These questions give children opportunities for close reading and ask them to make deeper connections between ideas. Here, too, children must cite text evidence to support their ideas.

**PERFORMANCE TASK** Each lesson culminates in a performance task in which children are asked to demonstrate understanding of the exemplar text. Within each task, children are expected to complete a short writing assignment as well as engage in a speaking and listening activity. Where applicable, the performance task matches the performance-task suggestion provided in Appendix B.

## Additional Lesson Features

**TEXT COMPLEXITY RUBRIC** To help you assess text complexity at a glance, a rubric is provided in every lesson. It identifies the overall complexity as Accessible, Complex, or More Complex. For selections that children read themselves, the rubric includes quantitative measures for the Lexile and the Guided Reading Level. It also shows qualitative measures on a four-point continuum with text-specific rationales.

**DOMAIN SPECIFIC VOCABULARY** These content-area, Tier 3 words are included only for texts with heavy discipline-specific content. Children are likely to use these words only within a specific discipline, such as *life cycle* in science.

**INDEPENDENT/SELF-SELECTED READING** This feature, included on the last page of every lesson, suggests two on-level developmentally and age appropriate books children might use for independent reading and additional application of the Standards addressed in the lesson.

**RESPOND TO SEGMENT—Classroom Collaboration** These activities are aimed to help children wrap-up each segment of text. Children summarize what they've already learned and address any questions they have before moving on.

## Tips for Getting Started

- **Review the list of text exemplars for your grade span.** The exemplars include a variety of classic and contemporary complex texts. Many of the texts will likely relate to cross-curricular topics already present in your current curriculum and can be used as supplementary material to further discuss a given topic.
- **Consider the needs and the reading levels of the children in your classroom.** Each list of exemplars covers a two-grade span, so some titles may not be at the right level for your class at a given point in the year. Use the text complexity rubric to help you select the exemplars that best suit your children's reading or listening comprehension abilities throughout the school year.
- **Work with your school librarian.** Your librarian can help you find copies of the exemplar texts, online magazine articles, and any poems and stories that are in the public domain.
- **Preview the exemplars.** As you prepare for a lesson, make notes to help you consider additional connections that children can make to the text and how you might best prepare them for reading or listening and discussion.

# Literature Discussion Groups

**The *Common Core ELA Exemplar Instructional Resource* can be effectively implemented with literature discussion groups. You can support children in collaborative discussion to further explore the text exemplars in ways that can foster higher-level thinking and the use of comprehension strategies, vocabulary acquisition, and speaking and listening skills—all essential for meeting the Common Core State Standards for English Language Arts. Use the following tips.**

## Before Reading

Divide children into small, mixed-proficiency groups, and schedule a time for the groups to meet each day. Assign roles to children, or allow them to choose their own. Possible roles include the following:

- **Discussion Director** moderates the discussion by asking questions provided by the teacher or by creating original questions to pose to the group.
- **Passage Finder** chooses passages that are particularly interesting, revealing, or challenging for the group to focus on.
- **Vocabulary Detective** identifies and records unknown words for the group to look up and discuss.
- **Connector** makes connections between the text and other texts and aspects of real-life, either in general terms or in relation to the children's experiences.
- **Summarizer** summarizes the segment of text read by the group or the teacher prior to the group's discussion and describes major characters, settings, and events or main ideas and details.

**Discuss Genre and Set Purpose** As groups begin to discuss the text, encourage them to

- identify elements of the text's genre and name other texts in that genre.
- consider the author's purpose in writing.
- review their purpose for reading.

## First Read

Have groups read a segment of the text.

- Ask children to take notes or flag sections of the text to later discuss and cite as text evidence.
- Have each group's Summarizer offer a summary of what was read. Others can add missing information as needed.
- Provide Discussion Directors with questions from the lesson, or have them make up their own questions.
- Guide children to use the context of the text to understand academic vocabulary.
- Monitor discussions to ensure groups stay focused and cite text evidence to support responses.

## Second Read

Have each group reread portions of the text to further analyze ideas and concepts.

- Guide groups to connect a segment to previous segments. Ensure they understand how the segments and ideas build throughout the text.
- Help groups focus on figurative language and literary elements, such as theme.
- Have groups support their responses with evidence from the text.
- Wrap up the discussion by having children summarize what they've learned.

## OBJECTIVES

- Describe the relationship between key events and illustrations
- Recognize sequence
- Identify cause and effect
- Answer questions about key details
- Analyze text using text evidence

***Little Bear*** **is broken into three instructional segments.**

**SEGMENTS**



### Options for Reading

**Independent** Children read the book independently or in a small group and then answer questions posed by the teacher.

**Supported** Children read each segment independently or with a partner, and answer questions with teacher support.

### Common Core Connection

**RL.K.1** ask and answer questions about key details; **RL.K.3** identify characters, settings, and major events; **RL.K.7** describe the relationship between illustrations and the story

**RL.1.1** ask and answer questions about key details; **RL.1.3** describe characters, settings, and major events; **RL.1.7** use illustrations and details to describe characters, settings, or events

# *Little Bear*

by Else Holmelund Minarik

**SUMMARY** This book includes four different stories about the adventures of Little Bear, his mother, and his friends. In the end, the author shows how Little Bear's imagination helps to tie the four stories together.

**ABOUT THE AUTHOR** **Else Holmelund Minarik** was born in Denmark, but moved to the United States when she was four. She was a reporter and a teacher before becoming a popular children's book writer. Her book *Little Bear* was the beginning of the popular *I Can Read* series.

## Discuss Genre and Set Purpose

**FICTION** Read the Table of Contents and look through the book with children. Help them identify characteristics of a story, including make-believe characters, different settings, and events.

**SET PURPOSE** Help children set a purpose for reading, such as to find out about the different events in Little Bear's adventures and how the illustrations relate to them.

### TEXT COMPLEXITY RUBRIC

| Overall Text Complexity | | *Little Bear* FICTION<br>ACCESSIBLE |
|---|---|---|
| Quantitative Measures | Lexile | 370L |
| | Guided Reading Level | J |
| Qualitative Measures | Text Structure | no major shifts in chronology, occasional use of flashback |
| | Language Conventionality and Clarity | increased, clearly-assigned dialogue |
| | Knowledge Demands | clearly fantastical situation |
| | Purpose/Levels of Meaning | single level of simple meaning |

## SEGMENT 1 pp. 11–21

### Academic Vocabulary

Read each word with children and discuss its meaning.

**snow** (p. 11) • white flakes of ice that fall from the sky
**birthday** (p. 22) • the anniversary or date of the day you were born
**friends** (p. 23) • pals, people you like and enjoy being with
**beautiful** (p. 34) • very pretty

## FIRST READ Think Through the Text

Have children use text evidence to answer these questions.

**p. 11** • *What does Little Bear want? Why? He wants something to put on because he is cold. How do you know? In the text he says that he is cold and wants to put something on.* **RL.K.1, RL.1.1**

**pp. 12–17** • *What does Mother Bear make for Little Bear first? a hat next? a coat last? snow pants* **RL.K.1, RL.1.1**

**pp. 18–21** • *The last page says that he was not cold. Why isn't Little Bear cold now?* Sample answer: *He has his fur coat, which is his real fur. That keeps him warm.* **RL.K.3, RL.1.3**

## SECOND READ Analyze the Text

- Have children look back at the pictures on pages 11–15. Ask: *Where do the pictures show that the story takes place? inside Little Bear's house Where else does Little Bear go in the story? outside How do you know? The text says that Little Bear went out to play.* **RL.K.3, RL.1.3**
- Help children compare the things Little Bear wears at the beginning of the story with what he wears at the end. Say: *Let's reread pages 14–17. Where does Little Bear get his hat, coat, and pants? His mother made them for him.* **RL.K.1, RL.1.1**
- *Let's look back at pages 20–21. Where does Little Bear get the fur coat that keeps him warm? It's his own fur. How do you know? I can see it in the picture.* **RL.K.7, RL.1.7**

### ENGLISH LANGUAGE LEARNERS

**Use Pantomime**

Have children act out putting on a hat, coat, and snow pants. As they act out putting on each item, have them repeat Little Bear's words, "Hurray! Now I will not be cold."

### RESPOND TO SEGMENT 1

**Classroom Collaboration**

Have small groups work together to summarize what they have read so far. Encourage them to ask questions about what they did not understand.

## ENGLISH LANGUAGE LEARNERS

**Use Pantomime**

Have children act out in order what Little Bear did when he went to the moon. Read aloud the last three lines on page 46 as children act out each action. Then have children tell what Little Bear did using the signal words *first, next, last*.

## RESPOND TO SEGMENT 2

**Classroom Collaboration**

Have small groups work together to summarize what they have read. Have them ask questions about what they don't understand.

**Common Core Connection**

**RL.K.1** ask and answer questions about key details; **RL.K.3** identify characters, settings, and major events; **RL.K.7** describe the relationship between illustrations and the story; **W.K.2** use drawing, dictating, and writing to compose informative/explanatory texts; **W.K.5** respond to questions/suggestions from peers and add details to strengthen writing; **SL.K.5** add drawings or visual displays to descriptions to provide detail

**RL.1.1** ask and answer questions about key details; **RL.1.3** describe characters, settings, and major events; **RL.1.7** use illustrations and details to describe characters, settings, or events; **RL.1.10** read prose and poetry; **W.1.2** write informative/explanatory texts; **W.1.5** focus on a topic, respond to questions/suggestions from peers, and add details to strengthen writing; **SL.1.5** add drawings or visual displays to descriptions to clarify ideas, thoughts, and feelings

## FIRST READ Think Through the Text

Have children use text evidence to answer these questions.

**pp. 22–25** • *Who comes in first?* Hen *How do you know?* The text says "First, hen comes in." **RL.K.3, RL.1.3**

**pp. 26–34** • *Who comes in after Hen?* Duck *after Duck?* Cat *What clue word tells that they come after?* next *Who comes in last?* Mother Bear **RL.K.1, RL.1.1**

**pp. 35–49** • *How is Little Bear's moon just like the earth?* The trees, the birds, and the house look the same. **RL.K.3, RL.1.3**

## SECOND READ Analyze the Text

- *What causes Little Bear to make a pot of soup for his friends?* Sample answer: It is his birthday, and he does not have a birthday cake for them. *What words help give evidence for this answer?* I think my friends will come, but I do not see a birthday cake. **RL.K.3, RL.1.3**
- *How does Little Bear feel at the beginning of "Birthday Soup"?* worried *Why?* He has no cake for his friends. *How does he feel at the end of the story?* happy *How can you tell?* He says that he is happy, and the picture shows that he is hugging his mother. **RL.K.3, RL.1.3**
- *Tell about the most important events in the story "Little Bear Goes to the Moon." Use the words* first, next, *and* last *to tell about them. Identify the pictures that show each major event.* Sample answer: First, Little Bear tells Mother Bear he will go to the moon. This is shown in the pictures on pp. 36 and 38. Next, he jumps from a tree and pretends he lands on the moon. This is shown in the pictures on pp. 41–43. Last, he goes back home to have lunch on his pretend moon. This is shown in the pictures on pp. 45–47. **RL.K.7, RL.1.7**

## FIRST READD Think Through the Text

Have children use text evidence to answer these questions.

**pp. 50–52** • *What is Little Bear's first wish? He wishes he could sit on a cloud and fly all around.* **RL.K.1, RL.1.1**

**pp. 53–56** • *Look at the pictures on these pages. How do they help you understand the key events on these pages? They show the different wishes Little Bear has.* **RL.K.7, RL.1.7**

**pp. 57–63** • *How does the story end? Mother tells Little Bear a story and he can go to sleep.* **RL.K.3, RL.1.3**

## SECOND READ Analyze the Text

- Guide children to review pages 50–57. Ask: *How are Little Bear's first wishes different from his last wish?* Sample answer: *He can't have the first wishes, but he can have the last wish.* **RL.K.3, RL.1.3**
- Have children reread pages 58–63. Ask: *What is the first story Mother Bear tells Little Bear about himself? What is the last one? The first is about Little Bear playing in the snow. The last is about Little Bear making Birthday Soup.* **RL.K.3, RL.1.3**

# Independent/Self-Selected Reading

If children have already demonstrated comprehension of *Little Bear*, have them practice the skills using another independent reading book. Model selecting a book from the classroom library. Help children read the title of the book, the author's name, and any information about the book on the back or inside cover. Suggested titles:

- *Little Bear's Friend* by Else Holmelund Minarik
- *Get Up, Rick!* by F. Isabel Campoy **RL.1.10**

### WRITE & PRESENT

1. Assign each group one of the four stories to discuss. Have them reread the story together. Guide children to talk about how the key events are related to the corresponding illustrations in their story. **RL.K.7, RL.1.7**
2. Help individual children write sentences to tell one key event from the beginning, middle, and end of the one story they discussed. Have them then draw a picture for each sentence. **W.K.2, W.1.2**
3. Children work in small groups to share and edit their sentences and drawings before making final copies. **W.K.5, W.1.5**
4. Finally, children present their pictures and text to summarize their stories and show how their pictures are related to each sentence. Encourage them to ask and answer questions as children make their presentations. **SL.K.5, SL.1.5**
5. Individuals turn in their final pieces to the teacher.

*See Copying Masters, pp. 242–245*

### STUDENT CHECKLIST

**Writing**

- ✔ Write and draw to tell about story events.
- ✔ Use illustrations to add details to sentences about key events.
- ✔ Use correct language conventions.

**Speaking & Listening**

- ✔ Ask and answer questions to clarify what a speaker says.
- ✔ Express ideas and opinions clearly.
- ✔ Describe how illustrations are related to events in their writing.

## OBJECTIVES

- Recognize and describe the relationship between text and illustrations
- Identify the problem and solution in a story
- Answer questions about key details
- Analyze text using text evidence

***Are You My Mother?*** **is broken into three instructional segments.**

**SEGMENTS**

**SEGMENT 1** .......... pp. 3–21
**SEGMENT 2** ........ pp. 22–49
**SEGMENT 3** ........ pp. 50–63

### Options for Reading

**Independent** Children read the book independently or in a small group and then answer questions posed by the teacher.

**Supported** Children read a segment and answer questions with teacher support.

### Common Core Connection

**RL.K.1** ask and answer questions about key details; **RL.K.3** identify characters, settings, and major events; **RL.K.7** describe the relationship between illustrations and the story

**RL.1.1** ask and answer questions about key details; **RL.1.3** describe characters, settings, and major events; **RL.1.7** use illustrations and details to describe characters, settings, or events

# Are You My Mother?

by P. D. Eastman

**SUMMARY** This book tells the adventures of a baby bird in search of his mother. Baby bird falls out of his nest while mother bird is away looking for food. After searching for his mother, baby bird eventually ends up back in his nest with his mother.

**ABOUT THE AUTHOR** **P. D. (Philip Dey) Eastman** was a screenwriter, author, and illustrator. He wrote many children's books. In the early 1950s, he was hired by Dr. Seuss at Random House to write and illustrate books for a new series called Beginner Books. *Are You My Mother?*, published in 1960, was number 18 in that series.

## Discuss Genre and Set Purpose

**FICTION** Have children look through the book to find and identify characteristics of fiction, including make-believe characters and a setting that could be found in real life.

**SET PURPOSE** Help children set a purpose for reading, such as to find out what problem baby bird has and how it is solved.

### TEXT COMPLEXITY RUBRIC

| Overall Text Complexity | | *Are You My Mother?* FICTION<br>ACCESSIBLE |
|---|---|---|
| Quantitative Measures | Lexile | 80L |
| | Guided Reading Level | I |
| Qualitative Measures | Text Structure | simple, linear chronology |
| | Language Conventionality and Clarity | clear, direct language |
| | Knowledge Demands | simple theme |
| | Purpose/Levels of Meaning | single level of simple meaning |

SEGMENT 1 pp. 3–21

### Academic Vocabulary

Read each word with children and discuss its meaning.

**where** (p. 10) • a question word used to ask about location

**could** (p. 18) • the ability to do something

## FIRST READ Think Through the Text

Have children use text evidence to answer these questions.

**pp. 3–7** • *What does mother bird want to do?* get food for her baby RL.K.1, RL.1.1

**pp. 8–11** • *What does baby bird do when he first comes out of the egg?* *He looks for his mother.* *How can you tell?* *The picture shows him looking around and the text says, "He looked for her."* RL.K.7, RL.1.7

**pp. 12–17** • *What happened to baby bird when he went to look for his mother?* *He fell down to the ground.* RL.K.1, RL.1.1

**pp. 18–21** • *Did baby bird see his mother? How can you tell?* *No, the text says that he walked by her and did not see her.* RL.K.1, RL.1.1

## SECOND READ Analyze the Text

- Have children reread pages 3–6. Ask: *Who is this part of the story about?* mother bird *Where does it take place?* in a tree or a nest RL.K.3, RL.1.3
- Ask children to look back at page 9. Say: *The words say, "Out came the baby bird!" How does the picture give more information about what happened?* Sample answer: *The picture shows that baby bird came out of his egg. It shows what baby bird looks like.* RL.K.7, RL.1.7
- *Let's look back at pages 20–21. What is mother bird doing?* *She is getting a worm.* *How can you tell?* *The picture shows this.* RL.K.7, RL.1.7
- *Let's reread pages 20–21. Why doesn't baby bird know what his mother looks like?* *He has never seen her. By the time he came out of his egg, she had gone looking for food.* RL.K.1, RL.1.1
- *What problem is baby bird trying to solve?* *He is trying to find his mother.* RL.K.3, RL.1.3

### ENGLISH LANGUAGE LEARNERS

**Use Gestures/Act It Out**

Have children put their hand above their eyes (as if saluting) to act out looking for something. Then have them act out pages 12 and 13, looking up and looking down for mother bird. Ask volunteers to reread these two pages aloud.

### RESPOND TO SEGMENT 1

**Classroom Collaboration**

Have small groups work together to summarize what they have read so far. Encourage them to ask questions about what they did not understand or would like to know in the next segment.

## ENGLISH LANGUAGE LEARNERS

**Comprehensible Input**

Before reading on, confirm children's understanding of the problem in the story using yes/no questions, such as: *Does baby bird see his mother?* no *Does baby bird want to find his mother?* yes *Will baby bird go looking for his mother?* yes

## RESPOND TO SEGMENT 2

**Classroom Collaboration**

Have small groups work together to summarize what they have read. Have them ask questions about what they don't understand.

**Common Core Connection**

**RL.K.1** ask and answer questions about key details; **RL.K.3** identify characters, settings, and major events; **RL.K.7** describe the relationship between illustrations and the story; **RL.K.9** compare and contrast adventures and experiences of characters; **W.K.1** use drawing, dictating, and writing to compose opinion pieces; **SL.K.6** speak audibly and express thoughts, feelings, and ideas clearly

**RL.1.1** ask and answer questions about key details; **RL.1.3** describe characters, settings, and major events; **RL.1.7** use illustrations and details to describe characters, settings, or events; **RL.1.9** compare and contrast adventures and experiences of characters; **RL.1.10** read prose and poetry; **W.1.1** write opinion pieces; **SL.1.4** describe people, places, things, and events with details/express ideas and feelings clearly

## FIRST READ Think Through the Text

Have children use text evidence to answer these questions.

**pp. 22–34** • *What question does baby bird ask all of the animals he meets?* *Are you my mother?* *What is their answer?* no **RL.K.1, RL.1.1**

**pp. 34–43** • *What else does baby bird see that is not his mother?* *a car, a boat, and a plane* **RL.K.1, RL.1.1**

**pp. 44–49** • *How does baby bird change from page 44 to page 49?* Sample answer: *When he first sees the Snort, he thinks it is his mother. By the end he does not think it is his mother and wants to get away from it.* **RL.K.9, RL.1.9**

## SECOND READ Analyze the Text

- *How are the things that baby bird thinks are his mother different in this part of the book and in the beginning of the book?* *In the first part, he thinks different animals are his mother; in this part, he thinks different machines are his mother.* **RL.K.9, RL.1.9**
- Have children review pages 44–47. Then ask: *What does baby bird do when he sees the machine?* *He runs right up to the machine.* *How can you tell?* *I can read the words "He ran right up to it" and see what baby bird does in the pictures.* *Why does baby bird do this? How can you tell?* *He thinks the machine is his mother. I can read the words "There is my mother!"* **RL.K.7, RL.1.7**
- Have children review the pictures and words on pages 48–49. Then ask: *What information do you learn from the picture that you do not learn from the words on these pages?* Sample answer: *The picture shows that the machine is a power shovel. The words just say that it is a Snort.* **RL.K.7, RL.1.7**
- *Has baby bird solved his problem yet?* no *Why not?* *He has not found his mother.* **RL.K.3, RL.1.3**

## FIRST READD Think Through the Text

Have children use text evidence to answer these questions.

**pp. 50–53 •** *Baby bird has a new problem in this part of the story. What is his problem?* Sample answer: *The Snort picks him up and moves. Baby bird can't get down.* **RL.K.3, RL.1.3**

**pp. 54–59 •** *How does the Snort solve this new problem for baby bird? How can you tell? He puts baby bird down in his nest.* **RL.K.7, RL.1.7**

**pp. 60–63 •** *How does the story end? Mother comes back to the nest. Baby bird finds his mother.* **RL.K.3, RL.1.3**

## SECOND READ Analyze the Text

- Guide children to review pages 50–57. Ask: *How does baby bird feel in this part of the book? How can you tell?* Sample answer: *He feels afraid. He says that he wants to go home.* ***Do the pictures also show how he feels? Why or why not?*** Sample answer: *Yes, on page 56 he looks upset and is screaming.* **RL.K.7, RL.1.7**
- Have children reread page 3 and page 63. Say: *Think about baby bird in the beginning of the story and at the end. How is he different? In the beginning he is in an egg; at the end he is out of the egg. How is he the same? In both the beginning and the end he is with his mother.* **RL.K.9, RL.1.9**
- *How is baby bird's problem solved at the end of the story? The Snort puts baby bird back in his nest, and mother bird comes home.* **RL.K.1, RL.1.1**

## Independent/Self-Selected Reading

If children have already demonstrated comprehension of *Are You My Mother?*, have them practice the skills using another independent reading book. Model selecting a book from the classroom library. Help children read the title of the book, the author's name, and any information about the book on the back or inside cover. Suggested titles:

- *Make Way for Ducklings* by Robert McCloskey
- *Go, Dog, Go!* by P. D. Eastman **RL.1.10**

### WRITE & PRESENT

1. Have partners look back at favorite parts of the book, discuss what they learned from the words and the pictures, and tell why they like these parts best. **RL.K.7, RL.1.7**
2. Have each child draw a favorite part of the story. Help them write sentences to tell what the picture shows. Have them use words that are not shown in the picture, but give more information about the event. **W.K.1, W.1.1**
3. Have children share their writing with partners and get ideas for editing. **W.K.5, W.1.5**
4. Children present their pictures and text to tell about their favorite part of the story. Encourage listeners to ask and answer questions as others make their presentations. **W.K.5, W.1.5**
5. Individuals turn in their final opinion pieces to the teacher.

*See Copying Masters, pp. 242–245.*

### STUDENT CHECKLIST

#### Writing

- ✔ Write and draw to express opinions.
- ✔ Describe how the author uses text and pictures to tell details in a story.
- ✔ Use correct language conventions.

#### Speaking & Listening

- ✔ Ask and answer questions to clarify what a speaker says.
- ✔ Express ideas and opinions clearly.
- ✔ Share ideas about the relationship between text and pictures.

## OBJECTIVES

- Make predictions based on text evidence
- Identify relationships between text and illustrations
- Recognize the main idea
- Answer questions about key details
- Analyze text using text evidence

***Green Eggs and Ham*** **is broken into three instructional segments.**

### SEGMENTS

SEGMENT 1. . . . . . . . . pp. 3–27
SEGMENT 2. . . . . . . . pp. 28–51
SEGMENT 3. . . . . . . . pp. 52–63

### Options for Reading

**Independent** Children read the book independently or in a small group and then answer questions posed by the teacher.

**Supported** Children read each segment independently or with a partner, and answer questions with teacher support.

### Common Core Connection

**RL.K.1** ask and answer questions about key details; **RL.K.3** identify characters, settings, and major events; **RL.K.5** recognize common types of texts; **RL.K.7** describe the relationship between illustrations and the story

**RL.1.1** ask and answer questions about key details; **RL.1.3** describe characters, settings, and major events; **RL.1.7** use illustrations and details to describe characters, settings, or events; **RL.1.10** read prose and poetry

# *Green Eggs and Ham*

by Dr. Seuss

**SUMMARY** This rhyming book takes the reader on a silly adventure as Sam-I-am tries to convince his friend to try and like green eggs and ham. In the end, he succeeds.

**ABOUT THE AUTHOR** Dr. Seuss was born Theodor Seuss Geisel in 1904. He had a career as a cartoonist for several magazines before he wrote and illustrated his first book for Vanguard Press called *And to Think That I Saw It on Mulberry Street*. By the time he died in 1991, he had written and illustrated 44 children's books.

## Discuss Genre and Set Purpose

**FICTION** Look through the illustrations with children. Help them see that there are two make-believe characters in this story. Ask children to think about the illustrations and decide whether this story could happen in real life.

**SET PURPOSE** Help children set a purpose for reading, such as to find out if the main character will ever like green eggs and ham.

### TEXT COMPLEXITY RUBRIC

| Overall Text Complexity | | *Green Eggs and Ham* FICTION<br>ACCESSIBLE |
|---|---|---|
| Quantitative Measures | Lexile | 30L |
| | Guided Reading Level | J |
| Qualitative Measures | Text Structure | few, if any, shifts in point of view |
| | Language Conventionality and Clarity | clear, direct language |
| | Knowledge Demands | single theme |
| | Purpose/Levels of Meaning | single level of meaning |

## SEGMENT 1 pp. 3–27

**Academic Vocabulary**

Read each word with children and discuss its meaning.

**ham** (p. 10) • meat from a pig
**would** (p. 14) • will, a word that asks if you want to do something
**anywhere** (p. 16) • any place
**try** (p. 53) • make an attempt

## FIRST READ Think Through the Text

Have children use text evidence to answer these questions.

**pp. 3–9** • *What do you know about Sam from reading the text on these pages? What do you know from the pictures?* Sample answers: *I know from reading the text that the character's name is Sam, or Sam-I-am, and the other character, the friend, does not like him. I know from looking at the pictures that Sam keeps walking by the friend introducing himself while the friend is trying to read his newspaper.* **RL.K.7, RL.1.7**

**pp. 10–19** • *Do you think the friend will like green eggs and ham in a house or with a mouse? Why or why not?* Sample answer: *No, because he said he would not like them anywhere.* **RL.K.3, RL.1.3**

**pp. 19–27** • *What is Sam trying to do? He is trying to get the friend to eat green eggs and ham. Is he able to do it? no* **RL.K.1, RL.1.1**

## SECOND READ Analyze the Text

- Have children reread pages 16–20 aloud with you. Ask: *What kind of words does the author use to tell this story?* Sample answer: *rhyming words; it is like a poem* *Why do you think the author uses rhyming words? They are fun to read and listen to.* **RL.K.5, RL.1.10**
- *What is this part of the book mostly about?* Sample answer: *Sam cannot get the friend to eat green eggs and ham.* **RL.K.3, RL.1.3**
- Have children look at pages 26–27. *What do you predict will happen next?* Sample answer: *Sam will ask the friend if he will eat green eggs and ham somewhere else, but his friend will say no.* *Why do you think this? Use clues from the first part of the book to explain your answer.* Sample answer: *In the first part of the story Sam tries to get his friend to eat green eggs and ham in many different places, but his friend keeps saying no. I think this will keep happening in the next part of the story.* **RL.K.3, RL.1.3**

### ENGLISH LANGUAGE LEARNERS

**Use Sentence Frames**

Have children focus on the main idea by completing sentence frames such as the following using the language in the story. Then have children repeat the completed sentences.

- *I do not like green eggs and ____. ham*
- *I do not like them Sam-I-am. I do not like ____.* *green eggs and ham*
- *This story is about ____.* Sample answer: *someone who does not like green eggs and ham*

### RESPOND TO SEGMENT 1

**Classroom Collaboration**

Have small groups work together to summarize what they have read so far. Encourage them to ask questions about what they did not understand.

## ENGLISH LANGUAGE LEARNERS

**Explain Idioms**

Explain that the phrase "let me be" on page 30 means "leave me alone." Then give the following situations. Have children respond to each one with "Let me be" if they would not like it.

- *Your sister wants to sing and play when you want to sleep.* Let me be.
- *Your friend gives you a gift.* No response.
- *A friend will not stop tickling you.* Let me be.

Ask children to tell about other times they would say, "Let me be."

## RESPOND TO SEGMENT 2

**Classroom Collaboration**

Have small groups work together to summarize what they have read. Have them ask questions about what they don't understand.

**Common Core Connection**

**RL.K.9** compare and contrast adventures and experiences of characters; **W.K.2** use drawing, dictating, and writing to compose informative/explanatory texts; **W.K.5** respond to questions/suggestions from peers and add details to strengthen writing; **SL.K.1b** continue a conversation through multiple exchanges; **SL.K.3** ask and answer questions to seek help, get information, or clarify something not understood

**RL.1.2** retell stories and demonstrate understanding of the message or lesson; **RL.1.9** compare and contrast adventures and experiences of characters; **W.1.2** write informative/explanatory texts; **W.1.5** focus on a topic, respond to questions/suggestions from peers, and add details to strengthen writing; **SL.1.1b** build on others' talk in conversations by responding to others' comments; **SL.1.3** ask and answer questions about what a speaker says

## FIRST READ Think Through the Text

Have children use text evidence to answer these questions.

**pp. 28–31** • *Where are some different places that the character does not like green eggs and ham?* in a tree, in a car, in a house, with a mouse, here or there, anywhere **RL.K.1, RL.1.1**

**pp. 32–45** • *What are some examples of where the pictures show what the text says?* Sample answers: *On pages 33–34 the text says and pictures show "on a train"; on pages 36–37 the text says and pictures show "in the dark."* **RL.K.7, RL.1.7**

**pp. 45–51** • *Where else does the text say the character does not like green eggs and ham?* on a boat, with a goat, in the rain, on a train, in a box, or with a fox **RL.K.1, RL.1.1**

## SECOND READ Analyze the Text

- *What is the main idea for this part of the book?* Sam still wants his friend to like green eggs and ham, but his friend will not try them. **RL.K.3, RL.1.3**
- Have children look at the picture of the friend on page 31. *How does the friend feel?* angry *How do you know?* His face looks angry and he is holding up his fist. Then have them look at the friend on page 33. *How does the friend feel now?* afraid *How do you know?* His eyes are wide and his mouth is open as he looks at the train they may crash into. *How do these pictures add information to what you read in the text?* They help you know how the friend feels; the text does not tell you that. **RL.K.7, RL.1.7**
- *How is the text different from the pictures on pages 45–52? Where do you learn more details?* Sample answer: *The text just names the places where the character does not like green eggs and ham. The pictures show the car, train, goat and all of the things crashing into the water. The pictures give more details.* **RL.K.7, RL.1.7**
- Ask children to recall their predictions about what would happen in the second part of the book. Then ask: *Was your prediction correct? How do you know?* Sample answer: *Yes, I predicted the friend would still not like green eggs and ham, and he doesn't.* **RL.K.3, RL.1.3**
- *What do you predict will happen in the next part of the book?* Sample answer: *Sam will keep trying to get the friend to eat green eggs and ham, and the friend will keep saying no.* *Why do you think so?* In the first two parts of the book, this is what happened, so I think it will happen again. **RL.K.3, RL.1.3**

## FIRST READ Think Through the Text

Have children use text evidence to answer these questions.

**pp. 52–53 •** *What does Sam want the friend to do?* *try green eggs and ham* *How can you tell that the friend has never tried green eggs and ham?* *Sam says, "Try them and you may." He would not say that if the friend had tried them before.* **RL.K.3, RL.1.3**

**pp. 54–55 •** *What deal does the friend make with Sam?* *The friend will try green eggs and ham if Sam will stop bothering him about it.* *What words tell you this?* *If you will let me be, I will try them.* **RL.K.3, RL.1.3**

**pp. 56–57 •** *Look at the picture of the friend on page 57. What does the picture show about how the friend feels that the text does not tell?* *The friend seems to be disgusted as he looks at the green egg.* **RL.K.7, RL.1.7**

**pp. 58–63 •** *How did the friend's feelings change about green eggs and ham and about Sam?* *Now the friend likes green eggs and ham and he likes Sam* *How do you know?* *The text says that he likes green eggs and ham. The friend thanks Sam and the picture shows the friend happily putting his arm around Sam.* **RL.K.3, RL.1.3**

## SECOND READ Analyze the Text

- Ask children to recall their predictions about what would happen in the last part of the book. *Was your prediction correct? Why or why not?* Sample answer: *No, I predicted that the friend would not eat green eggs and ham, but instead he agreed to try them and found out that he liked them.* **RL.K.3, RL.1.3**
- Guide children to review pages 58–63. Ask: *How are the beginning and the end of the book the same?* Sample answer: *In both parts of the book Sam wants the friend to try green eggs and ham, but the friend refuses.* *How are they different?* Sample answer: *In the beginning his friend won't try green eggs and ham and says he will not like them. In the end he tries them and likes them.* **RL.K.9, RL.1.9**
- *What is the lesson the author wants you to learn?* Sample answers: *You should try new things. Don't judge something without first trying it.* **RL.1.10**

# Independent/Self-Selected Reading

If children have already demonstrated comprehension of *Green Eggs and Ham,* have them practice the skills using another independent reading book. Model selecting a book from the classroom library. Help children read the title of the book, the author's name, and any information about the book on the back or inside cover. Suggested titles:

- *The Cat in the Hat* by Dr. Seuss
- *One Fish Two Fish Red Fish Blue Fish* by Dr. Seuss **RL.1.10**

### WRITE & PRESENT

1. Have small groups refer to pages where Sam asks questions. Ask them to discuss how they made predictions about what the friend's answers would be. Then have them use the text on the following pages to model how they checked their predictions. **SL.K.1b, SL.1.1b**
2. Have children each choose one part of the book to write sentences that tell about a prediction they made, whether the prediction was correct, and how they knew. Suggest that they illustrate their writing. **W.K.2, W.1.2**
3. Have children share their writing and drawing with a partner. Ask them to add details to their writing based on their partner's suggestions. **W.K.5, W.1.5**
4. Children present their writing and any drawings to their classmates. Encourage classmates to ask and answer questions about the presentations. **SL.K.3, SL.1.3**

*See Copying Masters, pp. 242–245.*

### STUDENT CHECKLIST

#### Writing

- ✔ Write sentences that tell about a prediction made, whether the prediction was correct, and how children knew.
- ✔ Include one or more details about their prediction.
- ✔ Use correct language conventions.

#### Speaking & Listening

- ✔ Ask and answer questions to clarify what a speaker says.
- ✔ Express ideas and opinions clearly.
- ✔ Demonstrate a connection between information in the text and their own writing and drawing.

### OBJECTIVES

- Use text and illustrations to identify causes and effects
- Retell key details
- Use illustrations to identify and infer character actions and feelings
- Make predictions
- Analyze text using text evidence

**_Put Me in the Zoo_ is broken into three instructional segments.**

**SEGMENTS**

**SEGMENT 1** .........pp. 3–23
**SEGMENT 2** ........pp. 24–41
**SEGMENT 3** ........pp. 42–61

### Options for Reading

**Independent** Children read the book independently or with the teacher and then answer questions posed by the teacher.

**Supported** Children read a few pages and answer questions with teacher support.

### Common Core Connection

**RL.K.1** ask and answer questions about key details; **RL.K.3** identify characters, settings, and major events; **RL.K.4** ask and answer questions about unknown words; **RL.K.7** describe the relationship between illustrations and the story

**RL.1.1** ask and answer questions about key details; **RL.1.3** describe characters, settings, and major events; **RL.1.6** identify who is telling the story; **RL.1.7** use illustrations and details to describe characters, settings, or events

# Put Me in the Zoo

by Robert Lopshire

**SUMMARY** This book is about Spot, a talented leopard, who does tricks with his spots, such as changing their color and number and making them fly. He wants to live in the zoo, but discovers that performing in the circus would be a better way to show off his talents.

**ABOUT THE AUTHOR Robert Lopshire** worked for Dr. Seuss's *Beginner Readers* project in the late 1950s. Dr. Seuss bet Lopshire that he couldn't write an interesting book with the characters Dick, Jane, and Spot from old-time readers. That led to Lopshire's writing *Put Me in the Zoo*. He also wrote other Beginner Books.

## Discuss Genre and Set Purpose

**FICTION** Look at the book with children, and help them find and identify characteristics of fiction, including make-believe characters and a story setting.

**SET PURPOSE** Help children set a purpose for reading, such as to find out what causes the problem Spot has and the effects of how he tries to solve the problem.

**TEXT COMPLEXITY RUBRIC**

| Overall Text Complexity | | *Put Me in the Zoo* FICTION<br>ACCESSIBLE |
|---|---|---|
| Quantitative Measures | Lexile | 150L |
| | Guided Reading Level | F |
| Qualitative Measures | Text Structure | less familiar story concepts |
| | Language Conventionality and Clarity | literal, accessible language |
| | Knowledge Demands | clearly fantastical situation |
| | Purpose/Levels of Meaning | single level of simple meaning |

SEGMENT 1 pp. 3–23

**Academic Vocabulary**

Read the word with children and discuss its meaning.

**violet** (p. 21) • a dark purple color

FIRST READ
## Think Through the Text

Have children use text evidence to answer these questions.

**p. 5** • *What does Spot want to do? He wants to live in the zoo.* **RL.K.3, RL.1.3**

**pp. 8–9** • *Do the zookeepers want Spot to stay in the zoo? How do you know? They do not. They carry him out.* **RL.K.1, RL.1.1**

**p. 14** • *What trick does Spot do? He turns his spots blue.* **RL.K.1, RL.1.1**

**pp. 15–20** • *What other colors do his spots turn? They turn orange, green, and violet.* **RL.K.1, RL.1.1**

**p. 22** • *What has Spot done now? How do you know? He made his spots all different colors. The picture shows it.* **RL.K.7, RL.1.7**

SECOND READ
## Analyze the Text

- *Who is telling the story? How do you know? The leopard tells the story. I can tell from the word* I. **RL.K.1, RL.1.6**
- Guide children to revisit pages 4–5 to answer the question: *What causes Spot to want to live in the zoo? He sees how the zookeepers take care of the animals and feed them. He wants them to take care of him and feed him, too.* **RL.K.7, RL.1.7**
- Have children reread page 13. Then ask: *Why do the children think the zoo doesn't want Spot? They don't think he can do anything special. They don't think visitors to the zoo will want to look at him.* **RL.K.1, RL.1.3**
- Have children look at the pictures on pages 15–17. Ask: *What can you tell about the children's feelings? At first, they are so surprised by Spot's trick that they drop their popcorn. They have probably never seen a leopard change its colors. Then they get excited. This is something special to see.* **RL.K.7, RL.1.7**
- Ask children to reread page 21. Ask: *What clues in the pages before this one help you know what* violet *means? The other pages tell about Spot's spots turning other colors. That helps me know that violet must be a color, too. I can tell from the picture what violet looks like.* **RL.K.4, RL.1.1**

**ENGLISH LANGUAGE LEARNERS**

**Use Visuals**

Be sure children understand that a zoo is a place to see animals. Revisit pages 3–6. Point out and name key details such as *cage* and *zookeeper*. Invite children to repeat the words. Have them name animals they see in the pictures: *I see a lion. I see a seal.* Encourage them to name other zoo animals and tell about or act out what those animals do.

**RESPOND TO SEGMENT 1**

**Classroom Collaboration**

Have partners work together to create and present a summary, as well as raise questions that might be answered in the next segment.

## ENGLISH LANGUAGE LEARNERS

**Use Patterned Sentences and Gestures**
Help children understand what is happening in this section. For pages 24–31, have them repeat patterned sentences while pointing to the appropriate part of the relevant illustration: *I can put my spots on a ball* (point to ball). *I can put my spots on a wall* (point to wall) and so on. Then have them pretend to be Spot and use the pattern with other objects. *I can put my spots on a desk.*

## RESPOND TO SEGMENT 2

**Classroom Collaboration**

Have small groups work together to summarize what they have read. Have them ask questions about what they don't understand.

**Common Core Connection**

**RL.K.2** retell familiar stories; **RL.K.3** identify characters, settings, and major events; **RL.K.5** recognize common types of texts; **W.K.1** use drawing, dictating, and writing to compose opinion pieces; **W.K.5** respond to questions/suggestions from peers and add details to strengthen writing; **SL.K.6** speak audibly and express thoughts, feelings, and ideas clearly

**RL.1.2** retell stories and demonstrate understanding of the message or lesson; **RL.1.3** describe characters, settings, and major events; **RL.1.5** explain major differences between story books and informational books; **RL.1.10** read prose and poetry; **W.1.1** write opinion pieces; **W.1.5** respond to questions/suggestions from peers and add details to strengthen writing; **SL.1.6** produce complete sentences when appropriate to task and situation

## FIRST READ Think Through the Text

Have children use text evidence to answer these questions.

**p. 24** • *What other trick does Spot do?* He puts his spots on other things. **RL.K.3, RL.1.3**

**pp. 24–31** • *Name the things Spot puts his spots on.* He puts them on a ball, wall, cat, hat, zoo, and the children. **RL.K.1, RL.1.1**

**pp. 32–33** • *Do the spots stay on the children? How do you know?* The picture shows the spots are on Spot but not on the children. He says, "One, two, three," and they come back onto him. **RL.K.7, RL.1.7**

**pp. 36–41** • *What other trick does Spot do?* He changes the size of his spots. **RL.K.3, RL.1.3**

## SECOND READ Analyze the Text

- *Is this a book that tells facts about leopards or a made-up story about a leopard? How do you know?* It is a made-up story because leopards can't do tricks with their spots. **RL.K.5, RL.1.5**
- Revisit page 28. Ask: *What might happen if a zookeeper sees that Spot put his spots on the zoo?* Sample answer: The zookeeper might think Spot is special and want him to live in the zoo. **RL.K.1, RL.1.1**
- Pause after page 31 and ask: *What do you predict might happen next? Why do you think that?* Sample answer: Spot will do another trick. The author has already told about two tricks, so he will probably tell more. **RL.K.1, RL.1.1**
- Have children revisit pages 34–35. *What is different about how Spot looks? What caused this change?* He doesn't have his spots. He took them off so he could juggle. **RL.K.1, RL.1.1**
- Have children pause after reading page 41. Ask: *What is a word you think describes Spot? Explain why. Use ideas from the book.* Sample answer: He is clever. He knows how to do many different things. He can change the color and size of his spots. He can put his spots in different places. **RL.K.1, RL.1.3**

## FIRST READ Think Through the Text

Have children use text evidence to answer these questions.

**pp. 44–46** • *Retell what happens on these pages. First, Spot puts his spots in a box. Then he takes them out. The spots turn into the shape of socks.* **RL.K.2, RL.1.2**

**pp. 48–51** • *What does Spot do with his spots next? He makes them fly around in the sky.* **RL.K.1, RL.1.3**

**pp. 57–61** • *Where do the children think Spot should go? Why? He should go to the circus. He can do many tricks that people who come to the circus would like to see.* **RL.K.1, RL.1.1**

## SECOND READ Analyze the Text

- Have children revisit the picture on page 44. Ask: *What is funny about the box? It is funny because it says* Spot Box, *and it is where Spot puts his spots.* **RL.K.7, RL.1.7**
- Ask children to look back at the picture on page 52. *Describe what the picture shows. All the spots that were up in the air fell down to the ground. They are piled so high that they cover the children's bodies up to their necks.* **RL.K.7, RL.1.7**
- *On page 54, Spot is still hoping the zoo will take him. What causes him to think that? He has shown that he can do many tricks that zoo visitors would like to see.* **RL.K.1, RL.1.1**
- Guide children to look at the illustration on page 55. Ask: *What are the children doing? Why? They are clapping for Spot. They like his spots, and they like him, too.* **RL.K.7, RL.1.7**
- *Why is the circus a good place for Spot? How do you know? He can show off all his tricks such as juggling and balancing spots on his tail. The picture shows he is happy and having fun. The people like his show and are smiling.* **RL.K.1, RL.1.1**

## Independent/Self-Selected Reading

If children have already demonstrated comprehension of *Put Me in the Zoo,* have them practice the skills using another independent reading book. Model selecting a book from the classroom library. Help children read the title of the book, the author's name, and any information about the book on the back or inside cover. Suggested titles:

- *Hippo! No, Rhino!* by Jeff Newman
- *Circus* by Lois Ehlert **RL.1.10**

### WRITE & PRESENT

1. Make a two-column chart. Write: *What: Spot wants to live in the zoo* as the left column head. Discuss with children what causes Spot to think the zoo would be a good place for him. Tell them to think about what they read and also to revisit the pictures. Record their ideas in the right column under *Why.* **RL.K.1, RL.1.1**
2. Ask each child to write opinion sentences about whether the zoo would be a good place for Spot and why. Encourage them to use ideas from the chart. **W.K.1, W.1.1**
3. Have children share their writing with partners and get ideas for editing. **W.K.5, W.1.5**
4. Have children present their final sentences to the class. **SL.K.6, SL.1.6**
5. Individual children turn in their final sentences to the teacher.

*See Copying Masters, pp. 242–245.*

### STUDENT CHECKLIST

**Writing**

- ✔ Write about whether the zoo would be a good home for Spot.
- ✔ Clearly state an opinion.
- ✔ Include details to support the opinion.

**Speaking & Listening**

- ✔ Read in a clear voice.
- ✔ Read loudly enough for classmates to hear.
- ✔ Ask and answer questions to clarify what a speaker says.
- ✔ Express ideas and opinions clearly.

## OBJECTIVES

- Identify the central message or lesson of a story
- Identify and infer character traits based on story dialogue and events
- Identify reasons for character actions
- Analyze text using text evidence

***Frog and Toad Together* is broken into three instructional segments.**

**SEGMENTS**

**SEGMENT 1**..........pp. 4–17
**SEGMENT 2**.........pp. 18–41
**SEGMENT 3**.........pp. 42–64

### Options for Reading

**Independent** Children read the book independently or with the teacher and then answer questions.

**Supported** Children read a few pages and answer questions with teacher support.

### Common Core Connection

**RL.K.1** ask and answer questions about key details; **RL.K.3** identify character, settings, and major events; **RL.K.7** describe the relationship between illustrations and the story

**RL.1.1** ask and answer questions about key details; **RL.1.2** retell stories and demonstrate understanding of the message or lesson; **RL.1.3** describe characters, settings, and major events; **RL.1.7** use illustrations and details to describe characters, settings, or events

# *Frog and Toad Together*

by Arnold Lobel

**SUMMARY** This chapter book includes five stories about Toad and his friend Frog. Impetuous Toad and wise Frog explore experiences such as planning for a day, planting a garden, learning about will power, and dealing with fear.

**ABOUT THE AUTHOR** **Arnold Lobel** wrote and illustrated almost 100 children's books. His books have won many awards, including a Newbery Honor award for *Frog and Toad Together*. The *Frog and Toad* series was the basis of a 2003 Broadway musical.

## Discuss Genre and Set Purpose

**FICTION** Read the Table of Contents and look through the book with children. Help them identify characteristics of fiction, including make-believe characters, different settings, and events.

**SET PURPOSE** Help children set a purpose for reading, such as to figure out the lesson or message of these Frog and Toad stories.

**TEXT COMPLEXITY RUBRIC**

| Overall Text Complexity | | *Frog and Toad Together* FICTION<br>ACCESSIBLE |
|---|---|---|
| Quantitative Measures | Lexile | 330L |
| | Guided Reading Level | K |
| Qualitative Measures | Text Structure | simple, familiar story concepts |
| | Language Conventionality and Clarity | increased, clearly-assigned dialogue |
| | Knowledge Demands | clearly fantastical situation |
| | Purpose/Levels of Meaning | single level of simple meaning |

SEGMENT 1 pp. 4–17

### Academic Vocabulary

Read each word with children and discuss its meaning.

**list** (p. 4) • a line of words or sentences written down, one under the other

**seed** (p. 18) • a small part of a plant that can grow into a new plant

**afraid** (p. 22) • thinking something bad is about to happen

**brave** (p. 42) • acting like you have no fear

**dream** (p. 52) • a story that is in your mind while you sleep

## FIRST READ Think Through the Text

Have children use text evidence to answer these questions.

**p. 4** • *Why does Toad make a list?* It will help him remember all the things he needs to do. **RL.K.1, RL.1.1**

**pp. 6–7** • *Why does Toad cross things off his list?* He crosses off things he has done. **RL.K.1, RL.1.1**

**pp. 12–13** • *Why is Toad upset when his list flies away?* He thinks he won't know what to do if he loses his list. **RL.K.1, RL.1.1**

**p. 16** • *What does the picture show about Toad's feelings? Why does he feel the way he does?* He feels sad because he doesn't know what to do. **RL.K.7, RL.1.7**

**p. 17** • *What is the last thing Toad and Frog do?* They go to sleep. **RL.K.3, RL.1.3**

## SECOND READ Analyze the Text

- Revisit page 10. *What kind of character is Frog? What in the story lets you know?* He is kind and friendly. He tells Toad his list is nice. He is willing to do what his friend wants to do. **RL.K.3, RL.1.3**
- Have children reread pp. 12–15. *Why is this part of the story funny?* It is funny that Toad thinks he cannot do something unless it is on his list. **RL.K.1, RL.1.1**
- *On page 17, Toad writes "Go to sleep" on the ground. Why does he do that?* He lost his list so he uses a stick for a pencil and the ground for paper to make a list to write down and cross out the last thing he has to do. **RL.K.1, RL.1.1**
- *Do you think all the things Toad put on his list were necessary to write down? Explain.* No, they were not all necessary. Some things he would remember without writing them down, like getting up, dressing, and eating. **RL.K.1, RL.1.1**
- *What is the lesson the author wants to teach in this story?* It is good to have plans, but we should not depend on them too much. **RL.K.1, RL.1.2**

### ENGLISH LANGUAGE LEARNERS

**Use Sentence Frames**

Use simple yes/no questions to help children understand the plot. *Did Toad make a list? Did Toad erase* wake up? As children are able, have them complete sentence frames using story words and phrases: *Toad made a ___. In bed, Toad crossed out ___.*

### RESPOND TO SEGMENT 1

**Classroom Collaboration**

Have partners work together to create and present a summary, as well as raise questions that might be answered in the next segment.

## ENGLISH LANGUAGE LEARNERS

**Use Gestures**

Help children understand how Toad planted seeds. As you show each action, say the word or phrase. For example, say: *plant*. Mime planting a seed. Continue with other actions such as *shouting, singing, reading poems,* and *playing music*. Have children imitate your actions and repeat the words. Then point to the pictures and have children say the words for the actions.

### RESPOND TO SEGMENT 2

**Classroom Collaboration**

Have small groups work together to summarize what they have read. Have them ask questions about what they don't understand.

**Common Core Connection**

**RL.K.3** identify character, settings, and major events; **RL.K.4** ask and answer questions about unknown words; **RL.K.9** compare and contrast adventures and experiences of characters; **W.K.2** use drawing, dictating, and writing to compose informative/explanatory texts; **W.K.5** respond to questions/suggestions from peers and add details to strengthen writing; **SL.K.6** speak audibly and express thoughts, feelings, and ideas clearly

**RL.1.2** retell stories and demonstrate understanding of the message or lesson; **RL.1.3** describe characters, settings, and major events; **RL.1.9** compare and contrast adventures and experiences of characters; **RL.1.10** read prose and poetry; **W.1.2** write informative/explanatory texts; **W.1.5** focus on a topic, respond to questions/suggestions from peers, and add details to strengthen writing; **SL.1.6** produce complete sentences when appropriate to task and situation

## FIRST READ Think Through the Text

Have children use text evidence to answer these questions.

**pp. 21–22** • *What does Toad do when his flower seeds do not grow right away? Does it work? He yells, "Now seeds, start growing." It does not work.* **RL.K.3, RL.1.3**

**pp. 24–27** • *Retell what things Toad tries next to make the seeds grow. He tells stories, sings songs, reads poems, and plays music.* **RL.K.1, RL.1.2**

**pp. 28–29** • *What happens at the end of the story? The seeds grow and make a beautiful garden.* **RL.K.3, RL.1.3**

**p. 32** • *What is the problem in this story? Toad and Frog can't stop eating cookies. They will get sick.* **RL.K.3, RL.1.3**

**p. 40** • *What does Frog do to solve the problem with the cookies? He gives the rest to the birds to eat.* **RL.K.3, RL.1.3**

## SECOND READ Analyze the Text

- *The stories, poems, and music Toad shares with his seeds are not what really make the flowers grow. What makes them grow? What page of the story helps you know that? What really makes the seeds grow is sun, rain, and time. On page 23 Frog tells Toad that.* **RL.K.1, RL.1.1**
- *The friends try different ways to make themselves stop eating the cookies. Why does the last way work when the others don't? When the friends put the cookies in a box, tie them up, and put them on a shelf, they are still there. When they feed them to the birds, they are gone.* **RL.K.1, RL.1.1**
- *What kind of an eater is Toad? What kind of an eater is Frog? Explain how you know. Toad eats too much. He keeps eating even if it will make him sick. Frog is a sensible eater. He knows it is a good idea to use will power.* **RL.K.9, RL.1.9**
- *What do you think will happen after Toad bakes a cake? Why?* Sample answer: *He will eat too much cake. I think this because he tells Frog he can keep all the will power. This means that Toad doesn't want to use will power.* **RL.K.1, RL.1.1**
- *What lesson can we learn from Frog and Toad in "Cookies"?* Sample answer: *We can learn that it is okay to enjoy things we like, but we should not overdo it.* **RL.K.1, RL.1.2**

SEGMENT 3 pp. 42–64

## FIRST READ Think Through the Text

Have children use text evidence to answer these questions.

**p. 44** • *Why do Frog and Toad decide to climb the mountain?* They want to see if they are brave. RL.K.1, RL.1.1

**p. 46** • *What is an avalanche? How do you know?* It is when rocks roll down a mountain. The author says that many large stones were rolling down the mountain and the picture shows it. RL.K.4, RL.1.1

**pp. 52–53** • *What does the author tell us that explains the picture?* Toad is dreaming that he is on a stage. RL.K.7, RL.1.7

**pp. 54–59** • *What are some things we learn that Toad is good at doing?* He can play the piano, walk on a high wire, and dance. RL.K.1, RL.1.1

**p. 62** • *What makes Toad wake up from his dream?* Frog wakes him up. RL.K.1, RL.1.1

## SECOND READ Analyze the Text

- Revisit the pictures on pp. 45–49. *How does Toad feel? How does Frog feel? Explain how the pictures help you know.* They are both afraid. You can tell from the looks on their faces. You can tell because they are running away from danger. RL.K.7, RL.1.7
- *Do you think Frog and Toad are brave or not? Explain.* Sample answer: *I think they are brave. They don't give up. They keep climbing until they get to the top of the mountain even though scary things happen.* RL.K.1, RL.1.1
- *Why does Frog look smaller and smaller as Toad performs?* Toad becomes more and more proud. He starts to think he is bigger and better than Frog. RL.K.1, RL.1.1
- *Explain what happens at the end of the story.* Toad gets upset because he is afraid he is going to lose his friend. Then Frog wakes him up. Toad realizes how important his friend is to him. RL.K.3, RL.1.3
- *What is the author's message in "The Dream"?* Sample answer: *It is important to think about how our actions affect the feelings of others.* RL.K.1, RL.1.2

# Independent/Self-Selected Reading

If children have already demonstrated comprehension of *Frog and Toad Together,* have them practice the skills using another independent reading book. Model selecting a book from the classroom library. Help children read the title of the book, the author's name, and any information about the book on the back or inside cover. Suggested titles:

- *George and Martha* by James Marshall
- *Frog and Toad Are Friends* by Arnold Lobel RL.1.10

### WRITE & PRESENT

1. Have small groups refer to the text to identify and discuss a lesson they learned about friendship from each of the stories. Encourage them to ask and answer questions they have about text details. RL.K.1, RL.1.2
2. Individual children write and draw about an important lesson they learned about friendship from reading Toad and Frog's adventures. Tell them to begin with the big idea about what they learned. Ask them to include examples and details from the story to explain the lesson. W.K.2, W.1.2
3. Have children share their drawing or writing with partners and get ideas for editing. W.K.5, W.1.5
4. Have children show their pictures and read their lessons about friendship to the class. SL.K.6, SL.1.6
5. Individual children turn in their final drawings and writing to the teacher.

*See Copying Masters, pp. 242–245.*

### STUDENT CHECKLIST

**Writing**

- ✔ Draw or write an idea about being a good friend.
- ✔ Include details from the story about how to be a good friend.
- ✔ Use correct language conventions.

**Speaking & Listening**

- ✔ Read in a clear voice.
- ✔ Read loudly enough for classmates to hear.
- ✔ Ask and answer questions to clarify what a speaker says.

## OBJECTIVES

- Compare and contrast story elements
- Retell a story
- Interpret illustrations
- Make predictions
- Analyze text using text evidence

**_Owl at Home_ is broken into three instructional segments.**

**SEGMENTS**



### Options for Reading

**Independent** Children read the book independently or with the teacher and then answer the teacher's questions.

**Supported** Children read a story and answer questions with teacher support.

# *Owl at Home*

## by Arnold Lobel

**SUMMARY** The book includes five stories about Owl. Each involves a humorous situation created by the way Owl understands things, from bumps in his bed to the moon overhead.

**ABOUT THE AUTHOR Arnold Lobel** wrote and illustrated almost 100 books. Many of them feature animals who help readers learn about how to be a good friend. In addition to fantasies, Lobel also wrote poetry. Lobel's book *Fables* won the Caldecott Medal in 1981.

## Discuss Genre and Set Purpose

**FICTION** Look at the book with children, flipping through the pages and viewing the illustrations. Read the title and the name of the author/illustrator. Ask children to tell how they know this book tells a story, rather than gives information and facts.

**SET PURPOSE** Help children set a purpose for reading, such as to find out what kinds of experiences Owl has that real owls do not.

### TEXT COMPLEXITY RUBRIC

| Overall Text Complexity | | ***Owl at Home*** FICTION<br>ACCESSIBLE |
|---|---|---|
| Quantitative Measures | Lexile | 370L |
| | Guided Reading Level | J |
| Qualitative Measures | Text Structure | one consistent point of view |
| | Language Conventionality and Clarity | some figurative language |
| | Knowledge Demands | clearly fantastical situation |
| | Purpose/Levels of Meaning | single level of complex meaning |

### Common Core Connection

**RL.K.1** ask and answer questions about key details; **RL.K.3** identify characters, settings, and major events; **RL.K.4** ask and answer questions about unknown words; **RL.K.5** recognize common types of texts; **RL.K.7** describe the relationship between illustrations and the story; **RL.K.9** compare and contrast adventures and experiences of characters

**RL.1.1** ask and answer questions about key details; **RL.1.3** describe characters, settings, and major events; **RL.1.5** explain major differences between story books and informational books; **RL.1.7** use illustrations and details to describe characters, settings, or events; **RL.1.9** compare and contrast adventures and experiences of characters

## SEGMENT 1 pp. 5–18

### Academic Vocabulary

Read each word with children and discuss its meaning.

**whirled** (p. 13) • turned quickly
**whooshed** (p. 13) • made a rushing sound
**guest** (p. 13) • a visitor
**pleasant** (p. 21) • giving happiness

## FIRST READ Think Through the Text

Have children use text evidence to answer these questions.

**p. 5 •** *What season is it? How does the author let you know? It is winter. The author says it is cold and snowy. He shows Owl sitting by a fire.* RL.K.3, RL.1.3

**pp. 6–8 •** *What are the banging and pounding sounds Owl hears? He hears the wind and snow beating against his door.* RL.K.1, RL.1.1

**pp. 9–12 •** *What do the pictures show? They show the wind and snow coming into Owl's house and making it cold.* RL.K.7, RL.1.7

**pp. 12–13 •** *What does the word* flap *mean? How do you know? It means to go up and down. The picture shows what it means.* RL.K.4, RL.1.1

**pp. 15–16 •** *How does Owl get his home warm again? He keeps the door closed. Then he makes a new fire.* RL.K.1, RL.1.1

## SECOND READ Analyze the Text

- Have children reread page 13. Ask: *How do you think Owl feels? What makes you think so?* Sample answer: *He is angry. He was nice to invite winter in. Now, winter is messing up his house.* RL.K.1, RL.1.1
- *What do you think Owl will do the next time he hears the wind and snow pounding at his door? Why do you think so? He will not open the door. He told Winter not to come back.* RL.K.1, RL.1.1
- *Did the author want to teach facts about winter or tell a story? tell a story Which parts of this story could happen in real life? If someone opens a door in winter, it does make the house feel cold.* RL.K.5, RL.1.5
- Help children recall the adventures and experiences of Owl in "The Guest." Then ask them to think about the owl in "The Owl and the Pussy-Cat" or another character in a book they read recently. Ask: *How are the characters alike? How are they different?* Sample answer: *Both owls do things that real owls can't do, such as talk and have adventures. They are different because one owl is at home and one is on a boat.* RL.K.9, RL.1.9

### ENGLISH LANGUAGE LEARNERS

**Use Visuals**

Have children use the pictures to understand the story. For example, point to the picture on page 5. Ask: *Is Owl warm or cold?* Look at the picture on page 10 and ask the same question. Encourage children to use other words to describe what is happening: *Owl is ___. happy, peaceful, cold, upset, angry*

### RESPOND TO SEGMENT 1

**Classroom Collaboration**

Have partners work together to create and present a summary, as well as raise questions that might be answered in the next segment.

## ENGLISH LANGUAGE LEARNERS

**Use Gestures**

Guide children in acting out the story. As you read page 31 aloud, act out getting out a kettle, putting it on your lap, and beginning to cry. Have children imitate what you do as you reread the page. Continue in this manner for other key parts of the story. Then ask questions: *What does Owl get out? Where does he put it? What does he do next?*

## RESPOND TO SEGMENT 2

**Classroom Collaboration**

Have small groups work together to summarize what they have read. Have them ask questions about what they don't understand.

**Common Core Connection**

**RL.K.1** ask and answer questions about key details; **RL.K.2** retell familiar stories; **RL.K.3** identify characters, settings, and major events; **RL.K.9** compare and contrast adventures and experiences of characters; **W.K.2** use drawing, dictating, and writing to compose informative/explanatory texts; **W.K.5** respond to questions/suggestions from peers and add details to strengthen writing; **SL.K.4** describe familiar people, places, things, and events/provide detail

**RL.1.1** ask and answer questions about key details; **RL.1.2** retell stories and demonstrate understanding of the message or lesson; **RL.1.3** describe characters, settings, and major events; **RL.1.9** compare and contrast adventures and experiences of characters; **RL.1.10** read prose and poetry; **W.1.2** write informative/explanatory texts; **W.1.5** focus on a topic, respond to questions/suggestions from peers and add details to strengthen writing; **SL.1.4** describe people, places, things, and events with details/express ideas and feelings clearly

### Academic Vocabulary

Read each word with children and discuss its meaning.

**kettle** (p. 31) • a pot for boiling water

**tear** (p. 31) • a drop of water that comes from your eye

**tea** (p. 31) • a drink made by boiling dried leaves

**sobbed** (p. 35) • cried hard

## FIRST READ Think Through the Text

Have children use text evidence to answer these questions.

**p. 19 •** ***When does the story happen? How do you know?*** *It happens at night. I know because Owl is in bed and it's dark in his room.* **RL.K.3, RL.1.3**

**pp. 19–29 •** ***Retell what happens to Owl.*** *He is ready to go to sleep. He sees bumps in his bed. He cannot figure out what they are. He can't get to sleep. He goes downstairs and sleeps in his chair.* **RL.K.2, RL.1.2**

**pp. 31–33 •** ***Why does Owl want to think of sad things?*** *He wants to make himself cry. He wants to use his tears as tea water.* **RL.K.3, RL.1.3**

**pp. 32–36 •** ***What is one sad thing he thinks about?*** Sample answer: *He thinks about books that have missing pages, so no one can read them.* **RL.K.1, RL.1.1**

**pp. 37–38 •** ***Why did Owl stop crying?*** *The kettle was full of water.* **RL.K.3, RL.1.3**

## SECOND READ Analyze the Text

- ***How do you think Owl feels when he leaves his bed and goes downstairs? Explain why.*** Sample answer: *He feels afraid because he doesn't know what the bumps are.* **RL.K.3, RL.1.3**
- ***What are the bumps in Owl's bed?*** *They are his feet.* ***Which sentence is a hint that lets you know?*** Sample answer: *One hint is the last sentence on page 23.* **RL.K.1, RL.1.1**
- ***How could Owl solve the mystery?*** Sample answer: *He could reach down and feel the bumps under the covers. He would feel his hand on his feet and know what the bumps are.* **RL.K.1, RL.1.1**
- ***Why are chairs with broken legs sad?*** *No one can sit in them.* ***What is something else sad that Owl could have thought about?*** Sample answer: *He could have thought about mittens that are useless because one is lost.* **RL.K.1, RL.1.1**
- ***How do you know that Owl has made tear-water tea before?*** *On page 39, Owl says that tear-water tea is always good. He wouldn't know that if he hadn't had it before.* **RL.K.1, RL.1.1**

**Academic Vocabulary**

Read each word with children and discuss its meaning.

**following** (p. 54) • coming after

**sailed** (p. 58) • moved smoothly

## FIRST READ Think Through the Text

Have children use text evidence to answer these questions.

**pp. 41–42** • *What is Owl's problem? If he is upstairs, he wants to be downstairs. If he is downstairs, he wants to be upstairs.* **RL.K.2, RL.1.3**

**pp. 43–45** • *How does he try to solve the problem? He tries running up and down the stairs faster and faster.* **RL.K.3, RL.1.3**

**p. 54** • *What does Owl think the moon is doing? He thinks it is leaving the seashore and coming home with him.* **RL.K.3, RL.1.3**

## SECOND READ Analyze the Text

- Have children reread pages 43–45. *Could Owl ever run fast enough to be upstairs and downstairs at the same time? Explain. He couldn't. It isn't possible to be in two places at once.* **RL.K.1, RL.1.1**
- *Explain why the ending of the story is funny. Now Owl is not upstairs or downstairs. He is in the middle.* **RL.K.1, RL.1.1**
- Review pages 60–61. *Explain what Owl thinks has happened. He thinks the moon has gone back to the seashore.* **RL.K.1, RL.1.1**
- *How does Owl feel at the beginning, middle, and end of the story? Why? He feels happy at the beginning because he thinks the moon is his friend. He feels worried in the middle because he thinks the moon is coming home with him. He is happy in the end because he sees the moon outside of his house.* **RL.K.3, RL.1.3**
- Help children retell "Owl and the Moon." Then ask them to recall the adventures of the owl in "The Owl and the Pussy-Cat" or those of another character in a recently read book. Ask: *How are their adventures alike?* Sample answer: *Both adventures happen at night.* **RL.K.9, RL.1.9**

## Independent/Self-Selected Reading

If children have already demonstrated comprehension of *Owl at Home*, have them practice the skills using another independent reading book. Suggested titles:

- *Mouse Tales* by Arnold Lobel
- *Harold and the Purple Crayon* by Crockett Johnson **RL.1. 10**

### WRITE & PRESENT

1. Make a T-chart. Head one side *Owl at Home* and the other "The Owl and the Pussy-Cat" or the title of another book children have read recently. Have children recall elements of each, such as characters, setting, and events. Record their ideas in the appropriate spaces of the chart. **RL.K.3, RL.1.3**
2. Have each child use the chart to note similarities and differences between the two pieces of literature. Have them draw and write about how the experiences and adventures of the two owls are the same and different. **W.K.2, W.1.2**
3. Have children share their drawings or writing with partners to get ideas for editing. **W.K.5, W.1.5**
4. Have children show or read their work to the class. **SL.K.4, SL.1.4**
5. Individual children turn in their final letters to the teacher.

*See Copying Masters, pp. 242–245.*

### STUDENT CHECKLIST

**Writing**

- ✔ Draw and write about the owls in *Owl at Home* and "The Owl and the Pussy-Cat."
- ✔ Include at least one way the owls' adventures are the same and one way they are different.
- ✔ Use correct language conventions.

**Speaking & Listening**

- ✔ Describe events including details.
- ✔ Ask and answer questions to clarify what a speaker says.
- ✔ Express ideas and opinions clearly.

## OBJECTIVES

- Explain major differences between story books and poetry
- Use illustrations and details to describe characters, settings, or events
- Ask and answer questions about key details

***Pancakes for Breakfast*** **is broken into three instructional segments.**

**SEGMENTS**



### Options for Reading

**Independent** Children read the book independently or with a partner and then answer questions posed by the teacher.

**Supported** Children read a segment and answer questions with teacher support.

### Common Core Connection

**RL.K.1** ask and answer questions about key details; **RL.K.3** identify characters, settings, and major events; **RL.K.4** ask and answer questions about unknown words; **RL.K.7** describe the relationship between illustrations and the story

**RL.1.1** ask and answer questions about key details; **RL.1.3** describe characters, settings, and major events; **RL.1.7** use illustrations and details to describe characters, settings, or events

# Pancakes for Breakfast

by Tomie dePaola

**SUMMARY** This wordless picture book is about what a farm woman has to do to get the ingredients for a pancake breakfast.

**ABOUT THE AUTHOR** **Tomie dePaola** has written or illustrated nearly 250 books in 40 years in publishing. His books have won many honors, including the Caldecott Honor and the Newbery Honor. He lives in New Hampshire with his dog and works out of a 200-year-old barn.

## Discuss Genre and Set Purpose

**FICTION** Look at the book with children. Guide them to note that it is a wordless picture book. As you page through the book, elicit some of the characteristics of a story book, or fiction: It has made-up characters and a plot. A plot is what happens in the story.

**SET PURPOSE** Help children set a purpose for reading, such as to find out what happens first, next, and last in the plot of the story.

**TEXT COMPLEXITY RUBRIC**

| Overall Text Complexity | | *Pancakes for Breakfast* FICTION<br>ACCESSIBLE |
|---|---|---|
| Quantitative Measures | Lexile | N/A |
| | Guided Reading Level | N/A |
| Qualitative Measures | Text Structure | simple, linear chronology |
| | Language Conventionality and Clarity | clear, direct language |
| | Knowledge Demands | single perspective |
| | Purpose/Levels of Meaning | single level of simple meaning |

SEGMENT 1 pp. 5–13

### Academic Vocabulary

Read each word with children and discuss its meaning.

**sift** (p. 11) • to pass through a screen to break up larger parts

**ingredients** (p. 11) • the parts of a mixture

**batter** (p. 11) • a thick mixture used to make things such as cakes

## FIRST READ Think Through the Illustrations

Have children use illustrations to answer these questions.

**p. 5** • ***Look at the picture on this page. Where does this story take place?*** *in a red house in the winter in the country* **RL.K.3, RL.1.3**

**pp. 6–7** • ***Who are the characters in the story?*** *There is a woman, a dog, and a cat.* **RL.K.3, RL.1.3**

**pp. 8–9** • ***What is the woman in the story thinking about doing? How do you know?*** *She is thinking about pancakes. The picture shows a thought bubble with a stack of pancakes.* **RL.K.7, RL.1.7**

**pp. 10–11** • ***What is the woman reading?*** *a cookbook with a recipe for pancakes* ***What ingredients does she need?*** *flour, baking powder, butter, sugar, salt, eggs, milk* **RL.K.1, RL.1.1**

**pp. 12–13** • ***What is the woman missing? How will she get the missing ingredient?*** *She does not have any eggs. She goes to the barn to get the eggs from the chickens.* **RL.K.1, RL.1.1**

## SECOND READ Analyze the Illustrations

- Ask children to look back over pages 5-13. *How can you tell what is happening in the story? You have to look at the pictures to see what is happening.* **RL.K.7, RL.1.7**
- Guide children to look back at page 9. Help them read the directions for making pancakes. Then ask: *What does the woman have to do first? Sift all dry ingredients into a bowl.* Then ask children to look at the series of illustrations on pages 10 and 11. Ask: *What is the woman doing in these pictures? Getting out the bowl and the flour and then sifting the flour.* **RL.K.1, RL.1.1**
- *How does the first illustration on page 11 help you understand the meaning of the word sift? It shows the woman using a kitchen tool to break up the flour into the bowl.* **RL.K.4, RL.1.1**
- *On page 12 the woman goes out to get eggs from the chickens. What do you think she will do next? She will go back to the kitchen to finish making the pancakes.* **RL.K.1, RL.1.1**

### ENGLISH LANGUAGE LEARNERS

**Use Visuals**

Help children use the illustrations to build vocabulary. Point to the dog and cat on pages 6 and 7, say their names, and have children repeat after you. Then ask children to point to other things in the pictures and say their names.

### RESPOND TO SEGMENT 1

**Classroom Collaboration**

Have partners work together to identify the main character in the story and describe what she is doing. Have them discuss what has already happened and what they think will happen in the next part of the story.

**ENGLISH LANGUAGE LEARNERS**

**Use Gestures**

Have children act out the story events. For example, ask them to pretend to wake up in the morning or walk outside to get eggs. As children act out the events, ask them to describe what they are doing.

**RESPOND TO SEGMENT 2**

**Classroom Collaboration**

Have small groups work together to summarize what they have read so far. Encourage them to ask questions about what they did not understand.

**Common Core Connection**

**RL.K.1** ask and answer questions about key details; **RL.K.3** identify characters, settings, and major events; **RL.K.5** recognize common types of texts; **RL.K.7** describe the relationship between illustrations and the story; **W.K.2** use drawing, dictating, and writing to compose informative/explanatory texts; **W.K.5** respond to questions/suggestions from peers and add details to strengthen writing; **SL.K.6** speak audibly and express thoughts, feelings, and ideas clearly

**RL.1.1** ask and answer questions about key details; **RL.1.3** describe characters, settings, and major events; **RL.1.7** use illustrations and details to describe characters, settings, or events; **RL.1.10** read prose and poetry; **W.1.2** write informative/explanatory texts; **W.1.5** focus on a topic, respond to questions/suggestions from peers, and add details to strengthen writing; **SL.1.4** describe people, places, things, and events with details/express ideas and feelings clearly

## FIRST READ Think Through the Illustrations

Have children use the illustrations to answer these questions.

**pp. 14–17** • *What ingredient is the woman in the story missing now? What does she do to get some? The woman is out of milk. She goes out to the barn and milks the cow to get some more milk.* **RL.K.1, RL.1.1**

**pp. 18–19** • *Look at the clock in the picture. What does it tell you about how long it takes the woman to churn the butter? The clock shows that a lot of time has passed. That means the woman took a long time to churn the butter.* **RL.K.7, RL.1.7**

**pp. 20–23** • *Now that the woman has all the ingredients to make the pancakes, what is she still missing? She does not have any syrup to put on top of her pancakes. How do you know? The woman looks unhappy as she holds a jug that says* maple syrup. **RL.K.3, RL.1.3**

## SECOND READ Analyze the Illustrations

- Guide children to look at the illustrations on pages 18–19. Explain that the barrel-like object with the long stick is called a butter churn and that it was used long ago to make butter. *How do you think the woman is feeling as she makes butter? How can you tell?* Sample answer: *The woman's face looks happy at first and then it looks sad. I think that she is working for a long time and she is feeling tired.* **RL.K.3, RL.1.3**
- *Do you think this story takes place now or long ago? Why do you think so?* Sample answer: *It takes place long ago. The woman wears a long dress, has to get eggs from chickens and milk from cows, and uses a churn to make butter. This is how people did things long ago.* **RL.K.3, RL.1.3**
- Have children look at the other characters in the story, the cat and dog. *What are they doing as the woman is working? They are watching her work, but also watching the food. What do you think will happen when the woman goes out to get the syrup?* Sample answer: *The dog and cat might try to eat the food.* **RL.K.3, RL.1.3**
- Display and read the poem "Mix a Pancake," on Copying Master p. 180. Ask: *How is "Mix a Pancake" like this book? They are both about the steps in making pancakes.* **RL.K.1, RL.1.1**

## FIRST READ Think Through the Illustrations

Have children use the illustrations to answer the following questions.

**pp. 24–25** • *What is the woman thinking about as she walks back home? She is thinking about making and eating her pancakes. How do you know? The thought bubbles in the pictures show what the woman is thinking.*
RL.K.1, RL.1.1

**pp. 26–27** • *What happens next in the story? When the woman gets home, she finds that the dog and the cat have eaten all of her ingredients.*
RL.K.3, RL.1.3

**pp. 28–32** • *How does the woman solve this last problem? The woman smells the food from next door. She goes next door to have breakfast.*
RL.K.3, RL.1.3

## SECOND READ Analyze the Illustrations

- Guide children to review the last part of the story. Ask: *After the woman got all of her ingredients, what happened? After she got everything, the dog and the cat ate all the food. There was nothing left for her to make pancakes. Was the woman still able to have pancakes for breakfast? How did she get them? The woman went across to her neighbors' house because they were having pancakes.* RL.K.3, RL.1.3
- Say: *Think about all the work that went into making those pancakes, and all the trouble the woman had. How do you think she felt after she ate the pancakes? She probably felt happy.* RL.K.7, RL.1.7
- Ask children to look back through the book to ask questions about anything they didn't understand. Then encourage them to try to find the answers to their questions by looking carefully at the pictures. RL.K.1, RL.1.1

## Independent/Self-Selected Reading

If children have already demonstrated comprehension of *Pancakes for Breakfast,* have them practice the skills using another independent reading book. Model selecting a book from the classroom library. Help children read the title of the book, the author's name, and any information about the book on the back or inside cover. Suggested titles:

- *Goodnight, Gorilla* by Peggy Rathman
- *The Snowy Day* by Ezra Jack Keats RL.1.10

### WRITE & PRESENT

1. Provide small groups with copies of the poem "Mix a Pancake." (See p. 180.) Have them discuss how they know that it is a poem and that *Pancakes for Breakfast* is a story book. Encourage them to ask and answer any questions they have about illustrations or other details. RL.K.5, RL.1.1
2. Individual children write to explain how they can distinguish between a story book and a poem. Have children draw a picture to support their writing. W.K.2, W.1.2
3. Children within each group share their writing and edit their work to add details about *Pancakes for Breakfast* and "Mix a Pancake." W.K.5, W.1.5
4. Have children share their writing with the class and then turn in their final drafts to the teacher. SL.K.6, SL.1.4

*See Copying Masters, p. 242–245.*

### STUDENT CHECKLIST

#### Writing

- ✔ Write about how to distinguish between a story book and a poem.
- ✔ Include details about illustrations.
- ✔ Use correct language conventions.

#### Speaking & Listening

- ✔ Participate effectively in a collaborative discussion.
- ✔ Ask and answer questions about details in illustrations.
- ✔ Demonstrate a connection between illustrations and their own writing.

### OBJECTIVES

- Use illustrations and details to describe characters and major events
- Ask and answer questions about key details
- Analyze text using text evidence

***Hi! Fly Guy* is broken into three instructional segments.**

**SEGMENTS**



**Options for Reading**

**Independent** Children read the book independently or with a partner and then answer questions posed by the teacher.

**Supported** Children read a segment and answer questions with teacher support.

**Common Core Connection**

**RL.K.1** ask and answer questions about key details; **RL.K.3** identify characters, settings, and major events; **RL.K.7** describe the relationship between illustrations and the story

**RL.1.1** ask and answer questions about key details; **RL.1.3** describe characters, settings, and major events; **RL.1.7** use illustrations and details to describe characters, setting, or events

# *Hi! Fly Guy*

by Tedd Arnold

**SUMMARY** This humorous story is about a boy who becomes friends with a fly and enters it in a pet competition, in spite of being told repeatedly that a fly cannot be a pet.

**ABOUT THE AUTHOR** Tedd Arnold is the author of more than 50 books for children. He took his first art lessons in an abandoned dentist's office in Florida. He later got a fine arts degree from the University of Florida. Among his hobbies, Arnold enjoys coin collecting and playing tennis.

## Discuss Genre and Set Purpose

**FICTION** Look at the story with children. Discuss how they can tell that *Hi! Fly Guy* is a story and not poetry or informational text. Guide them to point out the cartoon-like illustrations, especially those of the smiling fly.

**SET PURPOSE** Help children set a purpose for reading, such as to find out who Fly Guy is and what happens to him.

**TEXT COMPLEXITY RUBRIC**

| Overall Text Complexity | | *Hi! Fly Guy* FICTION<br>ACCESSIBLE |
|---|---|---|
| Quantitative Measures | Lexile | 280L |
| | Guided Reading Level | H |
| Qualitative Measures | Text Structure | simple, linear chronology |
| | Language Conventionality and Clarity | increased, clearly-assigned dialogue |
| | Knowledge Demands | experience includes unfamiliar aspects |
| | Purpose/Levels of Meaning | single level of simple meaning |

## SEGMENT 1 pp. 1–9

**Academic Vocabulary**

Read each word with children and discuss its meaning.

**amazing** (p. 4) • wonderful

**surprised** (p. 9) • amazed because something is not expected

**pest** (p. 12) • something that annoys or bothers

**rescue** (p. 13) • the act of saving from a bad situation

## FIRST READ Think Through the Text

Have children use text evidence to answer these questions.

**pp. 1–3** • *Who are the characters in the story? a boy and a fly How do you know? Page 1 shows and tells about a fly. Page 3 shows and tells about a boy.* **RL.K.3, RL.1.3**

**p. 2** • *What is the fly looking for? something to eat* **RL.K.1, RL.1.1**

**pp. 4–5** • *What is the boy looking for? The boy is looking for a pet. How do you know? The text on page 4 says that he was looking to catch something for The Amazing Pet Show.* **RL.K.1, RL.1.1**

**pp. 8–9** • *Why does the boy say that the fly is the smartest pet in the world? The boy thinks that the fly knows his name. Why does the fly say* buzz*? He was angry, and buzz is what flies say.* **RL.K.1, RL.1.1**

## SECOND READ Analyze the Text

- *Look at the illustration on pages 4 and 5. What can you tell about the kind of pet the boy wants?* Sample answer: *The boy has a cage, a jar, a fishing pole, and other things that could help him catch different kinds of pets. It looks like he wants to catch any kind of pet he happens to find.* **RL.K.1, RL.1.1**
- *Look at the illustration on page 7. How does the boy feel when he catches the fly? How do you know? He feels happy; I can tell because he is smiling as he looks at the jar holding the fly.* **RL.K.7, RL.1.7**
- *How does the fly feel when he gets caught? Explain all the ways you know. The text says that the fly was mad and that he stomped his foot. The picture shows an angry fly stomping his foot. The word* BUZZ *is printed in large orange capital letters surrounded with red to show you how he said* buzz. **RL.K.7, RL.1.7**

### ENGLISH LANGUAGE LEARNERS

**Use Visuals**

Point to different illustrations and ask questions to help children understand the plot. For example, for pages 4 and 5, ask: *Is the boy going to catch a pet or going home? He is going to catch a pet.* Then ask children to use clues from the pictures to explain their answers.

### RESPOND TO SEGMENT 1

**Classroom Collaboration**

Have small groups work together to summarize what they have read so far. Encourage them to ask questions about what they did not understand.

## ENGLISH LANGUAGE LEARNERS

**Use Peer-Supported Learning**

Have partners with different English language proficiency work together to ask and answer questions about the pets on pages 18–19. For example, *What is the animal with the long neck?* *a giraffe*

## RESPOND TO SEGMENT 2

**Classroom Collaboration**

Have partners work together to create and present a summary, as well as raise questions that might be answered in the next segment.

**Common Core Connection**

**RL.K.1** ask and answer questions about key details; **RL.K.3** identify characters, settings, and major events; **RL.K.4** ask and answer questions about unknown words; **RL.K.7** describe the relationship between illustrations and the story; **RL.K.9** compare and contrast adventures and experiences of characters; **W.K.2** use drawing, dictating, and writing to compose informative/explanatory texts; **W.K.5** respond to questions/suggestions from peers and add details to strengthen writing; **SL.K.2** confirm understanding of a text read aloud, information presented orally, or through other media by asking/answering questions and requesting clarification

**RL.1.1** ask and answer questions about key details; **RL.1.3** describe characters, settings, and major events; **RL.1.4** identify words and phrases that suggest feelings or appeal to senses; **RL.1.7** use illustrations and details to describe characters, setting, or events; **RL.1.9** compare and contrast adventures and experiences of characters; **RL.1.10** read prose and poetry; **W.1.2** write informative/explanatory texts; **W.1.5** focus on a topic, respond to questions/suggestions from peers, and add details to strengthen writing; **SL.1.2** ask and answer questions about details in a text read aloud, information presented orally, or through other media

## FIRST READ Think Through the Text

Have children use text evidence to answer these questions.

**pp. 10–12** • *How do Buzz's parents feel about Buzz having a fly for a pet? How do you know? Buzz's parents don't like him having a fly for a pet. His dad says that flies are pests, not pets. He tries to swat the fly.* **RL.K.3, RL.1.3**

**pp. 13–14** • *What makes Buzz's parents change their mind about his pet? When the fly says* Buzz *they say that he is smart. Now they think Buzz can have a fly for a pet.* **RL.K.1, RL.1.1**

**pp. 15–16** • *What evidence shows that Fly Guy is also happy about being Buzz's pet? After Buzz feeds Fly Guy, the story says that he is happy and the picture shows that he is stuffed full.* **RL.K.7, RL.1.7**

## SECOND READ Analyze the Text

- Have children look at pages 12 and 13. Say, *Both Buzz and his dad think Fly Guy is smart. Do you agree? Why or why not? Use examples from the text to tell why you think so.* Sample answer: *Fly Guy is smart because he flies on Buzz's nose to keep from getting swatted. He also says* Buzz *when Buzz speaks to him.* **RL.K.1, RL.1.1**
- Ask children to look back at the word *buzz* on pages 8, 12, and 14. *How does Fly Guy feel when he says* buzz *the first time? angry the second time? scared the third time? happy What clues does the type give you to help you figure this out? The color and size of the word* buzz *and the speech balloon help you know how Fly Guy feels. For example, when Fly Guy is angry, the speech balloon is red, but when he is happy, it is green.* **RL.K.4, RL.1.4**
- Guide children to look back at the first and second chapters. Say, *In the first chapter, Buzz is looking for a smart pet and the fly is looking for something to eat. Do they both get what they are looking for? How do you know?* Sample answer: *They both get what they are looking for. Buzz gets a smart pet in Fly Guy because Fly Guy can say Buzz's name. Fly Guy is looking for food, and Buzz gives him a hot dog, so Fly Guy is happy.* **RL.K.9, RL.1.9**

**SEGMENT 3** pp. 17–30

## FIRST READD Think Through the Text

Have children use text evidence to answer these questions.

**pp. 17–20 •** *What makes Buzz tell Fly Guy that he can't be a pet? The judges say that a fly is not a pet.* **RL.K.3, RL.1.3**

**pp. 21–25 •** *What does Fly Guy do next? Why? Fly Guy does some amazing tricks because he likes Buzz and wants to show the judges that flies can be pets.* **RL.K.1, RL.1.1**

**pp. 26–27 •** *Why do the judges let Fly Guy in the show? Fly Guy knows his jar, so they decide that he is a pet after all.* **RL.K.1, RL.1.1**

## SECOND READ Analyze the Text

- *What do the judges think of Fly Guy by the end? How do you know? The judges think that Fly Guy is very smart. They give him an award for being the smartest pet.* **RL.K.7, RL.1.7**
- *Guide children to review the third chapter. Ask: Why does Fly Guy do all of those tricks to impress the judges? When the judges tell Buzz that he can't have Fly Guy in the show, it makes him sad. Fly Guy wants to get into the show to make Buzz happy because he likes Buzz.* **RL.K.1, RL.1.1**
- Ask: *How do you think Buzz and Fly Guy feel about each other at the end of the book? What does the author say in the story that tells how they feel?* Sample answer: *They probably like each other a lot. The author says that it began a "beautiful friendship."* **RL.K.1, RL.1.4**

# Independent/Self-Selected Reading

If children have already demonstrated comprehension of *Hi! Fly Guy,* have them practice the skills using another independent reading book. Model selecting a book from the classroom library. Help children read the title of the book, the author's name, and any information about the book on the back or inside cover. Suggested titles:

- *Super Fly Guy* by Tedd Arnold
- *Dick Whittington and His Cat* by Marcia Brown **RL.1.10**

### WRITE & PRESENT

1. Have partners discuss how the illustrations help them better understand story events and how Buzz and Fly Guy feel at the beginning, middle, and end of the story. **RL.K.7, RL.1.7**
2. Have individual children write and draw to show story events and how Buzz and Fly Guy feel at the beginning, middle, and end. **W.K.2, W.1.2**
3. Partners reconvene to share and edit their work. **W.K.5, W.1.5**
4. Children present their pictures and text and show how the pictures relate to each sentence. Have them ask and answer questions during the presentations. **SL.K.2, SL.1.2**
5. Individual children turn in their final writing to the teacher.

*See Copying Masters, pp. 242–245.*

### STUDENT CHECKLIST

#### Writing

- ✔ Write and draw to show how Buzz and Fly Guy feel at the beginning, middle, and end.
- ✔ Include details from story text and illustrations.
- ✔ Use correct language conventions.

#### Speaking & Listening

- ✔ Participate in collaborative conversations.
- ✔ Ask and answer questions about details in the text and illustrations.
- ✔ Logically present claims and findings.
- ✔ Describe details in their own writing that relate to events and characters in *Hi! Fly Guy.*

### OBJECTIVES

- Understand that poetry is a type of writing
- Examine repetition in poetry
- Analyze text using text evidence

### Options for Reading

**Independent** Children read independently or with the teacher and then answer questions posed by the teacher.

**Supported** Children read each line and answer questions with teacher support. Then they read the entire poem independently or with a partner. Encourage children to read at least a few words on their own.

### Common Core Connection

**RL.K.1** ask and answer questions about key details; **RL.K.3** identify characters, settings, and major events; **RL.K.10** engage in group reading activities with purpose and understanding; **RF.K.2a** recognize and produce rhyming words; **W.K.2** use drawing, dictating, and writing to compose informative/explanatory texts; **W.K.5** respond to questions/suggestions from peers and add details to strengthen writing; **SL.K.6** speak audibly and express thoughts, feelings, and ideas clearly

**RL.1.1** ask and answer questions about key details; **RL.1.3** describe characters, settings, and major events; **RL.1.10** read prose and poetry; **RF.1.4b** read on-level text orally with accuracy, appropriate rate, and expression; **W.1.2** write informative/explanatory texts; **W.1.5** focus on a topic, respond to questions/suggestions from peers, and add details to strengthen writing; **SL.1.6** produce complete sentences when appropriate to task and situation

# "As I Was Going to St. Ives"

**SUMMARY** This traditional nursery rhyme ends with a riddle. It is part of a collection titled *Mother Goose Nursery Rhymes*, which includes hundreds of stories, songs, and poems that have been passed down orally from generation to generation. This rhyme first appeared in print around 1730.

## Discuss Genre and Set Purpose

**POETRY** Look at the poem. Guide children to identify characteristics of a poem such as the short lines and the rhymes at the end of the first two lines and last two lines. Tell children that this poem is also a riddle or brain teaser because it has a puzzling question at the end for the reader to solve.

**TEXT FOCUS: Repetition** Explain to children that many poems use repetition. They may repeat certain words or sentence patterns. Poems may also have repeated beginning sounds or ending sounds. Poets may use repetition to emphasize important ideas or merely make the poem sound fun when read aloud.

**SET PURPOSE** Help children set a purpose for reading, such as to find all the ways that repetition is used in this poem.

### TEXT COMPLEXITY RUBRIC

| Overall Text Complexity | | "As I Was Going to St. Ives" POETRY<br>ACCESSIBLE |
|---|---|---|
| Quantitative Measures | Lexile | N/A |
| | Guided Reading Level | N/A |
| Qualitative Measures | Text Structure | less familiar poetic structure |
| | Language Conventionality and Clarity | clear, direct language |
| | Knowledge Demands | single theme |
| | Purpose/Levels of Meaning | single level of simple meaning |

**Academic Vocabulary**

Read each word with children and discuss its meaning.

**wife** (line 3) • a woman who is married

**kits** (line 5) • baby kittens

## FIRST READ Think Through the Text

Have children use text evidence to answer these questions.

- *Where does the rhyme take place?* on the way to St. Ives *How do you know?* The text says "As I was going to St. Ives." RL.K.3, RL.1.3
- *What is this poem mostly about?* Sample answer: who the speaker meets on the way to St. Ives RL.K.1, RL.1.1

## SECOND READ Analyze the Text

- Tell children that this rhyme is a riddle. *What do you have to figure out?* how many are going to St. Ives Give children time to solve it. Then explain: *Only one, the speaker, is going; the rhyme never says that the man with the wives is going to St. Ives.* RL.K.1, RL.1.1
- Reread the rhyme aloud, and have children listen for repetition. Then ask: *Which words rhyme?* Ives/wives *What is repeated in rhyming words?* the ending sounds Then say *kits, cats, sacks. What sound is repeated?* the /k/ sound *Why do you think the poet uses repetition of sounds?* to make the poem sound fun when read aloud RF.K.2a, RL.1.1
- *What number word is repeated?* seven *What sentence pattern is repeated?* And every _____ had seven _____. *Why do you think the poet uses repetition of words and sentence patterns?* to emphasize the idea that there were many kits, cats, sacks, and wives RL.K.1, RL.1.1

## Practice Fluency

**EMPHASIZE RATE** Explain that detailed poems should be read slowly enough so the listener can understand the details, but quickly enough to make the poem fun. Read the poem aloud slowly, then quickly, and then at a moderate rate. Ask children which reading let them both understand the details and hear the fun sounds in the rhyme. RL.1.10

## Independent/Self-Selected Reading

If children have demonstrated comprehension of "As I Was Going to St. Ives," have them use another rhyme to practice skills. Suggested titles:

- *Pocketful of Posies* compiled by Salley Mavor
- *Favorite Nursery Rhymes from Mother Goose* illustrated by Scott Gustafson RL.1.10

### WRITE & PRESENT

1. Have partners refer to the text to discuss its use of repetition. Encourage children to ask and answer questions about details in the rhyme. RL.K.1, RL.1.1
2. Individual children write about at least two ways that the rhyme uses repetition and why each way is used. W.K.2, W.1.2
3. Have children share their writing with their partner. Ask them to add details and edit their writing based on the partner's suggestions. W.K.5, W.1.5
4. Invite children to take turns sharing their sentences with the class. SL.K.6, SL.1.6

*See Copying Masters, pp. 242–245.*

### STUDENT CHECKLIST

**Writing**

- ✔ Write explanatory sentences.
- ✔ Include two ways that "As I Was Going to St. Ives" uses repetition and why each way is used.
- ✔ Use correct language conventions.

**Speaking & Listening**

- ✔ Participate effectively in a collaborative discussion.
- ✔ Ask and answer questions about a rhyme's use of repetition.
- ✔ Demonstrate a connection between features in the rhyme and their own writing.

### OBJECTIVES

- Understand that poetry is a type of writing
- Examine the use of rhythm and rhyme in poetry
- Analyze text using text evidence

### Options for Reading

**Independent** Children read the poem independently or with a partner and then answer questions posed by the teacher.

**Supported** Children read each line and answer questions with teacher support. Then they read the entire poem independently or with a partner. Encourage children to read at least a few words on their own.

### Common Core Connection

**RL.K.1** ask and answer questions about key details; **RL.K.5** recognize common types of texts; **RL.K.10** engage in group reading activities with purpose and understanding; **RF.K.2a** recognize and produce rhyming words; **W.K.2** use drawing, dictating and writing to compose informative/explanatory texts; **W.K.5** respond to questions/suggestions from peers and add details to strengthen writing; **SL.K.6** speak audibly and express thoughts, feelings, and ideas clearly

**RL.1.1** ask and answer questions about key details; **RL.1.10** read prose and poetry; **RF.1.4b** read on-level text orally with accuracy, appropriate rate, and expression; **W.1.2** write informative/explanatory texts; **W.1.5** focus on a topic, respond to questions/suggestions from peers, and add details to strengthen writing; **SL.1.4** describe people, places, things, and events with details/express ideas and feelings clearly

# "Mix a Pancake"

by Christina Rossetti

**SUMMARY** This simple, playful poem is often chanted as a pat-a-cake game with very young children. It explains the steps in making a pancake.

**ABOUT THE AUTHOR** **Christina Rossetti** was a 19th-century British poet who grew up in a family of artists. She wrote about love, nature, and fantasy, in addition to penning her well-known verses for children. Rossetti's most famous collection is titled *Goblin Market and Other Poems*.

## Discuss Genre and Set Purpose

**POETRY** Ask children to look at the poem and explain how they can tell it is a poem and not a story book. Guide them to find and identify some characteristics of poetry in "Mix a Pancake," such as: words are arranged in lines; some words rhyme; some words are repeated.

**TEXT FOCUS: Rhythm** Remind children that most poems have a rhythm, or beat. Explain that poets create rhythm with the words they choose. Some words have strong beats; some do not. Putting strong and weak beats together in a certain order creates a rhythm. Repeating the same words also helps create a rhythm. Point out that rhythm makes reading poetry aloud more fun.

**SET PURPOSE** Help children set a purpose for reading, such as to feel and enjoy the rhythm of the poem.

**TEXT COMPLEXITY RUBRIC**

| Overall Text Complexity | | "Mix a Pancake" POETRY<br>ACCESSIBLE |
|---|---|---|
| Quantitative Measures | Lexile | N/A |
| | Guided Reading Level | N/A |
| Qualitative Measures | Text Structure | simple, familiar poetic structure |
| | Language Conventionality and Clarity | literal, accessible language |
| | Knowledge Demands | simple theme |
| | Purpose/Levels of Meaning | single level of simple meaning |

**Academic Vocabulary**

Read each word with children and discuss its meaning.

**pancake** (line 1) • a flat, thin cake of batter that is cooked in a pan

**stir** (line 2) • to mix together

**toss** (line 5) • to send into the air

## FIRST READ Think Through the Text

Have children use text evidence to answer these questions.

- *What does the poem say are the first two steps in making a pancake?* *mix and stir* RL.K.1, RL.1.1
- Reread the poem chorally with children. Then ask: *What rhyming words do you hear?* *pan/can* *Where do you hear them?* *at the end of lines 3 and 6* *What word is repeated?* *pancake* *Where is it repeated?* *at the end of lines 1, 2, 4, and 5* RF.K.2a, RL.1.1

## SECOND READ Analyze the Text

- Have children clap out the rhythm of the first three lines as they read them aloud. Then have them repeat with the next three lines. *How is the rhythm of lines 4–6 like the rhythm of lines 1–3?* *Both are two claps, two claps, three claps; the rhythm is the same.* RL.K.1, RF.1.4b
- Guide children to summarize the pattern of rhythm, rhyme, and repetition in the poem. *Lines 1–2 have two claps and end with* pancake. *Line 3 has three claps and ends with a rhyming word. This pattern repeats in the next three lines.* RL.K.1, RL.1.1
- Read *Pancakes for Breakfast* by Tomie DePaola. Ask: *How is this book like "Mix a Pancake"?* *They both include the steps in making pancakes.* RL.K.1, RL.1.1

## Practice Fluency

**EMPHASIZE RHYTHM** Remind children that when they read poetry aloud, they may enjoy it more if they emphasize its rhythm. Read the poem's first three lines, ignoring the rhythm. Reread them, emphasizing the beat. Ask children which reading was better. Have them tell why. RF.1.4b

## Independent/Self-Selected Reading

If children have demonstrated comprehension of "Mix a Pancake," have them practice recognizing rhythm in another poem. Model choosing a poem. Help children read the title and the poet's name. Suggested titles:

- *Random House Book of Poetry* compiled by Jack Prelutsky
- *Favorite Poems of Childhood* edited by Philip Smith RL.1.10

### WRITE & PRESENT

1. Provide small groups with *Pancakes for Breakfast* or a similar story book. Have them discuss how they know that it is a story book and "Mix a Pancake" is a poem. Encourage them to ask and answer any questions they have about text details. RL.K.5, RL.1.1
2. Individual children write or dictate sentences that explain how they can distinguish between text that is a story book and text that is a poem. W.K.2, W.1.2
3. Children within each group share their writing and edit their work to add details about *Pancakes for Breakfast* and "Mix a Pancake." W.K.5, W.1.5
4. Have children share their writing with the class, and then turn in their final drafts to the teacher. SL.K.6, SL.1.4

*See Copying Masters, pp. 242–245.*

### STUDENT CHECKLIST

**Writing**

- ✔ Write about how to distinguish between text that is a story book and text that is a poem.
- ✔ Include details about texts.
- ✔ Use correct language conventions.

**Speaking & Listening**

- ✔ Participate effectively in a collaborative discussion.
- ✔ Ask and answer questions about text details.
- ✔ Demonstrate a connection between texts and their own writing.

## OBJECTIVES

- Understand that poetry is a type of writing
- Examine word choice and the use of rhythm to create mood in poetry
- Analyze text using text evidence

### Options for Reading

**Independent** Children read independently or with the teacher and then answer questions posed by the teacher.

**Supported** Children read each line and answer questions with teacher support. Then they read the entire poem independently or with a partner. Encourage children to read at least a few words on their own.

### Common Core Connection

**RL.K.1** ask and answer questions about key details; **RL.K.3** identify characters, settings, and major events; **RL.K.5** recognize common types of texts; **W.K.2** use drawing, dictating, and writing to compose informative/explanatory texts; **W.K.5** respond to questions/suggestions from peers and add details to strengthen writing; **SL.K.6** speak audibly and express thoughts, feelings, and ideas clearly

**RL.1.1** ask and answer questions about key details; **RL.1.3** describe characters, settings, and major events; **RL.1.4** identify words and phrases that suggest feelings or appeal to senses; **RL.1.6** identify who is telling the story; **RL.1.10** read prose and poetry; **RF.1.4b** read on-level text orally with accuracy, appropriate rate, and expression; **W.1.2** write informative/explanatory texts; **W.1.5** focus on a topic, respond to questions/suggestions from peers, and add details to strengthen writing; **SL.1.4** describe people, places, things, and events with details/express ideas and feelings clearly

# "Singing-Time"

## by Rose Fyleman

**SUMMARY** Through rhyme and rhythm, this poem describes the joy of waking up in the morning. The poet uses familiar morning rituals and the repetition of the words "I sing" to evoke the delight of a new day.

**ABOUT THE POET** **Rose Fyleman** was born in England in 1877. A singer and schoolteacher, Fyleman could not find appropriate poetry for her students so she wrote her own to use in the classroom.

## Discuss Genre and Set Purpose

**POETRY** Ask children to look at the poem and explain how they can tell it is a poem and not another kind of text. Remind them poetry is a kind of writing that uses words to express feelings. As you read the poem, discuss words and phrases, such as *I sing*, that express feelings.

**TEXT FOCUS: Mood** Remind children that every poem has a mood, or overall feeling. Poems may have different kinds of moods: happy, sad, angry, and so on. Explain that, to create a mood, poets choose their words carefully. They may also use a certain rhythm, or "beat," that helps the reader understand the poem's mood.

**SET PURPOSE** Help children set a purpose for reading the poem, such as to feel the mood of the poem and understand how it is created. RL.K.5

### TEXT COMPLEXITY RUBRIC

| Overall Text Complexity | | "Singing-Time" POETRY |
|---|---|---|
| | | ACCESSIBLE |
| Quantitative Measures | Lexile | N/A |
| | Guided Reading Level | N/A |
| Qualitative Measures | Text Structure | simple, familiar poetic structure |
| | Language Conventionality and Clarity | clear, direct language |
| | Knowledge Demands | common everyday experience |
| | Purpose/Levels of Meaning | single level of simple meaning |

### Academic Vocabulary

Read each word with children and discuss its meaning.

**wake** (line 1) • to stop sleeping

**early** (line 1) • near the beginning of an event, such as morning

**poke** (line 3) • to push out

## FIRST READ Think Through the Text

Have children use text evidence to answer these questions.

- *Where does the poem take place? in a bed How do you know? The text says "I sit up in bed."* RL.K.3, RL.1.3
- *Who is the speaker in the poem?* Sample answers: *the poet; the person waking up How do you know? The poem uses the word* I. RL.1.6
- *What is this poem mostly about?* Sample answer: *what the speaker does when she wakes up in the morning* RL.K.1, RL.1.1

## SECOND READ Analyze the Text

- *How do you think the speaker of the poem feels when she wakes up? happy How do you know?* Sample answer: *People sing when they are happy.* RL.K.3, RL.1.3
- Remind children that mood is the feeling of the poem. *What is the mood of this poem? happy What words help create this mood?* Sample answer: *The words* and I sing *are repeated three times.* RL.K.3, RL.1.4
- Reread the poem, and encourage children to clap out the rhythm. Then ask: *How does the rhythm help create the mood?* Sample answer: *The rhythm is bouncy and fun; it makes you feel happy.* RL.K.1, RL.1.1

## Practice Fluency

**EMPHASIZE RATE** Explain that the rate at which a poem is read aloud should match its mood. Discuss how a sad poem and a happy poem might be read aloud. Read aloud "Singing-Time" first slowly, then quickly. Ask children which reading matches the mood. Then read the poem chorally. RF.1.4b

## Independent/Self-Selected Reading

If children have demonstrated comprehension of "Singing-Time," have them use another poem to practice recognizing mood. Model selecting a book from the classroom library and choosing a poem from the table of contents. Read aloud the title and the poet's name. Suggested titles:

- *Mary Middling and Other Silly Folk* by Rose Fyleman
- *The 20th Century Children's Poetry Treasury* by Jack Prelutsky RL.1.10

### WRITE & PRESENT

1. Have small groups discuss the elements that create a happy mood in "Singing-Time," such as its rhythm and repetition. Guide them to ask and answer questions about the poem's elements. RL.K.1, RL.1.1
2. Then guide children to each write or dictate sentences that explain how rhythm and repetition help create the mood. Suggest they use colored pencils or special type in their writing to show the mood. W.K.2, W.1.2
3. Have children share their writing with their group. Ask them to add details and edit their writing based on the group's suggestions. W.K.5, W.1.5
4. Invite children to take turns sharing their sentences with the class. SL.K.6, SL.1.4

*See Copying Masters, pp. 242–245.*

### STUDENT CHECKLIST

**Writing**

- ✔ Write explanatory sentences.
- ✔ Include details that tell how rhythm and repetition help create the mood.
- ✔ Use correct language conventions.

**Speaking & Listening**

- ✔ Participate effectively in collaborative discussion.
- ✔ Ask and answer questions about the poem's elements.
- ✔ Demonstrate a connection between features in the poem and their own writing.

## OBJECTIVES

- Understand that poetry is a type of writing
- Examine visual presentation in poetry
- Examine rhyme in poetry
- Analyze text using text evidence

### Options for Reading

**Independent** Children read independently or with the teacher and then answer questions posed by the teacher.

**Supported** Children read each line and answer questions with teacher support. Then they read the entire poem independently or with a partner. Encourage children to read at least a few words on their own.

### Common Core Connection

**RL.K.1** ask and answer questions about key details; **RL.K.3** identify characters, settings, and major events; **RL.K.5** recognize common types of texts; **RL.K.10** engage in group reading activities with purpose and understanding; **RF.K.2a** recognize and produce rhyming words; **W.K.2** use drawing, dictating, and writing to compose informative/explanatory texts; **W.K.5** respond to questions/suggestions from peers and add details to strengthen writing; **SL.K.6** speak audibly and express thoughts, feelings, and ideas clearly

**RL.1.1** ask and answer questions about key details; **RL.1.3** describe characters, settings, and major events; **RL.1.6** identify who is telling the story; **RL.1.10** read prose and poetry; **RF.1.4b** read on-level text orally with accuracy, appropriate rate, and expression; **W.1.2** write informative/explanatory texts; **W.1.5** focus on a topic, respond to questions/suggestions from peers, and add details to strengthen writing; **SL.1.4** describe people, places, things, and events with details/express ideas and feelings clearly

# "Halfway Down"

## by A. A. Milne

**SUMMARY** Through rhyme and visual presentation, this poem tells about sitting in the middle of a staircase. This poem is from the collection *When We Were Very Young* which was written for and about A. A. Milne's young son, Christopher Robin.

**ABOUT THE AUTHOR** A. A. Milne is best known for his *Winnie the Pooh* books, which are stories about the adventures of his son, Christopher Robin, his stuffed bear, Winnie the Pooh, and other animal friends. Born in England in 1896, Milne also wrote poetry, plays, and mystery stories.

## Discuss Genre and Set Purpose

**POETRY** Ask children to look at the poem and explain how they can tell it is a poem and not a story or informational text. Then elicit that poetry is a kind of writing that uses language to paint a word picture. Many poems rhyme, but others do not. **RL.K.5**

**TEXT FOCUS: Visual Presentation** Explain that in some poems the words on the page are arranged in a way that adds to the meaning of the poem and makes it more fun to read. Before children read the poem, ask them to look at the lengths of the lines and the way they are arranged.

**SET PURPOSE** Help children set a purpose for reading, such as to listen for rhyming words and notice how the words are arranged on the page.

### TEXT COMPLEXITY RUBRIC

| Overall Text Complexity | | "Halfway Down" POETRY<br>ACCESSIBLE |
|---|---|---|
| Quantitative Measures | Lexile | N/A |
| | Guided Reading Level | N/A |
| Qualitative Measures | Text Structure | less familiar poetic structure |
| | Language Conventionality and Clarity | some figurative language |
| | Knowledge Demands | perspective includes unfamiliar aspects |
| | Purpose/Levels of Meaning | single level of complex meaning |

### Academic Vocabulary

Read each word with children and discuss its meaning.

**halfway** (line 1) • in the middle
**nursery** (line 17) • a room for a baby or small child
**instead** (line 24) • in place of

## FIRST READ Think Through the Text

Have children use text evidence to answer these questions.

- *Where does the poem take place?* on a staircase *How do you know?* *The text says halfway down the stairs.* RL.K.3, RL.1.3
- *Who is the speaker in the poem?* Sample answers: *the poet; the person on the stairs* *How do you know?* *The poem uses the words* I *and* my. RL.1.6

## SECOND READ Analyze the Text

- *How does the way the lines are arranged on the page help you know where the poem takes place?* *The way the lines are arranged on the page looks a little like a flight of stairs.* RL.K.3, RL.1.3
- *What is the difference between the first and second stanzas?* Sample answer: *The first stanza says halfway down, but the second one says halfway up. In the first stanza the speaker talks about himself, but in the second stanza he talks about the stairs.* RL.K.1, RL.1.1
- Reread the poem aloud, and then ask: *What are the rhyming words you hear?* *sit/it, top/stop, down/town, head/instead* *Why do you think the poet uses rhyming words?* Sample answer: *They make the poem fun to listen to or read aloud.* RF.K.2a, RL.1.10

## Practice Fluency

**EMPHASIZE EXPRESSION** Point out that reading with expression makes listening to a poem more enjoyable. Read the first six lines aloud in a monotone. Then reread them with expression. Ask children which reading was better. Then have volunteers reread the poem expressively. RL.K.10, RF.1.4b

## Independent/Self-Selected Reading

If children have already demonstrated comprehension of "Halfway Down," have them use another poem to practice recognizing and understanding visual presentation. Model selecting a book and choosing one of the poems. Read aloud the title and poet's name. Suggested titles:

- *When We Were Very Young* by A. A. Milne
- *Now We Are Six* by A. A. Milne RL.1.10

### WRITE & PRESENT

1. Have small groups discuss the elements that make "Halfway Down" fun to read, such as its rhyme and visual presentation. Guide them to ask and answer questions about the poem's elements. RL.K.1, RL.1.1
2. Guide each child to write or dictate to explain how the rhyme and visual presentation make the poem fun to read. W.K.2, W.1.2
3. Have children share their writing with their group. Ask them to add details and edit their writing based on the group's suggestions. W.K.5, W.1.5
4. Invite children to take turns sharing their sentences with the class. SL.K.6, SL.1.4

*See Copying Masters, pp. 242–245.*

### STUDENT CHECKLIST

**Writing**

- ✔ Write explanatory sentences.
- ✔ Include details that tell how the rhyme and visual presentation make the poem fun to read.
- ✔ Use correct language conventions.

**Speaking & Listening**

- ✔ Participate effectively in collaborative discussion.
- ✔ Ask and answer questions about the poem's elements.
- ✔ Demonstrate a connection between features in the poem and their own writing.

## OBJECTIVES

- Understand that poetry is a type of writing
- Examine the use of visual imagery in poetry
- Analyze text using text evidence

### Options for Reading

**Independent** Children read the poem independently or with a partner and then answer questions posed by the teacher.

**Supported** Children read each line and answer questions with teacher support. Then they read the entire poem independently or with a partner. Encourage children to read at least a few words on their own.

### Common Core Connection

**RL.K.1** ask and answer questions about key details; **RL.K.3** identify characters, settings, and major events; **RF.K.2a** recognize and produce rhyming words; **W.K.2** use drawing, dictating, and writing to compose informative/explanatory texts; **W.K.5** respond to questions/suggestions from peers and add details to strengthen writing; **SL.K.6** speak audibly and express thoughts, feelings, and ideas clearly

**RL.1.1** ask and answer questions about key details; **RL.1.2** retell stories and demonstrate understanding of the message or lesson; **RL.1.3** describe characters, settings, and major events; **RL.1.4** identify words and phrases that suggest feelings or appeal to senses; **RL.1.6** identify who is telling the story; **RL.1.10** read prose and poetry; **RF.1.4b** read on-level text orally with accuracy, appropriate rate, and expression; **W.1.2** write informative/explanatory texts; **W.1.5** focus on a topic; respond to questions/suggestions from peers, and add details to strengthen writing; **SL.1.4** describe people, places, things, and events with details/express ideas and feelings clearly

# "Drinking Fountain"

by Marchette Chute

**SUMMARY** This humorous poem describes the difficulty of getting a drink from a water fountain. The water comes up too high or too low, but never just right to get a drink.

**ABOUT THE AUTHOR** **Marchette Chute** is the American author of many children's poems, as well as children's versions of many Shakespeare plays. She received the Women's National Book Award and in 1975 was elected to the American Academy of Arts and Letters. She died in 1994.

## Discuss Genre and Set Purpose

**POETRY** Ask children to look at "Drinking Fountain" and explain how they can tell it is a poem and not a story book. Guide them to find and identify some characteristics of poetry: words are arranged in lines; some words rhyme; the words have a rhythm or beat.

**TEXT FOCUS: Visual Imagery** Explain to children that poets use words to create a picture in the reader's mind. The poet may use interesting or exact verbs to help the reader picture exactly what is happening. Tell children that picturing what is happening in the poem can help them understand and enjoy it more.

**SET PURPOSE** Help children set a purpose for reading the poem, such as trying to picture exactly what is happening in the poem.

### TEXT COMPLEXITY RUBRIC

| Overall Text Complexity | | "Drinking Fountain" POETRY<br>ACCESSIBLE |
|---|---|---|
| Quantitative Measures | Lexile | N/A |
| | Guided Reading Level | N/A |
| Qualitative Measures | Text Structure | simple, familiar poetic structure |
| | Language Conventionality and Clarity | literal, accessible language |
| | Knowledge Demands | simple theme |
| | Purpose/Levels of Meaning | single level of simple meaning |

**Academic Vocabulary**

Read the word with children and discuss its meaning.

**fountain** • a structure or machine from which water flows

## FIRST READ Think Through the Text

Have children use text evidence to answer these questions.

- *Who is the speaker in the poem?* Sample answers: *the poet; the person getting a drink* *How do you know?* *The poem uses the word* I. RL.1.6
- *What is the speaker trying to do?* *drink from a water fountain* RL.K.1, RL.1.1
- *What problems does the speaker have doing this?* *First the water goes up too high, and then it doesn't go up enough.* RL.K.3, RL.1.3
- *Which words rhyme?* *drink/think, goes/nose, small/all* RF.K.2a

## SECOND READ Analyze the Text

- Reread the first stanza. Ask: *What do you think the poet means when she says that it doesn't work the way you'd think?* Sample answer: *It should be simple to get a drink out of a water fountain, but it isn't in this poem.* RL.K.1, RL.1.2
- Reread the second stanza. Ask: *Can water really go and hit someone in the nose?* *no* *How does using these words help you understand what is happening in the poem?* Sample answer: *This helps me picture how hard the fountain makes the water spurt out.* Guide children to describe other images that they get from the poem. RL.K.1, RL.1.4

## Practice Fluency

**EMPHASIZE ACCURACY** Explain that it is important to read each word of a poem accurately. Read the poem's first stanza, replacing *drink* with *rink* and *think* with *thank*. Discuss the effect of reading inaccurately: It can change the meaning so the poem no longer makes sense, or change the rhyme so the words sound wrong. Reread the stanza accurately to illustrate the difference. Then reread the poem chorally. RF.1.4b

## Independent/Self-Selected Reading

If children have already demonstrated comprehension of "Drinking Fountain," have them use another poem to practice the skills. Model selecting a book and choosing a poem. Suggested titles:

- *Read-Aloud Rhymes for the Very Young* selected by Jack Prelutsky
- *Sing a Song of Popcorn* selected by Beatrice Schenk de Regniers RL.1.10

### WRITE & PRESENT

1. Have partners refer to the text to discuss its visual imagery. Encourage children to ask and answer questions about details in the poem. RL.K.1, RL.1.1
2. Have individual children select one scene and write and draw to describe it. W.K.2, W.1.2
3. Have children share their writing with their group. Ask them to add details and edit their writing based on the group's suggestions. W.K.5, W.1.5
4. Invite children to take turns sharing their sentences with the class. SL.K.6, SL.1.4

*See Copying Masters, pp. 242–245.*

### STUDENT CHECKLIST

**Writing**

- ☑ Write explanatory sentences.
- ☑ Include details about one scene using images from "Drinking Fountain."
- ☑ Use correct language conventions.

**Speaking & Listening**

- ☑ Participate effectively in collaborative discussion.
- ☑ Ask and answer questions about the poem's visual images.
- ☑ Demonstrate a connection between features in the poem and their own writing.

## OBJECTIVES

- Understand that poetry is a type of writing
- Examine word choice to create mood in poetry
- Analyze text using text evidence

### Options for Reading

**Independent** Children read independently or with the teacher and then answer questions posed by the teacher.

**Supported** Children read each line and answer questions with teacher support. Then they read the entire poem independently or with a partner. Encourage children to read at least a few words on their own.

### Common Core Connection

**RL.K.1** ask and answer questions about key details; **RL.K.5** recognize common types of texts; **W.K.2** use drawing, dictating, and writing to compose informative/explanatory texts; **W.K.5** respond to questions/suggestions from peers and add details to strengthen writing; **SL.K.2** confirm understanding of a text read aloud, information presented orally, or through other media by asking/answering questions and requesting clarification; **SL.K.6** speak audibly and express thoughts, feelings, and ideas clearly

**RL.1.1** ask and answer questions about key details; **RL.1.4** identify words and phrases that suggest feelings or appeal to senses; **RL.1.6** identify who is telling the story; **RL.1.10** read prose and poetry; **RF.1.4b** read on-level text orally with accuracy, appropriate rate, and expression; **W.1.2** write informative/explanatory texts; **W.1.5** focus on a topic, respond to questions/suggestions from peers, and add details to strengthen writing; **SL.1.2** ask and answer questions about details in a text read aloud, information presented orally, or through other media; **SL.1.4** describe people, places, things, and events with details/express ideas and feelings clearly

# "Poem"

## by Langston Hughes

**SUMMARY** This poem reflects on the loss of a beloved friend. Yet, only the friend's physical presence is gone. The friend remains through the poet's love and memories.

**ABOUT THE AUTHOR** **Langston Hughes** was a major African-American poet whose work helped shape the Harlem Renaissance of the 1920s. Among his many awards are the NAACP Spingarn Medal and the Harmon Gold Medal for Literature.

## Discuss Genre and Set Purpose

**POETRY** Ask children to look at the poem and explain how they can tell it is a poem and not another kind of text. Remind them that poetry is a kind of writing that uses words whose sounds and meanings express feelings. As you read the poem, discuss words and phrases, such as *I loved my friend*, that express feelings. **RL.K.5, RL.1.4**

**TEXT FOCUS: Mood** Remind children that every poem has a mood or overall feeling. Poems may have different kinds of moods: happy, sad, angry, and so on. Explain that, to create a mood, poets choose their words carefully. They also pay attention to the tone of the poem. Tone is the "voice" that you imagine the poem being read in.

**SET PURPOSE** Help children set a purpose for reading the poem, such as to feel the mood of the poem and understand how it is created.

### TEXT COMPLEXITY RUBRIC

| Overall Text Complexity | | "Poem" POETRY<br>ACCESSIBLE |
|---|---|---|
| Quantitative Measures | Lexile | N/A |
| | Guided Reading Level | N/A |
| Qualitative Measures | Text Structure | less familiar poetic structure |
| | Language Conventionality and Clarity | clear, direct language |
| | Knowledge Demands | single perspective |
| | Purpose/Levels of Meaning | single level of simple meaning |

**Academic Vocabulary**

Read the word with students and discuss its meaning.

**soft** (line 5) • quiet, spoken in a low voice

## FIRST READD Think Through the Text

Have children use text evidence to answer these questions.

- *What is this poem mostly about?* Sample answer: *the love the speaker had for a friend who went away* RL.K.1, RL.1.1
- *Who is the speaker in the poem?* *the poet* *How do you know?* *The poem uses the words* I, my, *and* me. RL.1.6

## SECOND READ Analyze the Text

- Remind children that mood is the feeling of the poem. *What is the mood of this poem?* *sad* *How do you know?* Sample answer: *The speaker says that the friend that he loved went away. He misses his friend.* RL.K.1, RL.1.1
- *Why does* I loved my friend *begin and end the poem?* Sample answer: *It is the most important idea of the poem.* *How does this line help to create the mood?* Sample answer: *It uses the past tense, loved, so you can tell the speaker is sad that the friend is gone.* RL.K.1, RL.1.4
- Remind children that tone is the "voice" of the poem. Reread the poem in a loud voice and then in a soft voice. Ask: *Which voice matched the poem's tone?* *the soft voice* *Why?* *It shows how the speaker feels. When people are sad, they often speak softly.* SL.K.2, SL.1.2

## Practice Fluency

**EMPHASIZE RATE** Explain that the rate at which a poem is read aloud should match its mood. Discuss the differences in how a sad poem and a happy poem might be read aloud. Read aloud "Poem" slowly. Then read it quickly. Ask children which reading matched the mood of the poem. RF.1.4b

## Independent/Self-Selected Reading

If children have demonstrated comprehension of "Poem," have them use another poem to practice recognizing mood. Model selecting a book of poetry and choosing a poem. Read the title and the poet's name. Suggested titles:

- *Poetry for Young People: Langston Hughes* by Langston Hughes
- *A Child's Introduction to Poetry* compiled by Michael Driscoll RL.1.10

### WRITE & PRESENT

1. Have small groups discuss the elements that create a sad mood in "Poem," such as its tone and repetition. Guide them to ask and answer questions about the poem's elements. RL.K.1, RL.1.1
2. Then guide children to each write or dictate sentences that explain how tone and repetition help create the mood. Suggest that they use colored pencils or special type in their writing to show the mood. W.K.2, W.1.2
3. Have children share their writing with their group. Ask them to add details and edit their writing based on the group's suggestions. W.K.5, W.1.5
4. Invite children to take turns sharing their sentences with the class. SL.K.6, SL.1.4

*See Copying Masters, pp. 242–245.*

### STUDENT CHECKLIST

**Writing**

- ✓ Write explanatory sentences.
- ✓ Include details that tell how tone and repetition help create the mood.
- ✓ Use correct language conventions.

**Speaking & Listening**

- ✓ Participate effectively in collaborative discussion.
- ✓ Ask and answer questions about the poem's elements.
- ✓ Demonstrate a connection between features in the poem and their own writing.

### OBJECTIVES

- Understand that poetry is a type of writing
- Examine rhyme and rhythm in poetry
- Analyze text using text evidence

### Options for Reading

**Independent** Children read the poem independently or with a partner and then answer questions posed by the teacher.

**Supported** Children read each line and answer questions with teacher support. Then they read the entire poem independently or with a partner. Encourage children to read at least a few words on their own.

### Common Core Connection

**RL.K.1** ask and answer questions about key details; **RL.K.5** recognize common types of texts; **RF.K.2a** recognize and produce rhyming words; **W.K.2** use drawing, dictating, and writing to compose informative/explanatory texts; **W.K.5** respond to questions/suggestions from peers and add details to strengthen writing; **SL.K.1a** follow rules for discussions; **SL.K.6** speak audibly and express thoughts, feelings, and ideas clearly

**RL.1.1** ask and answer questions about key details; **RL.1.4** identify words and phrases that suggest feelings or appeal to senses; **RL.1.6** identify who is telling the story; **RF.1.4b** read on-level text orally with accuracy, appropriate rate, and expression; **W.1.2** write informative/explanatory texts; **W.1.5** focus on a topic, respond to questions/suggestions from peers, and add details to strengthen writing; **SL.1.1a** follow rules for discussions; **SL.1.6** produce complete sentences when appropriate to task and situation

# "Wouldn't You?"

## by John Ciardi

**SUMMARY** In this short poem, the poet remarks that he would like the wind to blow him up and down in the air. By choosing the title "Wouldn't You?," he invites the reader to consider the same adventure.

**ABOUT THE AUTHOR** **John Ciardi** is an American writer who felt that poetry was misunderstood. He worked throughout his life to expose the public to this genre. Ciardi is best known for his humorous children's poetry, which he started writing to entertain his own children.

## Discuss Genre and Set Purpose

**POETRY** Ask children to look at "Wouldn't You?" and tell how they know the text is a poem and not an informational book. Help them identify its short length, as well as how it is broken up into lines. RL.K.5

**TEXT FOCUS**: **Rhyme and Rhythm** Remind children that rhyming words have the same ending sounds. Point out that many poems use rhyming words, but some do not. Explain that some poems also have a rhythm, or beat, and that poets often use rhyme and rhythm as a way to create a song-like quality so that a poem will be more fun to read. RF.K.2a

**SET PURPOSE** Help children set a purpose for reading, such as finding out why the poet selected the title "Wouldn't You?" or listening for rhyming words. RF.K.2a

### TEXT COMPLEXITY RUBRIC

| Overall Text Complexity | | "Wouldn't You?" POETRY<br>ACCESSIBLE |
|---|---|---|
| Quantitative Measures | Lexile | N/A |
| | Guided Reading Level | N/A |
| Qualitative Measures | Text Structure | simple, familiar poetic structure |
| | Language Conventionality and Clarity | contemporary, familiar language |
| | Knowledge Demands | common everyday experience |
| | Purpose/Levels of Meaning | single level of simple meaning |

### Academic Vocabulary

Read the word with children and discuss its meaning.

**blow** (line 8) • cause to move by wind

## FIRST READ Think Through the Text

Have children use text evidence to answer these questions.

- *Who is the speaker in the poem?* the poet *How do you know?* He uses the words I and I'd. RL.K.1, RL.1.6
- *What will help the poet go high and low?* Sample answer: the wind; the wind will blow. RL.K.1, RL.1.1
- *What are the rhyming words that you hear in the poem?* go, low, blow RF.K.2a, RL.1.1

## SECOND READ Analyze the Text

- *Why do you think the poet chose "Wouldn't You?" as the title for this poem?* Sample answer: He wants us to think like he does; it helps us get interested in what he is going to say. RL.K.1, RL.1.1
- Reread the poem. Encourage children to clap the rhythm. Then ask: *How is the rhythm of the poem like the movement of blowing wind?* Sample answer: The words flow smoothly like the wind. RL.K.1, RL.1.4
- *Why do you think the author repeats the words* As the wind? Sample answer: They are important because the poem is about the wind. Reread the three repeated lines again. *How are the sounds of these words like the sound of the wind?* Sample answer: The w at the beginning sounds like the wind; they are soft sounds. RL.K.1, RL.1.4

## Practice Fluency

**EMPHASIZE RHYTHM** Remind children that rhyme and rhythm give many poems a song-like quality. Point out that stressing these elements when reading aloud can make the poem fun to listen to. Read the poem without rhythm. Then read the poem so that the rhythm is smooth and breezy. Have children tell which sounds better and why. Then choral read the poem, emphasizing its rhythm. RF.1.4b

## Independent/Self-Selected Reading

If children have already demonstrated comprehension of "Wouldn't You?," have them read other poems to practice recognizing rhyme and rhythm. Model selecting a book and choosing a poem. Suggested titles:

- *Doodle Soup* by John Ciardi
- *You Read to Me, I'll Read to You* by John Ciardi RL.1.10

### WRITE & PRESENT

1. Have small groups discuss how rhyme and rhythm help make "Wouldn't You?" fun to read. Encourage them to ask and answer questions about why they would or would not like to have the wind blow them around in the air. Remind them to be good listeners and speakers and follow the rules of discussion. SL.K.1a, SL.1.1a
2. Individual children write or dictate sentences that explain how rhyme and rhythm help make "Wouldn't You?" fun to read. Tell them to be sure to include at least one example of rhyme or rhythm in their sentences. W.K.2, W.1.2
3. Have children share their writing with their group. Ask them to add details and edit their writing based on the group's suggestions. W.K.5, W.1.5
4. Invite children to take turns sharing their writing with the class. SL.K.6, SL.1.4

*See Copying Masters, pp. 242–245.*

### STUDENT CHECKLIST

#### Writing

- ✔ Write sentences that explain how rhyme and rhythm help make the poem fun to read.
- ✔ Include at least one example of rhyme or rhythm.
- ✔ Use correct language conventions.

#### Speaking & Listening

- ✔ Participate effectively in collaborative discussion.
- ✔ Ask and answer questions about their writing.
- ✔ Demonstrate a connection between the poem and their own writing.

## OBJECTIVES

- Understand that poetry is a type of writing
- Describe haiku poetry
- Analyze text using text evidence

### Options for Reading

**Independent** Children read the poem independently or with a partner and then answer questions posed by the teacher.

**Supported** Children read each line and answer questions with teacher support. Then they read the entire poem independently or with a partner. Encourage children to read at least a few words on their own.

### Common Core Connection

**RL.K.1** ask and answer questions about key details; **RL.K.5** recognize common types of texts; **RL.K.10** engage in group reading activities with purpose and understanding; **W.K.1** use drawing, dictating, and writing to compose opinion pieces; **W.K.5** respond to questions/suggestions from peers and add details to strengthen writing; **SL.K.2** confirm understanding of a text read aloud, information presented orally, or through other media by asking/answering questions and requesting clarification; **SL.K.6** speak audibly and express thoughts, feelings, and ideas clearly

**RL.1.1** ask and answer questions about key details; **RL.1.10** read prose and poetry; **RF.1.4b** read on-level text orally with accuracy, appropriate rate, and expression; **W.1.1** write opinion pieces; **W.1.5** focus on a topic, respond to questions/suggestions from peers, and add details to strengthen writing; **SL.1.2** ask and answer questions about details in a text read aloud, information presented orally, or through other media; **SL.1.4** describe people, places, things, and events with details/express ideas and feelings clearly

# "Laughing Boy"

by Richard Wright

**SUMMARY** Using a haiku format, the poet describes the joy a young boy feels in a snowstorm as the flakes land on his outstretched hands.

**ABOUT THE AUTHOR** **Richard Wright** is a well-known African-American novelist. He became fascinated with haiku in the later years of his life and wrote more than 4,000 of the three-line poems.

## Discuss Genre and Set Purpose

**POETRY** Ask children to tell how all poems are alike. Lead them to conclude that they are usually short, and the poet shares a specific feeling or message. Then invite children to examine "Laughing Boy." Explain that it is an example of a kind of poem called haiku. Point out that haikus do not use rhyming words. **RL.K.5**

**TEXT FOCUS: Haiku** Tell children that haikus are three-line poems that generally describe something in nature and follow a patterned format. Explain that haikus have a pattern of five syllables in line 1, seven in line 2, and five in line 3.

**SET PURPOSE** Help children set a purpose for reading the poem, such as to find out why the boy is laughing or to count the syllables in each line of the haiku.

### TEXT COMPLEXITY RUBRIC

| Overall Text Complexity | | "Laughing Boy" POETRY<br>ACCESSIBLE |
|---|---|---|
| Quantitative Measures | Lexile | N/A |
| | Guided Reading Level | N/A |
| Qualitative Measures | Text Structure | less familiar poetic structure |
| | Language Conventionality and Clarity | literal, accessible language |
| | Knowledge Demands | common everyday experience |
| | Purpose/Levels of Meaning | single level of simple meaning (single theme) |

## Academic Vocabulary

Read the word with children and discuss its meaning.

**palms** (line 2) • the part of the hand from fingertips to wrist when the hand is opened and facing up

## FIRST READ Think Through the Text

Have children use text evidence to answer these questions.

- *What time of year is the poet describing?* winter RL.K.1, RL.1.1
- *Why are the boy's hands white?* *The boy is holding out his hands, and the snow is falling on them.* RL.K.1, RL.1.1
- *Even before reading this poem, why might you think it is a haiku?* *It has 3 lines.* RL.K.5

## SECOND READ Analyze the Text

- *How do you think the boy feels about the snow?* *He likes it.* *How do you know?* Sample answer: *He's laughing. Someone who is laughing is happy.* RL.K.1, RL.1.1
- Remind children that a haiku has a certain number of syllables in each line. Chorally read the first line in the haiku with children, holding up your fingers to count each syllable. *How many syllables are in the first line?* five *the second line?* eight *the last line?* five Point out that most haikus have seven syllables in the second line, but the poet, Richard Wright, took liberties with the haiku pattern. RL.K.10, RL.1.10

## Practice Fluency

**EMPHASIZE ACCURACY** Tell children that a haiku is so short that it is very important to read each word correctly. Reread "Laughing Boy" and replace *snow* with *show* and *white* with *write*. Ask children how the poem changed. Lead them to understand that the poem no longer makes sense. Then read the poem together, focusing on accuracy. RF.1.4b

## Independent/Self-Selected Reading

If children have already demonstrated comprehension of "Laughing Boy," have them compare other poems to practice recognizing and understanding a haiku format. Select a book that contains a variety of poems, including several haikus. Read aloud the titles and the poets' names. Suggested titles:

- *In the Eyes of the Cat* selected by Demi
- *Rainbow Soup: Adventures in Poetry* by Brian P. Cleary RL.1.10

### WRITE & PRESENT

1. Have small groups discuss the elements of haiku and whether they like this type of poem. Encourage them to ask and answer questions to clarify anything they don't understand. SL.K.2, SL.1.2
2. Individual children write or dictate an opinion piece about whether they like haikus. Tell them to be sure to include two reasons to support their opinions. W.K.1, W.1.1
3. Have children share their writing with their group. Ask them to add details and edit their writing based on the group's suggestions. W.K.5, W.1.5
4. Invite children to take turns sharing their writing with the class. SL.K.6, SL.1.4

*See Copying Masters, pp. 242–245.*

### STUDENT CHECKLIST

**Writing**

- ✔ Write an opinion piece.
- ✔ Include two reasons with details to support their opinions.
- ✔ Use correct language conventions.

**Speaking & Listening**

- ✔ Participate effectively in collaborative discussion.
- ✔ Ask and answer questions about the haiku elements.
- ✔ Demonstrate a connection between the poem and their own writing.

## OBJECTIVES

- Understand that poetry is a type of writing
- Examine rhyme in text
- Analyze text using text evidence

### Options for Reading

**Independent** Children read the poem independently or with a partner and then answer questions posed by the teacher.

**Supported** Children read each line and answer questions with teacher support. Then they read the entire poem independently or with a partner. Encourage children to read at least a few words on their own.

# "By Myself"

## by Eloise Greenfield

**SUMMARY** Using rhyming couplets, the poet identifies what she imagines herself to be when her eyes are closed. Yet when she opens her eyes, the poet is happy to be herself.

**ABOUT THE AUTHOR** **Eloise Greenfield** was born in 1929. She was an avid reader and visited the library often as a child. Greenfield, an African-American author and poet, has published over 30 children's books, including biographies, poetry, and picture books.

## Discuss Genre and Set Purpose

**POETRY** Review with children that a poem is a special kind of writing in which a poet wants to share one feeling or idea. Discuss how some poems rhyme, while others do not. RL.K.5

**TEXT FOCUS: Rhyme** Tell children that rhyming words have the same ending sounds. Provide these examples: *cat/hat* and *book/hook*. Say more word pairs, like *man/can, big/bit,* and *box/fox*. Have children clap if the words rhyme. Discuss that poets often use rhyming words to make the text more interesting and make it sound more like a song. RF.K.2a

**SET PURPOSE** Help children set a purpose for reading the poem, such as to find out what the author likes to do when she is by herself or to listen for rhyming words.

### TEXT COMPLEXITY RUBRIC

| Overall Text Complexity | | "By Myself" POETRY<br>ACCESSIBLE |
|---|---|---|
| Quantitative Measures | Lexile | N/A |
| | Guided Reading Level | N/A |
| Qualitative Measures | Text Structure | less familiar poetic structure |
| | Language Conventionality and Clarity | some figurative language |
| | Knowledge Demands | contemporary, familiar language |
| | Purpose/Levels of Meaning | single level of complex meaning |

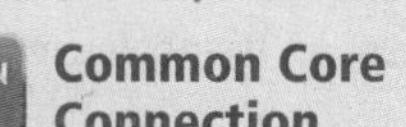

### Common Core Connection

**RL.K.1** ask and answer questions about key details; **RL.K.5** recognize common types of texts; **RF.K.2a** recognize and produce rhyming words; **W.K.2** use drawing, dictating, and writing to compose informative/explanatory texts; **W.K.5** respond to questions/suggestions from peers and add details to strengthen writing; **SL.K.6** speak audibly and express thoughts, feelings, and ideas clearly

**RL.1.1** ask and answer questions about key details; **RL.1.10** read prose and poetry; **RF.1.4b** read on-level text orally with accuracy, appropriate rate, and expression; **W.1.2** write informative/explanatory texts; **W.1.5** focus on a topic, respond to questions/suggestions from peers, and add details to strengthen writing; **SL.1.4** describe people, places, things, and events with details/express ideas and feelings clearly

**Academic Vocabulary**

Read each word with children and discuss its meaning.

**dimple** (line 4) • a hollow or small hole
**gospel** (line 7) • relating to church
**gong** (line 8) • a instrument that is a large, metal disk

## FIRST READD Think Through the Text

Have children use text evidence to answer these questions.

- *What kinds of things does the poet say she is when her eyes are closed?* Sample answers: *a twin; a squeaky noise* RL.K.1, RL.1.1
- *What does the poet like to be when her eyes are open?* herself RL.K.1, RL.1.1
- *What are some rhyming words in the poem?* Sample answer: *toys/noise, song/gong* RF.K.2a, RL.1.1

## SECOND READ Analyze the Text

- *What is the poet doing when she closes her eyes?* Sample answer: *She is pretending to be other things.* RL.K.1, RL.1.1
- Reread lines 3–4. *What do you notice about the way the lines end?* *The words rhyme.* *Why do you think the poet made them rhyme?* Sample answer: *Rhyme makes the poem more fun to read.* RF.K.2a, RL.1.1
- Reread the last two lines. Ask: *What do you think the poet means?* Sample answer: *She is happy with who she is. She can pretend to be different things, but she likes being herself the best.* RL.K.1, RL.1.1

## Practice Fluency

**EMPHASIZE RATE** Tell children that the rate at which they read a rhyming poem is important because listeners need to clearly hear and understand the rhyming words. Model reading the poem aloud at a moderate rate—not too fast or too slow, pausing after each line to stress the rhyming words. Then read the poem chorally. RF.1.4b

## Independent/Self-Selected Reading

If children have already demonstrated comprehension of "By Myself," have them read other poems to practice recognizing rhyme. Model selecting a book and choosing a poem from the table of contents. Read aloud the title and the poet's name. Suggested titles:

- *Under the Sunday Tree* by Eloise Greenfield
- *Yellow Elephant: A Bright Bestiary* by Julie Larios RL.1.10

### WRITE & PRESENT

1. Have small groups identify the pairs of rhyming words in "By Myself." Challenge them to brainstorm other words that rhyme. RF.K.2a
2. Remind children that the poet likes who she is. Then invite children to write or dictate sentences that tell why they like themselves. Challenge them to make two of the sentences rhyme. Have each child draw a picture to accompany their writing. W.K.2, W.1.2
3. Have children share their writing with their group. Ask them to add details and edit their writing based on the group's suggestions. W.K.5, W.1.5
4. Invite children to take turns sharing their sentences with the class. Help children identify rhyming sentences. SL.K.6, SL.1.4

*See Copying Masters, pp. 242–245.*

### STUDENT CHECKLIST

**Writing**

- ✓ Write sentences that tell why they like themselves.
- ✓ Include two sentences that rhyme.
- ✓ Use correct language conventions.

**Speaking & Listening**

- ✓ Participate effectively in collaborative discussion.
- ✓ Ask and answer questions about rhyming words.

## OBJECTIVES

- Understand that poetry is a type of writing
- Examine rhythm and rhyme in text
- Use text evidence to explore visual imagery in text

### Options for Reading

**Independent** Children read the poem independently or with the teacher and then answer questions posed by the teacher.

**Supported** Children read a few lines and answer questions with teacher support. Children then reread the lines independently or with a partner. Encourage children to read at least a few lines on their own.

### Common Core Connection

**RL.K.1** ask and answer questions about key details; **RL.K.3** identify characters, settings, and major events; **RL.K.5** recognize common types of texts; **RF.K.2a** recognize and produce rhyming words; **W.K.3** use drawing, dictating, and writing to narrate; **SL.K.1b** continue a conversation through multiple exchanges

**RL.1.1** ask and answer questions about key details; **RL.1.3** describe characters, settings, and major events; **RL.1.10** read prose and poetry; **RF.1.4b** read on-level text orally with accuracy, appropriate rate, and expression; **W.1.3** write narratives; **SL.1.1b** build on others' talk in conversation by responding to others' comments

# "Covers"

by Nikki Giovanni

**SUMMARY** This rhyming poem uses a slightly humorous tone as it tells about things that cover other things, such as glass that covers windows and clouds that cover the sky. The poet uses both concrete images (a blanket covering a person) and abstract images (nighttime covering creeping things).

**ABOUT THE AUTHOR** Nikki Giovanni is an American poet. She has written many books of poetry and holds the Langston Hughes Medal for Outstanding Poetry.

## Discuss Genre and Set Purpose

**POETRY** Tell children that poetry is a kind of writing which arranges words in a special way to create visual images and a certain mood or feeling. Many poems rhyme, but some do not.

**TEXT FOCUS: Rhythm and Rhyme** Tell children that rhyming poems have words with the same ending sound. Poems also have a rhythm, or beat. As you read the poem aloud, discuss with children how the rhyming words and rhythm let them know this is a poem. RL.K.5

**SET PURPOSE** Help children set a purpose for reading the poem, such as to enjoy its images and rhythm and rhyme.

### TEXT COMPLEXITY RUBRIC

| Overall Text Complexity | | "Covers" POETRY<br>COMPLEX |
|---|---|---|
| Quantitative Measures | Lexile | N/A |
| | Guided Reading Level | N/A |
| Qualitative Measures | Text Structure | less familiar poetic structure |
| | Language Conventionality and Clarity | some figurative language |
| | Knowledge Demands | experience includes unfamiliar aspects |
| | Purpose/Levels of Meaning | single level of complex meaning |

### Academic Vocabulary

Read each word with children and discuss its meaning.

**cover** (line 3) • to protect something or hide something from sight
**nighttime** (line 5) • after dark or at night
**creep** (line 6) • to move slowly or quietly
**asleep** (line 8) • sleeping

## FIRST READ Think Through the Text

Have children use text evidence to answer these questions.

- *What covers windows?* glass *Why? to keep cold out* RL.K.1, RL.1.1
- *Why do clouds cover the sky?* to make a rainy day RL.K.1, RL.1.1
- *What covers me when I'm asleep?* a blanket RL.K.1, RL.1.1

## SECOND READ Analyze the Text

- Read the poem aloud. Then guide children to describe the kinds of visual images they get from the poem. Sample answer: *The poem says glass covers the windows to keep the cold away. I can picture a warm place inside with frost on the windows.* RL.K.1, RL.1.1
- Reread the poem aloud. Discuss what might creep at night. Ask: *How does the nighttime cover things?* Sample answer: *The darkness makes things hard to see.* RL.K.3, RL.1.3
- Help children recognize the rhyming words. Read the poem again, inviting children to clap to the beat of the rhythm. RF.K.2a

## Practice Fluency

**EMPHASIZE RHYTHM** Remind children that when they read poetry aloud, they may enjoy it more if they emphasize the rhythm or beat of the text. Read the first two lines of the poem, ignoring the rhythm. Reread the lines together and emphasize the beat. Then ask children which reading they preferred. RF.1.4b

## Independent/Self-Selected Reading

If children have already demonstrated comprehension of "Covers," have them practice recognizing rhythm and rhyme using another poem. Model selecting a book from the classroom library and choosing one poem from the table of contents. Read aloud the title of the poem and the author's name. Suggested titles:

- *Tomie dePaola's Book of Poems* by Tomie dePaola
- *The Sun Is So Quiet* by Nikki Giovanni RL.1.10

### WRITE & PRESENT

1. Have small groups refer to the text to discuss its visual imagery. Encourage children to ask and answer questions about details from the poem. RL.K.1, RL.1.1
2. Individual children draw and write to describe one or more scenes from "Covers." W.K.3, W.1.3
3. Children within each group share their descriptions with each other and edit their writing. SL.K.1b, SL.1.1b
4. Individual children turn in their final drafts to the teacher.

*See Copying Masters, pp. 242–245.*

### STUDENT CHECKLIST

#### Writing

- Write about and draw one or more scenes using images from "Covers."
- Include details.
- Use correct language conventions.

#### Speaking & Listening

- Participate effectively in a collaborative discussion.
- Ask and answer questions about the poem's details.
- Describe details in their own writing and drawing that relate to scenes in "Covers."

## OBJECTIVES

- Understand that poetry is a type of writing
- Explore how repeated words and phrases give clues about the poet's message
- Analyze text using text evidence

### Options for Reading

**Independent** Children read independently or with the teacher and then answer questions posed by the teacher.

**Supported** Children read each line and answer questions with teacher support. Then they read the entire poem independently or with a partner. Encourage children to read at least a few words on their own.

### Common Core Connection

**RL.K.1** ask and answer questions about key details; **W.K.1** use drawing, dictating, and writing to compose opinion pieces; **W.K.5** respond to questions/suggestions from peers and add details to strengthen writing; **SL.K.2** confirm understanding of a text read aloud, information presented orally, or through other media by asking/answering questions and requesting clarification; **SL.K.6** speak audibly and express thoughts, feelings, and ideas clearly
**RL.1.1** ask and answer questions about key details; **RL.1.4** identify words and phrases that suggest feelings or appeal to senses; **RL.1.10** read prose and poetry; **RF.1.4b** read on-level text orally with accuracy, appropriate rate, and expression; **W.1.1** write opinion pieces; **W.1.5** focus on a topic, respond to questions/suggestions from peers, and add details to strengthen writing; **SL.1.2** ask and answer questions about details in a text read aloud, information presented orally, or through other media; **SL.1.4** describe people, places, things, and events with details/express ideas and feelings clearly

# "It Fell in the City"

by Eve Merriam

**SUMMARY** This poem describes the changes in a city when snow falls throughout the night. The repetitive phrase *all turned white* helps readers visualize how a colorful place changes.

**ABOUT THE AUTHOR** Eve Merriam, born in 1916, began writing poetry around the age of eight. She fell in love with the written word and devoted herself to all forms of writing. Her true love was poetry, of which she wrote or compiled over 20 books.

## Discuss Genre and Set Purpose

**POETRY** Remind children that poetry uses words to create a picture in the reader's mind. As you read the poem, discuss how the repetition of the phrase *all turned white* helps the reader see changes in a city.

**TEXT FOCUS: Repetition** Remind children that most poems are short, and poets have to express a feeling or share an important message in just a few words. Explain that poets often repeat words and phrases so they stand out, which helps the reader know they might be important to the poet's message.

**SET PURPOSE** Help children set a purpose for reading the poem, such as to find out what fell in the city or to listen for repeated words.

### TEXT COMPLEXITY RUBRIC

| Overall Text Complexity | | "It Fell in the City" POETRY ACCESSIBLE |
|---|---|---|
| Quantitative Measures | Lexile | N/A |
| | Guided Reading Level | N/A |
| Qualitative Measures | Text Structure | simple, familiar poetic structure |
| | Language Conventionality and Clarity | some figurative language |
| | Knowledge Demands | common everyday experience |
| | Purpose/Levels of Meaning | single level of simple meaning (single theme) |

**Academic Vocabulary**

Read the word with children and discuss its meaning.

**hydrants** (line 5) • pipes that tap water underground that are often used to fight fires

## FIRST READ Think Through the Text

Have children use text evidence to answer these questions.

- *What is falling in the city?* snow *How do you know?* Sample answer: *Snow is white. When snow falls, it covers everything and makes everything look white.* RL.K.1, RL.1.1
- *How long did the snow fall?* through the night RL.K.1, RL.1.1
- *What are some repeated words?* It fell in the city; all turned white. RL.K.1, RL.1.1

## SECOND READ Analyze the Text

- *What season is it?* winter *How do you know? Snow is falling.* RL.K.1, RL.1.1
- *Why do you think the author repeats the words* all turned white? Sample answer: *The words are the most important idea of the poem. What do you think the poet wants to tell you?* Sample answer: *Snow can change something as big as a city.* RL.K.1, RL.1.4
- Reread the poem again. Ask children to listen for other repeated words. *What words does the poet repeat?* It fell in the city *and* through the night. *Why are these words important?* Sample answer: *It tells us where the snow is falling; it shows why everything is turning white.* SL.K.2, SL.1.2

## Practice Fluency

**EMPHASIZE EXPRESSION** One aspect of reading with expression is phrasing. Discuss how a period and a comma show a reader where to pause. Point out that some lines do not have punctuation. Read the second stanza out loud, modeling how to pause at the periods and read smoothly on the return sweeps. Have children join you in rereading. RF.1.4b

## Independent/Self-Selected Reading

If children have demonstrated comprehension of "It Fell in the City," have them use another poem to practice the skills. Suggested titles:

- *Out Loud* by Eve Merriam
- *It Doesn't Always Have to Rhyme* by Eve Merriam RL.1.10

### WRITE & PRESENT

1. Have small groups discuss the poet's use of repeated words and phrases in the poem. Have them ask and answer questions about what they liked about the images in "It Fell in the City." RL.K.1, RL.1.1
2. Individual children write or dictate an opinion piece about what they liked about the poem. Tell them to be sure to include two reasons with details to support their opinions. Suggest that they include a drawing to show an image they especially liked. W.K.1, W.1.1
3. Have children share their writing in small groups. Ask them to add details and edit their writing based on the group's suggestions. W.K.5, W.1.5
4. Invite children to take turns sharing their writing and drawings with the class. SL.K.6, SL.1.4

*See Copying Masters, pp. 242–245.*

### STUDENT CHECKLIST

**Writing**

- ☑ Write an opinion piece.
- ☑ Include two reasons with details to support opinions.
- ☑ Use correct language conventions.

**Speaking & Listening**

- ☑ Participate effectively in collaborative discussion.
- ☑ Ask and answer questions about their writing.
- ☑ Demonstrate a connection between the poem and their own writing.

## OBJECTIVES

- Understand that poetry is a type of writing
- Examine the use of imagery in poetry
- Analyze text using text evidence

### Options for Reading

**Independent** Children read the poem independently or with a partner and then answer questions posed by the teacher.

**Supported** Children read each line and answer questions with teacher support. Then they read the entire poem independently or with a partner. Encourage children to read at least a few words on their own.

### Common Core Connection

**RL.K.1** ask and answer questions about key details; **RL.K.5** recognize common types of texts; **W.K.5** respond to questions/suggestions from peers and add details to strengthen writing; **W.K.7** participate in shared research and writing projects; **SL.K.6** speak audibly and express thoughts, feelings, and ideas clearly

**RL.1.1** ask and answer questions about key details; **RL.1.4** identify words and phrases that suggest feelings or appeal to senses; **RL.1.6** identify who is telling the story; **RL.1.10** read prose and poetry; **RF.1.4b** read on-level text orally with accuracy, appropriate rate, and expression; **W.1.5** focus on a topic, respond to questions/suggestions from peers, and add details to strengthen writing; **W.1.7** participate in shared research and writing projects; **SL.1.4** describe people, places, things, and events with details/express ideas and feelings clearly

# "Celebration"

by Alonzo Lopez

**SUMMARY** The poet vividly describes the activities he will enjoy during an American Indian celebration in his community. Strong action words describe the dancing, singing, feasting, and games the people will play during the night.

**ABOUT THE AUTHOR** **Alonzo Lopez** is an American-Indian poet who writes about his heritage. Born in Arizona, he is a member of the Tohono O'odham Nation.

## Discuss Genre and Set Purpose

**POETRY** Ask children to look at "Celebration" and explain how they can tell it is a poem. Lead them to identify characteristics of poetry, including its short length and placement of text. RL.K.5

**TEXT FOCUS: Imagery** Review with children that poets carefully choose words to help readers create a picture in their minds. Explain that a poet may use vivid verbs to help the reader more clearly understand the actions. Tell children that picturing what is happening in the poem can help them better understand the poet's message.

**SET PURPOSE** Help children set a purpose for reading the poem, such as to picture the celebration in their minds.

**TEXT COMPLEXITY RUBRIC**

| Overall Text Complexity | | "Celebration" POETRY |
|---|---|---|
| | | ACCESSIBLE |
| Quantitative Measures | Lexile | N/A |
| | Guided Reading Level | N/A |
| Qualitative Measures | Text Structure | less familiar poetic structure |
| | Language Conventionality and Clarity | clear, direct language |
| | Knowledge Demands | single theme |
| | Purpose/Levels of Meaning | single level of simple meaning (single theme) |

### Academic Vocabulary

Read each word with children and discuss its meaning.

**dusk** (line 2) • the time of day immediately after sunset
**feasting** (line 4) • eating a large meal with many people
**leaps** (line 7) • jumps
**stomps** (line 8) • the motion of walking heavily

## FIRST READ Think Through the Text

Have children use text evidence to answer these questions.

- *What is the poet telling about? a celebration that he will be going to* RL.K.1, RL.1.1
- *Who is the speaker in the poem?* Sample answer: *the poet* *How do you know? The poem uses the words* I *and* my. RL.1.6
- *What vivid verbs does the poet use? dancing, feasting, leaps, talk* RL.K.1, RL.1.4

## SECOND READ Analyze the Text

- *Close your eyes and think about the poet's words. What picture do you see in your mind?* Sample answer: *The tables are covered with food. Many people will be dancing around. Some will be dancing in a circle. Some will be stomping, and others will be leaping.* RL.K.1, RL.1.1
- *Do you think the celebration is important to the poet and the other people? How do you know?* Sample answer: *It is important because there are lots of people, and the celebration will be all night. The poet uses the words* my people. RL.K.1, RL.1.1

## Practice Fluency

**EMPHASIZE EXPRESSION** Tell children that they can use their voices to make a poem sound more interesting and fun. Read "Celebration" in a monotone. Remind children that Lopez chose words that describe vivid actions. Explain that the voice you used to read the poem was flat and boring. Then reread the first two sentences with more excitement and discuss how the second reading matches the action words. RF.1.4b

## Independent/Self-Selected Reading

If children have already demonstrated comprehension of "Celebration," have them use another poem to practice understanding imagery. Model selecting a book and choosing a poem. Suggested titles:

- *Falling Up* by Shel Silverstein
- *Song and Dance* selected by Lee Bennett Hopkins RL.1.10

### WRITE & PRESENT

1. Have small groups refer to the text to discuss its imagery. Encourage them to ask and answer questions about details in the poem. RL.K.1, RL.1.1
2. Have partners use a computer to research an American Indian celebration and write and illustrate sentences that describe it. Suggest that they use vivid verbs from the poem and other verbs to clearly tell the action. W.K.7, W.1.7
3. Have children share their writing with their group. Ask them to add details and edit their writing based on the group's suggestions. W.K.5, W.1.5
4. Invite children to take turns sharing their work with the class. Remind them to speak clearly and in a voice that can be clearly understood by others. SL.K.6, SL.1.4

*See Copying Masters, pp. 242–245.*

### STUDENT CHECKLIST

**Writing**

- ✔ Research American Indian celebrations.
- ✔ Write about an American Indian celebration using vivid action words.
- ✔ Use correct language conventions.

**Speaking & Listening**

- ✔ Participate effectively in collaborative discussion.
- ✔ Ask and answer questions about the poem's images.
- ✔ Demonstrate a connection between features in the poem and their own writing.

## OBJECTIVES

- Understand that poetry is a type of writing
- Explore the use of alliteration in poetry
- Analyze text using text evidence

### Options for Reading

**Independent** Children read independently or with the teacher and then answer questions posed by the teacher.

**Supported** Children read each sentence and answer questions with teacher support. Then they read the entire poem independently or with a partner. Encourage children to read at least a few words on their own.

# "Two Tree Toads"

by Jon Agee

**SUMMARY** Using rhythm, rhyme, and alliteration, this humorous poem is a tongue-twister that describes the problems a three-toed tree toad has tying a two-toed tree toad's shoes.

**ABOUT THE POET** **Jon Agee** began writing and illustrating his own stories as a child with his mother's help. He went on to attend art school at Cooper Union and begin a career as an illustrator. Most of Agee's writings depict characters in nonsensical situations or include wordplay.

## Discuss Genre and Set Purpose

**POETRY** Show children the poem and help them identify some characteristics of poetry, such as the smaller number of words on lines and its short length. Explain that poetry often uses rhythm and rhyme to tell about make-believe ideas as well as real things.

**TEXT FOCUS: Alliteration** Explain that poets choose words that add to a poem's rhythm and flow. One way they do this is to repeat sounds in different words. Explain that alliteration is the repeating of the same beginning sound. Discuss how alliteration makes a poem fun to listen to.

**SET PURPOSE** Help children set a purpose for reading the poem, such as to listen for repeated sounds or to find out what problem the two tree toads face.

### TEXT COMPLEXITY RUBRIC

| Overall Text Complexity | | "Two Tree Toads" POETRY<br>ACCESSIBLE |
|---|---|---|
| Quantitative Measures | Lexile | N/A |
| | Guided Reading Level | N/A |
| Qualitative Measures | Text Structure | simple, familiar poetic structure |
| | Language Conventionality and Clarity | more complex sentence structure |
| | Knowledge Demands | situation includes unfamiliar aspects |
| | Purpose/Levels of Meaning | single level of simple meaning |

### Common Core Connection

**RL.K.1** ask and answer questions about key details; **RL.K.3** identify characters, settings, and major events; **RL.K.4** ask and answer questions about unknown words; **W.K.2** use drawing, dictating, and writing to compose informative/explanatory texts; **W.K.5** respond to questions/suggestions from peers and add details to strengthen writing; **SL.K.1b** continue a conversation through multiple exchanges

**RL.1.1** ask and answer questions about key details; **RL.1.3** describe characters, settings, and major events; **RL.1.4** identify words and phrases that suggest feelings or appeal to senses; **RL.1.10** read prose and poetry; **RF.1.4b** read on-level text orally with accuracy, appropriate rate, and expression; **W.1.2** write informative/explanatory texts; **W.1.5** focus on a topic, respond to questions/suggestions from peers, and add details to strengthen writing; **SL.1.1b** build on others' talk in conversations by responding to others' comments

**Academic Vocabulary**

Read each word with children and discuss its meaning.

**sighed** (line 10) • let out a heavy breath in a loud way

**alas** (line 12) • by bad luck

## FIRST READ Think Through the Text

Have children use text evidence to answer these questions.

- *Who are the characters in this poem?* *a three-toed tree toad and a two-toed tree toad* RL.K.3, RL.1.3
- *What is this poem mostly about?* *The three-toed tree toad tries to tie the two-toed tree toad's shoe.* RL.K.3, RL.1.3
- *Did the shoe get tied?* *no* RL.K.1, RL.1.1

## SECOND READ Analyze the Text

- Remind children what alliteration is. Then reread the first two lines. Ask: *Which sound do you hear in many of the words?* /t/ *Which words have this repeated sound?* three, toed, tree, toad, tried, to, tie RL.1.4
- Write *toed* and *toad* on the board. Read the words, point out their spellings, and share their meanings. Invite children to ask and answer questions about these words. Repeat with *to* and *two*. RL.K.4
- Reread the poem. Have children listen for the repetition of /t/. Ask: *How does the repeated /t/ make this poem fun?* Sample answer: *Saying so many /t/ sounds is hard, so that makes it funny to read the poem.* RL.1.4

## Practice Fluency

**EMPHASIZE ACCURACY AND RATE** Point out to children that reading the words in a poem accurately is important so that listeners can understand the poet's message. Discuss how reading words accurately may be difficult when many of the beginning sounds in the words are repeated. Tell children that if they read at a slower rate, they will have more success reading the words correctly. RF.1.4b

## Independent/Self-Selected Reading

If children have already demonstrated comprehension of "Two Tree Toads," have them use another poem to practice skills. Suggested titles:

- *Orangutan Tongs: Poems to Tangle Your Tongue* by Jon Agee
- *Oh Say Can You Say?* by Dr. Seuss RL.1.10

### WRITE & PRESENT

1. Have children take turns reciting phrases or sentences from the poem that have alliteration. Ask them to discuss how the alliteration makes the poem fun to listen to. Encourage children to build on each others' comments. SL.K.1b, SL.1.1b
2. Individual children choose one animal and write or dictate sentences that use alliteration with the initial sound of the animal's name. Have them include details that tell what the animal looks like and how it acts. Then have them draw a picture of their animal. W.K.2, W.1.2
3. Have children share their writing with their group. Ask them to add details and edit their writing based on the group's suggestions. W.K.5, W.1.5
4. Invite children to share their sentences and illustrations with the class.

*See Copying Masters, pp. 242–245.*

### STUDENT CHECKLIST

**Writing**

- ✔ Choose an animal and write alliterative sentences using the initial sound of the animal's name.
- ✔ Include details that tell what the animal looks like and how it acts.
- ✔ Use correct language conventions.

**Speaking & Listening**

- ✔ Participate effectively in collaborative discussion.
- ✔ Build on the comments of others to extend the conversation.
- ✔ Demonstrate a connection between features in the poem and their own writing.

## OBJECTIVES

- Identify and describe characters, settings, and major events in a read-aloud story
- Ask and answer questions about key details in a text
- Analyze text using text evidence

***The Wonderful Wizard of Oz*** **is broken into three instructional segments.**

**SEGMENTS**



### Options for Reading

*Set aside 10–15 minutes to read aloud each day. Be sure to display the book's pictures and read with expression to model fluent reading.*

**Uninterrupted** Focus on the flow of the story by reading aloud without stopping for comments or questions.

**Interactive** Stop at appropriate places while reading to make comments and ask children questions. Invite children to share their own comments and questions.

### Common Core Connection

**RL.K.3** identify characters, settings, and major events; **SL.K.2** confirm understanding of a text read aloud, information presented orally, or through other media by asking/answering questions and requesting clarification; **SL.K.3** ask and answer questions to seek help, get information, or clarify something not understood

**RL.1.3** describe characters, settings, and major events; **SL.1.1c** ask questions to clear up confusion about topics and texts under discussion; **SL.1.2** ask and answer questions about details in a text read aloud, information presented orally, or through other media

# The Wonderful Wizard of Oz

by L. Frank Baum

**SUMMARY** This book tells the story of Dorothy, a Kansas farm girl, and her dog, Toto, who are swept away by a cyclone to the imaginary Land of Oz. There, the Scarecrow, Tin Woodman, and the Cowardly Lion join them on a journey to meet the powerful Wizard of Oz.

**ABOUT THE AUTHOR** L. Frank Baum wrote 14 Oz novels but his first, *The Wonderful Wizard of Oz*, published in 1900, became an American classic. Before he became a published author, Baum held many jobs including breeding poultry, selling fireworks, and owning a theater.

## Discuss Genre and Set Purpose

**FANTASY** Tell children that they will listen to a story about a girl and her dog in an imaginary land. Explain that they will hear about many characters, interesting settings, and unusual events. Ask children to think about which elements are possible in real life and which are not.

**SET PURPOSE** Help children set a purpose for listening, such as to find out the characters Dorothy meets along the way, where she goes, and what adventures she has.

**TEXT COMPLEXITY RUBRIC**

| Overall Text Complexity | | *The Wonderful Wizard of Oz* FANTASY<br>MORE COMPLEX |
|---|---|---|
| Quantitative Measures | Lexile | N/A |
| | Guided Reading Level | N/A |
| Qualitative Measures | Text Structure | unconventional story structure |
| | Language Conventionality and Clarity | complex and varied sentence structure |
| | Knowledge Demands | multiple themes |
| | Purpose/Levels of Meaning | multiple levels of complex meaning |

SEGMENT 1 pp. 9–84

### Academic Vocabulary

Read each word with children and discuss its meaning.

**shriek** (p. 14) • loud, high-pitched sound
**grateful** (p. 21) • thankful
**ordinary** (p. 35) • usual; not special
**misfortune** (p. 59) • an unlucky event
**broad** (p. 80) • wide

## FIRST READ Think Through the Text

Have children use text evidence to answer these questions.

**pp. 13–20** • *How do Dorothy and Toto get from the farm in Kansas to the Land of Oz?* *A cyclone picks up their house, carries it high in the air, and sets it down in the Land of Oz.* **RL.K.3, RL.1.3**

**pp. 21–23** • *Why are the Munchkins grateful to Dorothy?* *The Wicked Witch of the East kept the Munchkins as slaves. Dorothy's house lands on the witch and kills her so now the Munchkins are free.* **SL.K.2, SL.1.2**

**pp. 25–27** • *What is Dorothy's problem?* *Dorothy wants to go back to Uncle Henry and Aunt Em.* *What must Dorothy do to solve her problem?* *Dorothy must follow the yellow brick road to the City of Emeralds and ask the Great Wizard of Oz for help.* **SL.K.2, SL.1.2**

**pp. 38–70** • *Who are the three new friends that Dorothy and Toto meet along the yellow brick road?* *They meet the Scarecrow, the Tin Woodman, and the Cowardly Lion.* *What is each character's problem?* *The Scarecrow wants brains. The Tin Woodman wants a heart. The Cowardly Lion wants courage.* **RL.K.3, RL.1.3**

## SECOND READ Analyze the Text

- Reread pages 33–34. Then ask: *How is the land where the Munchkins live different from the forest?* Sample answer: *The yellow brick road is easy to walk on. The sun shines and the birds sing. The forest is dark and the land is rough and hard to walk on.* **RL.K.3, RL.1.3**
- Reread Dorothy's response to the Scarecrow about home on pages 44–45. Ask: *What does Dorothy mean when she says, "There is no place like home."* Sample answer: *No matter where we go, our own home is the place we like best.* **SL.K.2, SL.1.2**
- Remind children that crossing the gulf in the road is a major event. Guide them to ask questions about key details, such as: *How do the friends work together to escape from the Kalidahs?* Then support children in answering by drawing key details from the text. **SL.K.3, SL.1.1c**

### ENGLISH LANGUAGE LEARNERS

**Use Visuals and Sentence Frames**

To help children identify and describe characters, point to the characters in the illustration on page 13 and name them. Have children repeat each name and point to the corresponding character. Have children orally complete sentence frames such as: *The girl is* ____. *Dorothy* *She has a* ____. *dog*

### RESPOND TO SEGMENT 1

**Classroom Collaboration**

Have partners take turns summarizing what they have heard and asking and answering questions about anything they still don't understand.

## ENGLISH LANGUAGE LEARNERS

**Use Gestures**

To help children describe a major event, demonstrate pantomiming what happens and then have children imitate. For example, show how Dorothy throws water on the Wicked Witch of the West, causing the witch to melt. Have other children say what is being pantomimed.

**RESPOND TO SEGMENT 2**

**Classroom Collaboration**

Have partners work together to summarize what they have heard. Have them ask questions about what they don't understand.

**Common Core Connection**

**RL.K.3** identify characters, settings, and major events; **W.K.2** use drawings, dictating, and writing to compose informative/explanatory texts; **W.K.5** respond to questions/suggestions from peers and add details to strengthen writing; **SL.K.1b** continue a conversation through multiple exchanges; **SL.K.2** confirm understanding of a text read aloud, information presented orally, or through other media by asking/answering questions and requesting clarification; **SL.K.3** ask and answer questions to seek help, get information, or clarify something not understood

**RL.1.3** describe characters, settings, and major events; **RL.1.10** read prose and poetry; **W.1.2** write informative/explanatory texts; **W.1.5** focus on a topic, respond to questions/suggestions from peers and add details to strengthen writing; **SL.1.1b** build on others' talk in conversations by responding to others' comments; **SL.1.1c** ask questions to clear up confusion about topics and texts under discussion; **SL.1.2** ask and answer questions about details in a text read aloud, information presented orally, or through other media

**Academic Vocabulary**

Read each word with children and discuss its meaning.

**bounded** (p. 95) • jumped
**astonished** (p. 103) • surprised
**dazzled** (p. 115) • hurt the eyes with too much light
**meek** (p. 127) • shy
**rejoicing** (p. 159) • showing happiness; celebrating

## FIRST READ Think Through the Text

Have children use text evidence to answer these questions.

**pp. 121–122** • Reread the text on pages 121–122. Ask: *What words in the text tell about the Emerald City?* Sample answer: beautiful houses, sparkling emeralds, no horses nor animals *Why do people wear green spectacles, or glasses, in the Emerald City?* *If they don't, the brightness of Emerald City will blind them.* **RL.K.3, RL.1.3**

**pp. 128–135** • *Why are the friends disappointed after they meet with the Wizard of Oz? The friends find out they must kill the Wicked Witch of the West to get their wishes, and they don't think they can do this.* **SL.K.2, SL.1.2**

**pp. 140–149** • *How does the Wicked Witch of the West try to stop the friends? Does her plan work? She sends wolves, crows, black bees, and Winkies to stop them, but this does not work. Finally, the Wicked Witch calls for the Winged Monkeys. The monkeys stop the Scarecrow and Tin Woodman. They bring the Lion, Dorothy, and Toto back to the Wicked Witch's castle.* **SL.K.2, SL.1.2**

**pp. 154–155** • *How does Dorothy get rid of the Wicked Witch of the West? She throws a bucket of water on the witch and this causes the witch to melt away.* **RL.K.3, RL.1.3**

## SECOND READ Analyze the Text

- Review pages 127–134 with children. *What does the Wizard of Oz look like? How do you know? The Wizard of Oz can change what he looks like. For Dorothy, he looks like an enormous head, he is a lovely lady for Scarecrow, a terrible beast for the Tin Woodman, and a ball of fire for Lion.* **RL.K.3, RL.1.3**
- Reread the last paragraph on page 145. Ask: *Why is the Golden Cap so important to those who own it? The owner can call on the Winged Monkeys three times to obey any order they are given.* Remind children that Dorothy became the owner of the Golden Cap when she got rid of the witch. Ask: *How does Dorothy use the Golden Cap for the first time? When the friends are lost, Dorothy asks the Winged Monkeys to take them back to the Emerald City.* **SL.K.2, SL.1.2**

SEGMENT 3 pp. 177–261

**Academic Vocabulary**

Read each word with children and discuss its meaning.

**fierce** (p. 203) • wild and frightening
**wept** (p. 211) • cried
**scramble** (p. 234) • climb or crawl quickly
**gravely** (p. 261) • seriously

## FIRST READ Think Through the Text

Have children cite text evidence to answer these questions.

**pp. 183–184** • *What surprising thing do the friends find out about the Wizard of Oz? They find out he is just a little old man.* **SL.K.2, SL.1.2**

**pp. 207–208** • *What happens to the Wizard of Oz? He leaves Oz forever in a hot air balloon.* **RL.K.3, RL.1.3**

**pp. 257–259** • *How does Dorothy get back home? She claps the heels of the Silver Shoes together three times and says, "Take me home to Aunt Em!" Then she is carried through the air to Kansas.* **RL.K.3, RL.1.3**

## SECOND READ Analyze the Text

- Remind children that when the Wizard tells the friends how he tricked them, it is a major event. Reread pp. 185–188. Guide children to ask questions about the event. Suggest that they begin questions with the words *who*, *what*, *when*, *why*, or *how*. Support children in answering questions by drawing key details from the text. **SL.K.2, SL.1.2**
- Reread pages 254–257. Ask: *What kind of person is Glinda? How do you know?* Sample answer: *Glinda is good, kind, and helpful. She helps the Scarecrow, Tin Woodman, and the Lion get back to the places where they are rulers. She helps Dorothy get back to Kansas.* **RL.K.3, RL.1.3**
- Reread page 261. Ask: *How does Aunt Em feel when Dorothy comes home? How do you know?* Sample answer: *Aunt Em is happy. She hugs and kisses her.* **SL.K.2, SL.1.2**

# Independent/Self-Selected Reading

If children have demonstrated comprehension of *The Wonderful Wizard of Oz*, have them practice and apply skills using another book. Model selecting a book from the classroom library. Help children read the title of the book and the name of the author. Suggested titles:

- *Where the Wild Things Are* by Maurice Sendak
- *The Polar Express* by Chris Van Allsburg **RL.1.10**

### WRITE & PRESENT

1. Guide children in small groups to ask each other questions about the characters of Dorothy, Aunt Em, and Uncle Henry, the setting of the Kansas prairie, and major events such as the arrival of the cyclone. Then prompt and support them in answering the questions by drawing key details from the text. **SL.K.1b, SL.1.1b**
2. Individual children use the answers to their questions to draw a picture and write a description of one major event, including its setting and the characters involved. **W.K.2, W.1.2**
3. Children within each group share their descriptions with each other and edit their work. **W.K.5, W.1.5**
4. Individual children present their final ideas and illustrations to classmates. **SL.K.6**

*See Copying Masters, pp. 242–245.*

### STUDENT CHECKLIST

**Writing**

- ✔ Draw and write about one major event from the story.
- ✔ Include a description of the characters and the setting.
- ✔ Use correct language conventions.

**Speaking & Listening**

- ✔ Participate effectively in a collaborative discussion.
- ✔ Ask and answer questions about text details.
- ✔ Describe details in their own drawings and writing that demonstrate an understanding of the text.

## OBJECTIVES

- Ask and answer questions about events and key details in a read-aloud story
- Describe the concept of pioneer life
- Analyze text using text evidence

***Little House in the Big Woods*** **is broken into three instructional segments.**

**SEGMENTS**



### Options for Read Aloud

*Set aside 10–15 minutes to read aloud each day. Be sure to display the book's pictures and read with expression to model fluent reading.*

**Uninterrupted** Focus on the flow of the story by reading aloud without stopping for comments or questions.

**Interactive** Stop at appropriate places while reading to make comments and ask children questions. Also, invite children to share their own comments and questions.

### Common Core Connection

**RL.K.3** identify characters, settings, and major events; **SL.K.2** confirm understanding of a text read aloud, information presented orally, or through other media by asking/answering questions and requesting clarification; **SL.K.3** ask and answer questions to seek help, get information, or clarify something not understood

**RL.1.3** describe characters, settings, and major events; **SL.1.2** ask and answer questions about details in a text read aloud, information presented orally, or through other media; **SL.1.1c** ask questions to clear up confusion about topics and texts under discussion

# *Little House in the Big Woods*

by Laura Ingalls Wilder

**SUMMARY** This book narrates the adventures of five-year-old Laura Ingalls and her family, who live in a log cabin deep in the remote woods of Wisconsin in the 1870s.

**ABOUT THE AUTHOR** **Laura Ingalls Wilder** was born in a log cabin in Wisconsin in 1867 and spent most of her childhood moving from place to place. As an adult, Wilder began to write down stories of her childhood for her daughter. *Little House in the Big Woods* was her first book, published when she was 65 years old.

## Discuss Genre and Set Purpose

**HISTORICAL FICTION** Tell children that they will be listening to a story about a little girl and her family who lived a long time ago in a log cabin in the woods. Explain that the girl and her family were the first people to settle on the land they lived on. Tell children that the story is based on the author's own childhood almost 150 years ago.

**SET PURPOSE** Help children set a purpose for listening, such as to learn about events that take place in the life of a family living in a log cabin long ago.

**TEXT COMPLEXITY RUBRIC**

| Overall Text Complexity | | *Little House in the Big Woods* HISTORICAL FICTION<br>MORE COMPLEX |
|---|---|---|
| Quantitative Measures | Lexile | N/A |
| | Guided Reading Level | N/A |
| Qualitative Measures | Text Structure | complex, unfamiliar story concepts |
| | Language Conventionality and Clarity | many unfamiliar or high academic words |
| | Knowledge Demands | distinctly unfamiliar experience |
| | Purpose/Levels of Meaning | multiple levels of meaning |

## SEGMENT 1 pp. 1–82

### Academic Vocabulary

Read each word with children and discuss its meaning.

**swift** (p. 5) • fast
**mend** (p. 29) • fix
**sleek** (p. 48) • smooth
**savage** (p. 69) • wild
**chores** (p. 79) • household tasks or jobs

## FIRST READ Think Through the Text

Have children use text evidence to answer the following questions.

**pp. 1–2** • *Where does this story take place? in the Big Woods of Wisconsin When does this story take place? a long time ago* How do you know? *The text says that the family lives alone in the woods and that they must gather and prepare their own food. The pictures on the first two pages show a log cabin in the woods and people wearing old-fashioned clothing.* RL.K.3, RL.1.3

**pp. 5–23** • *What do the Ingalls do to get ready for the winter? Pa hunts and fishes to get food; they salt the meat and store it away; they gather vegetables from their garden to store in the cellar.* SL.K.2, SL.1.2

**pp. 33–44** • *What does the Ingalls family do for fun? They play games, play with dolls, and tell stories. Pa plays his fiddle.* SL.K.2, SL.1.2

**pp. 59–80** • *How do the Ingalls celebrate Christmas? Their relatives visit, they receive and give presents, and they eat special food.* SL.K.2, SL.1.2

## SECOND READ Analyze the Text

- Reread Ma's saying about work that appears on page 29. Have children ask questions about any words that are unfamiliar, and discuss the different chores that the family has. Then ask: *Why does Ma have this saying? to remind them of what needs to be done each day; to be sure that everything gets done* Ask: *How else do Laura and Mary help Ma? They wipe their dishes and make their bed.* SL.K.3, SL.1.1c
- Ask: *Why do the Ingalls need to store away food for winter? They live in the woods and do not have stores where they can buy food; they must hunt or grow all their food themselves.* SL.K.2, SL.1.2
- Remind children that Christmas is a major event in the book. Guide them to ask questions about key details related to the event. Suggest that children begin their questions with the words *who, what, where, when, why,* or *how*. Record their questions on the board. Then reread the questions and prompt and support children in answering questions by drawing key details from the text. SL.K.3, SL.1.1c

### Domain Specific Vocabulary

**venison** (p. 5) • meat from deer
**brine** (p. 14) • water with salt in it used for soaking food
**cracklings** (p.17) • the crispy fatty skin of roast pork
**churn** (p. 29) • to mix milk or cream so it becomes butter

### ELL ENGLISH LANGUAGE LEARNERS

**Using Pictures and Sentence Frames**

To be sure that children understand story characters and setting, have them draw a picture that shows the main character and where she lives. Then ask children to orally complete sentence frames such as: *The main character is_____. Laura She lives in a _____. log cabin in the woods*

### RESPOND TO SEGMENT 1

**Classroom Collaboration**

Have partners take turns summarizing what they have learned and asking and answering questions about anything they still don't understand.

**Domain Specific Vocabulary**

**samplers** (p. 96) • pieces of cloth embroidered with different stitches

## ENGLISH LANGUAGE LEARNERS

**Use Visuals and Sentence Frames**

Show children the picture on page 165 and ask yes/no questions about it, such as: *Is the family at their log cabin?* no *Is the family in a wagon going to town?* yes Then have children orally complete sentences such as: *The family is going to _______.* town

**RESPOND TO SEGMENT 2**

**Classroom Collaboration**

Have partners work together to summarize what they have heard. Have them ask questions about what they don't understand.

**Common Core Connection**

**W.K.2** use drawing, dictating, and writing to compose informative/explanatory texts; **W.K.5** respond to questions/suggestions from peers and add details to strengthen writing; **SL.K.1b** continue a conversation through multiple exchanges; **SL.K.6** speak audibly and express thoughts, feelings, and ideas clearly

**RL.1.10** read prose and poetry; **W.1.2** write informative/explanatory texts; **W.1.5** focus on a topic, respond to questions/suggestions from peers and add details to strengthen writing; **SL.1.1b** build on others' talk in conversations by responding to others' comments

**Academic Vocabulary**

Read each word with children and discuss its meaning.

**solemn** (p. 87) • serious

**stump** (p. 113) • the bottom part of a tree trunk after most of the tree has been cut off

**spacious** (p. 135) • having lots of space

**muzzle** (p. 159) • the nose and mouth of an animal

## FIRST READ Think Through the Text

Have children use text evidence to answer the following questions.

**pp. 83–85** • Have children think about how Laura and Mary spend their Sundays. Ask: *How is Sunday for Laura and Mary different than the rest of the days of the week?* On Sunday the girls don't do any work or chores; they sit and read or play quietly. **SL.K.2, SL.1.2**

**pp. 131–155** • *Why do the Ingalls go to visit Grandma and Grandpa?* to help gather maple syrup and to go to a dance **SL.K.2, SL.1.2**

**pp. 156–176** • Remind children that Laura and Mary go to town for the first time. Ask: *How is town different from where the Ingalls live?* The town has many buildings close together, but where they live in the woods, the log cabin is the only building. Ask: *What do Laura and Mary do in the store?* They look at all the different things. *What do Ma and Pa do?* They trade for things they need. **SL.K.2, SL.1.2**

## SECOND READ Analyze the Text

- Remind children that Pa tells "The Story of Grandpa's Sled and the Pig" after Laura says that she hates Sundays. *Why does Pa tell Laura this story?* to teach Laura a lesson; to show that she is not the only one who has trouble sitting still on Sundays; to show that Sunday rules were much stricter when Grandpa was a boy **SL.K.2, SL.1.2**
- Remind children that Pa leaves Ma and the girls alone when he goes to town to trade furs. Ask: *How is it different in the house when Pa is away?* It doesn't seem as safe. *What clues in the story help you to know this?* Ma locks the doors, and Laura and Mary have trouble falling asleep. **SL.K.2, SL.1.2**
- Remind children that going to town is a major event for the Ingalls. Guide them to ask questions about key details related to the event, such as: *How does Laura feel when she sees town for the first time?* Then prompt and support children in answering the questions by drawing key details from the text. For example: *How do you know how Laura feels? What does the text tell you?* **RL.K.3, RL.1.3**

**SEGMENT 3** pp. 177–238

### Academic Vocabulary

Read each word with students and discuss its meaning.

**primly** (p. 181) • politely
**harvest** (p. 199) • the gathering of crops
**stoop** (p. 201) • bend down
**scampering** (p. 215) • running quickly

## FIRST READ Think Through the Text

Have children cite text evidence to answer the following questions.

**pp. 177–182** • *How is summer different from winter for the Ingalls?* Sample answer: *In summer the Ingalls have visitors over for dinner; the grown-ups sit and talk and the children play outside.* **SL.K.2, SL.1.2**

**pp. 199–211** • Remind children that Pa and Uncle Henry share work during harvest time. Ask: *What do they do to their crops during the harvest? They cut and gather the crops; they get them ready for winter.* **SL.K.2, SL.1.2**

**pp. 232–236** • Remind children that Pa goes hunting one night. Ask: *Why doesn't Pa bring home fresh meat? He could not bring himself to shoot the animals that he saw.* **SL.K.2, SL.1.2**

## SECOND READ Analyze the Text

- Ask: *How are Laura and Mary different? Laura is noisy and likes to run around; Mary is quiet and well-behaved.* ***How do you know?*** *Laura gets in trouble in the text; Mary does not. Laura likes to play outside with other children; Mary likes to walk quietly and talk.* **SL.K.2, SL.1.2**
- Ask children to think about how hard Pa and Uncle Henry work to harvest their crops. Ask: *Why is Chapter 12 called "The Wonderful Machine"? The machine is able to thresh the grain faster and better than Pa and Uncle Henry; it saves them a lot of time and hard work.* **SL.K.2, SL.1.2**

## Independent/Self-Selected Reading

If children have demonstrated listening comprehension of *Little House in the Big Woods,* have them practice and apply skills using another book. Model selecting a book from the classroom library. Help children read the title of the book, the author's name, and any information about the book on the back or inside cover. Suggested titles:

- *Going to Town (My First Little House series)* by Laura Ingalls Wilder
- *Summertime in the Big Woods (My First Little House series)* by Laura Ingalls Wilder **RL.1.10**

### WRITE & PRESENT

1. Guide partners to ask each other questions about key events that occur in the text, such as the encounter with the bear. Then prompt and support them in answering the questions by drawing key details from the text. **SL.K.1b, SL.1.1b**
2. Individual children use the answers to their questions to draw and write about one key event from the story. **W.K.2, W.1.2**
3. Children work with partners to share and edit their work. **W.K.5, W.1.5**
4. Individual children present their final ideas and illustrations to classmates. **SL.K.6**

*See Copying Masters, pp. 242–245.*

### STUDENT CHECKLIST

**Writing**

- ✔ Draw and write about one key event from the story.
- ✔ Include a main idea and key details.
- ✔ Use correct language conventions.

**Speaking & Listening**

- ✔ Participate effectively in a collaborative discussion.
- ✔ Ask and answer questions about text details.
- ✔ Demonstrate a connection between the information from the text and their own writing and drawing.

## OBJECTIVES

- Describe characters, settings, and major events in a read-aloud story
- Use key details to make predictions about the text
- Analyze text using text evidence

***Mr. Popper's Penguins* is broken into three instructional segments.**

**SEGMENTS**

**SEGMENT 1. . . . . . . . .pp. 3–49**
**SEGMENT 2. . . . . . . . pp. 50–80**
**SEGMENT 3. . . . . . . pp. 81–139**

### Options for Reading

*Set aside 10–15 minutes to read aloud each day. Be sure to display the book's pictures and read with expression to model fluent reading.*

**Uninterrupted** Focus on the flow of the story by reading aloud without stopping for comments or questions.

**Interactive** Stop at appropriate places while reading to make comments and ask children questions. Also, invite children to share their own comments and questions.

### Common Core Connection

**RL.K.3** identify characters, settings, and major events; **RL.K.9** compare and contrast adventures and experiences of characters; **SL.K.2** confirm understanding of a text read aloud, information presented orally, or through other media by asking/answering questions and requesting clarification; **SL.K.3** ask and answer questions to seek help, get information, or clarify something not understood

**RL.1.3** describe characters, settings, and major events; **RL.1.9** compare and contrast adventures and experiences of characters; **SL.1.2** ask and answer questions about details in a text read aloud, information presented orally, or through other media; **SL.1.1c** ask questions to clear up confusion about topics and texts under discussion

# Mr. Popper's Penguins

by Richard and Florence Atwater

**SUMMARY** In this classic tale, house painter Mr. Popper loves reading about his favorite topic, exploring Antarctica. Then suddenly he finds himself owning a penguin from Antarctica, and his life changes forever.

**ABOUT THE AUTHOR Richard Atwater** and his wife, **Florence Atwater**, got the idea for *Mr. Popper's Penguins* after seeing a film about an Antarctic expedition. Mr. Atwater wrote a first version of the book before suffering a stroke. Mrs. Atwater then worked on a second version and had the book published in 1938. The following year, *Mr. Popper's Penguins* was named a Newbery Honor book.

## Discuss Genre and Set Purpose

**HUMOROUS FICTION** Explain that children will be listening to a story about Mr. Popper, who receives a gift of a penguin from Antarctica. Discuss with children how they can tell that this book tells a story that is made-up and what might be funny about Mr. Popper's situation.

**SET PURPOSE** Help children set a purpose for listening, such as to find out about the key events in the story of Mr. Popper and his penguin.

**TEXT COMPLEXITY RUBRIC**

| Overall Text Complexity | | *Mr. Popper's Penguins* HUMOROUS FICTION<br>COMPLEX |
|---|---|---|
| Quantitative Measures | Lexile | N/A |
| | Guided Reading Level | N/A |
| Qualitative Measures | Text Structure | complex, unfamiliar story concepts |
| | Language Conventionality and Clarity | more complex descriptions |
| | Knowledge Demands | distinctly unfamiliar experience |
| | Purpose/Levels of Meaning | multiple levels of meaning |

## SEGMENT 1 pp. 3–49

### Academic Vocabulary

Read each word with children and discuss its meaning.

**untidy** (p. 3) • messy; not neat

**flippers** (p. 18) • wide, flat arm-like parts of an animal's body that it uses to swim

**curious** (p. 18) • wanting to know about things

**strut** (p. 19) • a way of walking that shows pride in oneself

**pecking** (p. 24) • biting or poking something with a beak

### Domain Specific Vocabulary

**expeditions** (p. 6) • long trips by a group of people who want to discover something

**tobogganed** (p. 21) • slid as if on a sled

**rookery** (p. 48) • a place where there are many birds' nests

## FIRST READ Think Through the Text

Have children use text evidence to answer these questions.

**pp. 3–6** • *Who is the story about?* Mr. Popper *What is Mr. Popper's job?* house painter *What job does he wish he had?* scientist in the North or South Pole *Why?* He is interested in everything about the North and South Poles. RL.K.3, RL.1.3

**pp. 14–18** • *How does Mr. Popper get a penguin?* He writes to an Antarctic explorer who sends him a penguin as a gift. SL.K.2, SL.1.2

**pp. 31–43** • *Retell a part of the story that tells about a problem that the penguin, Captain Cook, causes the Popper family.* Sample answer: Mr. Popper asks a man to fix the refrigerator so the penguin can go in it to keep cool. The man thinks Mr. Popper is crazy. The penguin comes out and pecks the man. He runs away and tells the police. SL.K.2, SL.1.2

## SECOND READ Analyze the Text

- Ask: *How are Mr. and Mrs. Popper different?* She worries about money. He doesn't. She likes things tidy. He's messy. She doesn't want a pet. He does. RL.K.9, RL.1.9
- Guide children to think about the setting of the story. Ask: *How would you describe where the Poppers live?* It's quiet and nothing new ever happens; everyone does the same thing. *How do things change once Captain Cook arrives?* It's more exciting. RL.K.3, RL.1.3
- Point out that Mrs. Popper's feelings about the penguin change. Invite children to ask questions to clarify their understanding of those changes. Suggest that they ask questions that begin with *why* and *how*. Guide children in finding key details in the text that help answer their questions and clarify their understanding. SL.K.3, SL.1.1c
- Say: *Predict something that might happen when Mr. Popper takes Captain Cook for a walk. Why do you think so?* Sample answer: Captain Cook might walk up to people and peck them. He is curious and sometimes pecks people or things he is curious about. SL.K.2, SL.1.2

### ENGLISH LANGUAGE LEARNERS

**Use Visuals**

Call attention to the picture on page 18. Say *penguin* and have children repeat the word. Encourage children to give the name in their native language, such as *pingüino* in Spanish. Identify the animal's colors and have children repeat the words. Point to parts of its body and name them: *flippers*, *beak*, *tail*, *feet*. Have children echo the words. Then ask children to say words to describe the animal and its parts, if possible.

### RESPOND TO SEGMENT 1

**Classroom Collaboration**

Have partners work together to create and present a summary, as well as raise questions that might be answered in the next segment.

### Domain Specific Vocabulary

**climate** (p. 64) • weather over a long period of time

**aquarium** (p. 66) • a building that people can visit to see sea animals

### ENGLISH LANGUAGE LEARNERS

**Use Gestures**

Have children use gestures and facial expressions to act out Chapters X and XI. Help them show how Captain Cook feels before and after Greta arrives. Encourage children to use words such as: *sad*, *lonely*, *happy*, and *well* to tell about his feelings.

### RESPOND TO SEGMENT 2

**Classroom Collaboration**

Have small groups work together to summarize what they have heard. Have them ask questions about what they don't understand.

### Common Core Connection

**W.K.2** use drawing, dictating, and writing to compose informative/explanatory texts; **W.K.5** respond to questions/suggestions from peers and add details to strengthen writing; **SL.K.1b** continue a conversation through multiple exchanges; **SL.K.4** describe familiar people, places, things, and events/provide detail **RL.1.10** read prose and poetry; **SL.1.1b** build on others' talk in conversations by responding to others' comments; **W.1.2** write informative/explanatory texts; **W.1.5** focus on a topic, respond to questions/suggestions from peers, and add details to strengthen writing; **SL.1.4** describe people, places, things, and events with details/express ideas and feelings clearly

### Academic Vocabulary

Read each word with children and discuss its meaning.

**stroll** (p. 50) • a slow, easy walk

**waddling** (p. 51) • moving in little steps with the body moving from side to side

**plunge** (p. 60) • to rush ahead

**sulking** (p. 63) • letting others know you are sad or upset by being quiet.

## FIRST READ Think Through the Text

Have children use text evidence to answer these questions.

**pp. 53–56** • *Why do a reporter and cameraman stop Mr. Popper?* They *want to write a story about the penguin for the newspaper.* **SL.K.2, SL.1.2**

**pp. 62–65** • *How does Captain Cook look and act when the Poppers think he is sick?* *He looks unhappy. He isn't curious. He won't play. He is mean and tries to bite people.* **SL.K.2, SL.1.2**

**pp. 67–69** • *What makes the penguin get better?* *Mr. Popper gets another penguin, Greta, to be Captain Cook's friend.* **SL.K.2, SL.1.2**

**pp. 74–77** • *How are the baby penguins born?* *Greta lays eggs. She keeps them warm until they hatch.* **SL.K.2, SL.1.2**

## SECOND READ Analyze the Text

- Remind children of how people in the neighborhood act when they see Captain Cook. Ask: *Why might they act that way?* Sample answer: *They are afraid of him or annoyed with him. Some people have probably never seen a penguin, so they don't know what it is. Other people may not believe it is a penguin because they know penguins only live in cold places.* **RL.K.3, RL.1.3**
- *Why do the neighbors bring special foods for Captain Cook when he is not feeling well?* Possible answers: *They have gotten used to him and might even like him; they feel sorry for Mr. Popper.* **SL.K.2, SL.1.2**
- Have children think about events in the Poppers' house as the weather gets colder. Ask: *What is unusual about what happens in the house?* *The family wears coats and boots inside; there is snow in the house; the children sled indoors.* **RL.K.3, RL.1.3**
- Tell children that the next chapter is called "Money Worries." Ask: *What do you predict this chapter may be about? Why?* Sample answer: *The chapter might be about how Mrs. Popper worries about how to pay for taking care of all the penguins. She has been worried about money in the past, so she will probably worry again now that there are more.* **SL.K.2, SL.1.2**

**SEGMENT 3** pp. 81–139

### Academic Vocabulary

Read each word with children and discuss its meaning.

**trained** (p. 82) • taught to do something
**famous** (p. 108) • known by a lot of people
**decision** (p. 131) • choice; what someone picks
**voyage** (p. 135) • a long trip

## FIRST READ Think Through the Text

Have children use text evidence to answer these questions.

**p. 83** • *What is Mr. Popper's idea about how to get money? He wants to train the penguins to do tricks so they can perform in shows.* SL.K.2, SL.1.2

**pp. 92–98** • *What kinds of acts do the penguins do in their shows? They march, fight, and slide.* SL.K.2, SL.1.2

**pp. 138–139** • *What does Admiral Drake ask Mr. Popper to do at the end of the story? He asks him to come to the North Pole with the penguins and get them settled there.* SL.K.2, SL.1.2

## SECOND READ Analyze the Text

- Ask: *Why is the penguins' act a big success?* Sample answer: *People think it is funny to see animals doing things that people usually do, such as going down ladders. It is funny to see the penguins doing these things in a different way than humans do.* SL.K.2, SL.1.2
- *How might Mr. Popper be feeling when the weather gets warm? worried, sad Why?* Sample answer: *He feels worried because he knows the penguins need to be in a cold place and they won't be able to do their act any more. He feels sad that he will have to give them up.* RL.K.3, RL.1.3
- Have children think about what they have learned about what penguins need to live. Ask: *What will the penguins' home in the North Pole probably be like? It will be cold, so they won't need a special place like a refrigerator or ice rink. They'll catch fish to eat and slide on snow. They'll build nests with rocks they find on the land.* SL.K.2, SL.1.2

# Independent/Self-Selected Reading

If children have demonstrated listening comprehension of *Mr. Popper's Penguins*, have them practice the skills using another book. Model selecting a book from the classroom library. Suggested titles:

- *A Penguin Story* by Antoinette Portis
- *The Emperor's Egg* by Martin Jenkins RL.1.10

### WRITE & PRESENT

1. Have small groups of children review key events by asking and answering questions about the story. Encourage them to record their ideas in words or drawings on a piece of paper. SL.K.1b, SL.1.1b
2. Individual children pick one key event from what the group recorded and write sentences about it. Tell them to include at least two details in their sentences. Encourage children to make a picture to go with the writing. W.K.2, W.1.2
3. In groups, children work to edit their work. W.K.5, W.1.5
4. Children in each group present their final work in the order in which the events take place, so that the story makes sense. SL.K.4, SL.1.4
5. Individual children turn in their final art and writing to the teacher.

*See Copying Masters, pp. 242–245.*

### STUDENT CHECKLIST

#### Writing

- ✔ Draw and write about one key event from the story.
- ✔ Include at least two relevant details.
- ✔ Use correct language conventions.

#### Speaking & Listening

- ✔ Participate effectively in a collaborative discussion.
- ✔ Ask and answer questions about text details.
- ✔ Demonstrate a connection between the information from the text and the information presented in their writing.

## OBJECTIVES

- Ask and answer questions about key details
- Identify characters, setting, and main events
- Identify the points at which different characters are telling the story

***Finn Family Moomintroll*** **is broken into three instructional segments.**

**SEGMENTS**



### Options for Reading

*Set aside 10–15 minutes to read aloud each day. Be sure to display the book's pictures and read with expression to model fluent reading.*

**Uninterrupted** Focus on the flow of the story by reading aloud without stopping for comments or questions.

**Interactive** Stop at appropriate places while reading to make comments and ask children questions. Also, invite children to share their own comments and questions.

### Common Core Connection

**RL.K.1** ask and answer questions about key details; **RL.K.3** identify characters, settings, and major events; **RL.K.5** recognize common types of texts

**RL.1.1** ask and answer questions about key details; **RL.1.3** describe characters, settings, and major events; **RL.1.5** explain major differences between story books and informational books; **RL.1.6** identify who is telling the story

# *Finn Family Moomintroll*

by Tove Jansson

**SUMMARY** Spring has come to the valley, and Moomintroll, Snufkin, and Sniff find something amazing—a Hobgoblin's top hat that has magical powers. The top hat leads to many adventures and changes for the Moomins as spring turns into autumn.

**ABOUT THE AUTHOR** **Tove Jansson** was a Swedish-speaking Finnish author who is best known for her character Moomintroll and the Moomin family. The Moomin series is so popular that it has been translated worldwide and has inspired television series, movies, operas, and even theme parks. Tove Jansson died in 2001.

## Discuss Genre and Set Purpose

**FANTASY** Display the book and read the title together. Then read the chapter synopses and show children the illustrations. Discuss with children how they know this story is about make-believe characters and events.

**SET PURPOSE** Help children set a purpose for listening, such as to find out what Moomintroll and his friends do with the top hat they find.

**TEXT COMPLEXITY RUBRIC**

| Overall Text Complexity | | *Finn Family Moomintroll* FANTASY<br>MORE COMPLEX |
|---|---|---|
| Quantitative Measures | Lexile | N/A |
| | Guided Reading Level | N/A |
| Qualitative Measures | Text Structure | some unconventional story structure elements |
| | Language Conventionality and Clarity | increased unfamiliar or academic words |
| | Knowledge Demands | somewhat unfamiliar experience |
| | Purpose/Levels of Meaning | single level of complex meaning |

### Academic Vocabulary

Read each word with children and discuss its meaning.

**clambered** (p. 7) • to climb or move quickly but with difficulty

**lure** (p. 27) • to attract someone or something

## FIRST READ Think Through the Text

Have children use text evidence to answer these questions.

**pp. 1–3** • *Who is the main character in this story?* *Moomintroll* *Where does the story take place?* *Moomin Valley* RL.K.3, RL.1.3

**pp. 8–9** • *What do Moomintroll, Sniff, and Snufkin find at the top of the mountain?* *a tall black hat* *Do they know the hat is magical?* *no* *How do you know?* *The text says that they don't know that the hat will cast a spell on the Valley of the Moomins and that they will see strange things.* RL.K.3, RL.1.3

**pp. 22–23** • *What happens to Moomintroll when he hides in the Hobgoblin's hat?* *He changes shape. His fat parts become thin and everything that was small becomes big.* RL.K.1, RL.1.1

## SECOND READ Analyze the Text

- Reread pages 4–5. Explain that each chapter in this story focuses on a different character and tells about the events the way that character sees them. Ask: *Which character is this chapter going to be about?* *Moomintroll* *How do you know?* *The story tells us about Moomintroll waking up from his winter's sleep. We learn what he does and what he thinks.* RL.K.1, RL.1.6
- Reread pages 6–7. *Is this story about things that could happen in real life?* *no* *How do you know?* *The story describes spirits that haunt trees and an earthworm that talks.* RL.K.5, RL.1.5
- Review the dialogue between Moomintroll and Snork on the top of page 27. Point out that even though they don't say what "it" must be, we can figure out the meaning by thinking about what they were just talking about. *Ask: What do Moomintroll and Snork think must have changed Moomintroll?* *the hat* RL.K.3, RL.1.3
- Reread page 38. *Do you think Moomintroll is sure they have done the right thing by going after the hat?* *no* *How do you know?* *He says it's the first time they have done anything they couldn't tell mother and father about.* RL.K.3, RL.1.3

### ENGLISH LANGUAGE LEARNERS

**Use Comprehensible Input**

To ensure that children understand the most important words in the story, ask questions that can be answered using key story words, such as: *When does Moomintroll wake up?* *spring* *What does Moomintroll find?* *a hat*

### RESPOND TO SEGMENT 1

**Classroom Collaboration**

Have partners summarize what they have heard so far. Tell them to ask questions about anything they don't understand.

## ENGLISH LANGUAGE LEARNERS

**Use Visuals**

Use the illustrations to help children understand the characters and events. For example, show the illustration on page 40 and say *Muskrat is upset*. Make an upset face. Have children repeat. Then have them turn to a partner and say words or sentences to describe the illustration. Repeat for additional illustrations.

**RESPOND TO SEGMENT 2**

**Classroom Collaboration**

Have small groups work together to summarize what they have read so far. Have them ask questions about what they don't understand.

**Common Core Connection**

**RL.K.1** ask and answer questions about key details; **RL.K.3** identify characters, settings, and major events; **RL.K.9** compare and contrast adventures and experiences of characters; **RL.K.10** engage in group reading activities with purpose and understanding; **W.K.2** use drawing, dictating, and writing to compose informative/explanatory texts; **W.K.5** respond to questions/suggestions from peers and add details to strengthen writing; **SL.K.6** speak audibly and express thoughts, feelings, and ideas clearly

**RL.1.1** ask and answer questions about key details; **RL.1.3** describe characters, settings, and major events; **RL.1.9** compare and contrast adventures and experiences of characters; **RL.1.10** read prose and poetry; **W.1.2** write informative/explanatory texts; **W.1.5** focus on a topic, respond to questions/suggestions from peers, and add details to strengthen writing; **SL.1.6** produce complete sentences when appropriate to task and situation

**Academic Vocabulary**

Read each word with students and discuss its meaning.

**pandemonium** (p. 66) • noisy confusion

**suspicious** (p. 86) • questioning

## FIRST READ Think Through the Text

Have children use text evidence to answer these questions.

**pp. 48–52** • *What does the Moomin family find on the beach?* *a sailing-boat with oars and fishing tackle* ***What do they name it?*** The Adventure ***Where do they go with it?*** *to Lonely Island* **RL.K.1, RL.1.1**

**pp. 65–69** • *Why do the Hattifatteners attack the Moomins?* *They are looking for their barometer.* ***What happens to the Snork Maiden because of the attack?*** *Her hair gets burnt off.* **RL.K.3, RL.1.3**

**pp. 94–97** • *What is the Mameluke?* *a fish* **RL.K.1, RL.1.1**

**pp. 98–99** • *What happens to the Moomins' house?* *It becomes a jungle after Moominmamma drops a ball of poisonous pink perennials into the Hobgoblin's Hat.* **RL.K.1, RL.1.1**

## SECOND READ Analyze the Text

- Remind children that this story tells about the adventures of many different characters. Explain that good readers pay attention to which character the author is talking about by looking for clues, such as the words and thoughts of a character. Reread pages 40–41. Say: *Which character is the author telling a story about?* *Muskrat* ***What does Muskrat say that shows he doesn't like to be embarrassed?*** *The earth can crack and fire come down from heaven for all I care—that sort of thing doesn't disturb me—but I do not like to be put into a ridiculous situation.* **RL.K.1, RL.1.6**
- Review pages 46–48. Ask: *How is the Muskrat's experience with the hat like the experiences of the other characters?* *He dropped something into the hat and it changed.* ***How is it different?*** *The other characters have had harmless or amusing experiences with the hat. Muskrat is scared by what his false teeth change into.* **RL.K.9, RL.1.9**
- Reread pages 84–85. Ask: *Who is telling the story about the Hobgoblin?* *Snufkin* ***Why does he tell this story?*** *to frighten the others; to explain how Sniff found the hat* **RL.K.1, RL.1.6**

**SEGMENT 3** pp. 107–151

### Academic Vocabulary

Read each word with students and discuss its meaning.

**departure** (p. 131) • the action of leaving or going away

## FIRST READ Think Through the Text

Have children use text evidence to answer these questions.

**pp. 107–113** • *Who comes to stay with the Moomins?* Thingumy and Bob *What do they have that the Groke wants?* a suitcase **RL.K.3, RL.1.3**

**p. 121** • *How do the Moomins get rid of the hat?* The Groke takes it. **RL.K.3, RL.1.3**

**pp. 126–127** • *Why is Moomintroll sad?* Snufkin has gone away. *Why do Bob and Thingumy show Moomintroll what is inside the suitcase?* to cheer him up **RL.K.3, RL.1.3**

**pp. 140–143** • *Why does the Hobgoblin come to the Valley of the Moomins?* to get the King's Ruby from Bob and Thingumy **RL.K.3, RL.1.3**

## SECOND READ Analyze the Text

- Reread page 107. Ask: *Whose story is being told in this chapter?* Thingumy and Bob's *What kind of animals are Thingumy and Bob?* mice *What is strange about the way they talk?* They switch the first letters in their words. **RL.K.1, RL.1.6**
- Reread page 123. Say: *What time of year is it?* late August; the end of summer *What details does the author give to show how the seasons are starting to change?* Moomin Wood was full of glow-worms and the sea was disturbed. There was expectation in the air, and the harvest moon came up huge and yellow. **RL.K.3, RL.1.3**
- *Throughout the story, it seems like the Hobgoblin might be a scary or dangerous character. What kind of character does the Hobgoblin turn out to be?* He turns out to be honest and kind. *How do you know?* He won't take Thingumy and Bob's ruby because it would be stealing. He grants everyone's wishes. **RL.K.3, RL.1.3**

# Independent/Self-Selected Reading

If children have already demonstrated listening comprehension of *Finn Family Moomintroll*, have them practice and apply reading comprehension skills using another book. Model selecting a book from the classroom library. Help them read the title of the book, the author's name, and any information about the book on the back or inside cover. Suggested titles:

- *How the Ladies Stopped the Wind* by Bruce McMillan
- *The Tomten* by Astrid Lindgren **RL.1.10**

### WRITE & PRESENT

1. Remind children that story events are told through the thoughts and actions of different characters. Have children refer to the story to ask and answer questions about different events and the characters that tell them. **RL.K.1, RL.1.6**
2. Ask children to pretend they are a character from the story. Have them draw a picture of something they did in the story, such as finding the Hobgoblin's hat. Then ask them to write a paragraph describing what is happening in their picture. **W.K.2, W.1.2**
3. Have children share their drawing and writing with a partner. Ask them to add details to their writing based on their partner's suggestions. **W.K.5, W.1.5**
4. Individual children speak in audible complete sentences to present their work. **SL.K.6, SL.1.6**

*See Copying Masters, pp. 242–245.*

### STUDENT CHECKLIST

**Writing**

- ✔ Draw a picture of an event from the story.
- ✔ Write sentences from the point of view of a character in the story.
- ✔ Add details based on peer feedback.

**Speaking & Listening**

- ✔ Participate effectively in a collaborative discussion.
- ✔ Ask and answer questions about text details.
- ✔ Describe details in their writing and drawing.

## OBJECTIVES

- Use information from text and illustrations to describe character, setting, or events
- Identify major events in a text
- Analyze text using text evidence

***A Story, a Story*** **is broken into three instructional segments.**

**SEGMENTS**

**SEGMENT 1**..........pp. 4–13
**SEGMENT 2**.........pp. 14–25
**SEGMENT 3**.........pp. 26–34

### Options for Reading

*Display the book's pictures, and read with expression to model fluent reading.*

**Uninterrupted** Focus on the flow of the story by reading aloud without stopping for comments or questions.

**Interactive** Stop at appropriate places while reading to make comments and ask children questions. Also, invite children to share their own comments and questions.

### Common Core Connection

**RL.K.3** identify characters, setting, and major events; **RL.K.7** describe the relationship between illustrations and the story; **SL.K.2** confirm understanding of a text read aloud, information presented orally, or through other media by asking/answering questions and requesting clarification

**RL.1.3** describe characters, settings, and major events; **RL.1.7** use illustrations and details to describe characters, settings, or events; **SL.1.2** ask and answer questions about details in a text read aloud, information presented orally, or through other media

# *A Story, a Story*

by Gail E. Haley

**SUMMARY** This African folktale explains how Ananse, the Spider man, bought stories from Nyame, the Sky God. It describes the three deeds that Ananse successfully completed to make the purchase.

**ABOUT THE AUTHOR** **Gail E. Haley** has been writing and illustrating children's books for over thirty years. Many of her books are retellings of traditional folktales, and all are illustrated with her bold, fanciful drawings. *A Story, a Story* won the Caldecott Medal in 1971.

## Discuss Genre and Set Purpose

**FOLKTALE** Tell children you will be reading them a kind of story called a folktale. Briefly page through the book to show children the text and accompanying illustrations. Discuss with them how a story includes characters and a setting as well as a problem and the steps the main character takes to solve the problem.

**SET PURPOSE** Help children set a purpose for listening, such as to find out what happens in this story.

**TEXT COMPLEXITY RUBRIC**

| Overall Text Complexity | | *A Story, a Story* FOLKTALE<br>COMPLEX |
|---|---|---|
| Quantitative Measures | Lexile | N/A |
| | Guided Reading Level | N/A |
| Qualitative Measures | Text Structure | less familiar story structure |
| | Language Conventionality and Clarity | figurative, less accessible language |
| | Knowledge Demands | some cultural and literary knowledge useful |
| | Purpose/Levels of Meaning | multiple levels of meaning |

## SEGMENT 1 pp. 4–13

### Academic Vocabulary

Read each word with children and discuss its meaning.

**royal** (p. 4) • having to do with a king or queen
**spun** (p. 6) • made a web
**chuckled** (p. 8) • laughed quietly
**terrible** (p. 10) • very bad or unpleasant

## FIRST READ Think Through the Text

Have children use text evidence to answer these questions.

**pp. 4–7** • *Who is the story about?* *Ananse the Spider man* *Where does the story take place?* *in a warm place* *How do you know?* *The pictures show people wearing few clothes and living in huts.* **RL.K.7, RL.1.7**

**pp. 6–9** • *How does Ananse reach the Sky God?* *He spins a web to the sky.* *What does Ananse want from the Sky God?* *He wants to buy some of the Sky God's stories.* *What does the Sky God want from Ananse in return for the stories?* *He wants Ananse to bring him Osebo the leopard, Mmboro the hornet, and Mmoatia the fairy.* **SL.K.2, RL.1.2**

**pp. 10–13** • *How does Ananse catch Osebo the leopard?* *Ananse tricks Osebo into playing a game. Ananse ties up Osebo with a vine and hangs him in a tree.* **SL.K.2, SL.1.2**

## SECOND READ Analyze the Text

- Reread page 8, and display the picture on pages 8–9. Ask: *Why does the Sky God chuckle when Ananse says he will pay the price for the stories?* Sample answer: *Ananse looks like a weak old man. The Sky God does not believe that Ananse can do what he is being asked.* **SL.K.2, SL.1.2**
- Show children pages 12–13. Say: *The text tells how Ananse tied up Osebo the leopard. What does the picture show?* Sample answer: *The picture shows how Ananse used a vine creeper to tie Osebo's feet together and hang him in a tree.* **RL.K.7, RL.1.7**
- Show children pages 4–13. Ask: *What kind of person is Ananse? How do you know?* Sample answer: *Ananse is brave and smart. He figures out how to reach the Sky God and also how to capture the leopard.* **RL.K.3, RL.1.3**

### ENGLISH LANGUAGE LEARNERS

**Use Sentence Frames**

Point to Ananse on page 8 and the Sky God on page 9, and have children identify each character. Ask children to describe each character by completing the following sentence frames:

Ananse looks like_____. *an old man*

The Sky God looks like_____. *a king*

Then have children suggest additional sentences.

### RESPOND TO SEGMENT 1

**Classroom Collaboration**

Have small groups work together to create and present a short summary, as well as raise questions that might be answered in the next segment.

## ENGLISH LANGUAGE LEARNERS

**Use Visuals**

Help children identify the banana tree frond and the calabash in the picture on pages 14–15. Then have them use the picture to describe Ananse's actions in order.

### RESPOND TO SEGMENT 2

**Classroom Collaboration**

Have small groups work together to summarize what they have heard and ask questions about anything they don't understand.

**Common Core Connection**

**RL.K.3** identify characters, setting, and major events; **RL.K.7** describe the relationship between illustrations and the story; **RL.K.10** engage in group reading activities with purpose and understanding; **W.K.2** use drawing, dictating, and writing to compose explanatory text; **W.K.5** respond to questions/suggestions from peers and add details to strengthen writing; **SL.K.2** confirm understanding of a text read aloud, information presented orally, or through other media by asking/answering questions and requesting clarification; **SL.K.6** speak audibly and express thoughts, feelings, and ideas clearly

**RL.1.3** describe characters, settings, and major events; **RL.1.7** use illustrations and details to describe characters, settings, or events; **RL.1.10** read prose and poetry; **W.1.2** write informative/explanatory texts; **W.1.5** focus on a topic, respond to questions from peers, and add details to strengthen writing; **SL.1.2** ask and answer questions about details in a text read aloud, information presented orally, or through other media; **SL.1.6** produce complete sentences when appropriate to task and situation

**Academic Vocabulary**

Read each word with children and discuss its meaning.

**frond** (p. 14) • a long leaf with many smaller sections
**crept** (p. 14) • moved slowly and quietly
**tatter** (p. 17) • tear or shred
**flamboyant** (p. 21) • fancy, colorful
**furious** (p. 24) • angry

## FIRST READ Think Through the Text

Have children use text evidence to answer these questions.

**pp. 14–17** • *How does Ananse capture the hornets? He pours water over their nest and says they should fly into his calabash to stay dry. The hornets think it's raining, and they do as he says.* SL.K.2, SL.1.2

**pp. 18–21** • *What does Ananse make to attract Mmoatia the fairy? He makes a doll holding a bowl of yams.* SL.K.2, SL.1.2

**pp. 22–25** • *How does Mmoatia feel when she gets stuck? She is angry.* SL.K.2, SL.1.2

## SECOND READ Analyze the Text

- Show children pages 16–17. Ask: *Why do the hornets say "Thank you" to Ananse? They think he is saving them from getting wet in the rain.* SL.K.2, SL.1.2
- Reread pages 21–23. Ask: *Why does Ananse tie the vine around the doll's head? So the fairy will think the doll is a real baby.* SL.K.2, SL.1.2
- Guide children to spend time looking at the pictures on pages 18–25. Have them tell about something they did not understand when they first listened to the selection. Then ask children to talk about how the pictures helped them to better understand the characters, setting, and events in the story. RL.K.7, RL.1.7

## SEGMENT 3 pp. 26–34

### Academic Vocabulary

Read each word with children and discuss its meaning.

**captives** (p. 27) • prisoners
**command** (p. 30) • order
**proclaimed** (p. 30) • said for the public to know
**related** (p. 34) • told

## FIRST READ Think Through the Text

Have children use text evidence to answer these questions.

**pp. 26–27** • *How does Ananse get his captives up to the Sky God? He spins a web around them and then spins another web that he climbs to reach the sky.* **SL.K.2, SL.1.2**

**pp. 30–31** • *What does the Sky God say when he sees the things Ananse has brought? He says that the stories now belong to Ananse.* **RL.K.3, RL.1.3**

**pp. 32–33** • *What happens when Ananse opens the box of stories? They scatter all over the world.* **RL.K.3, RL.1.3**

## SECOND READ Analyze the Text

- Reread page 30. Ask: *What new name does the Sky God give the stories? Why does he give them this name? He calls them Spider Stories to show that they belong to Ananse the Spider man.* **SL.K.2, SL.1.2**
- *How do Ananse's actions change his village and the whole world? Before Ananse bought the stories, only the Sky God had stories. Since Ananse bought the stories, his village and the whole world have had stories.* **SL.K.2, SL.1.2**
- Guide children to compare and contrast the sky on pages 26–31 with the village on pages 32 and 33. Ask: *What do you see that is different? The sky is swirling and blue; the village is green and still. The sky people have fancy clothing; the village people are dressed simply. What do you see that is the same? Ananse is in both pictures. What are the people in the village doing? looking up at Ananse Why? to see what he has brought back* **RL.K.7, RL.1.7**

# Independent/Self-Selected Reading

If children have demonstrated comprehension of *A Story, a Story*, have them practice skills using an independent reading book. Model selecting a book from the classroom library. Help them read the title, the author's name, and any information on the cover. Suggest titles:

- *Anansi the Spider* by Gerald McDermott
- *Fairy Tales from Far and Wide* retold by Fiona Waters **RL.1.10**

### WRITE & PRESENT

1. Have small groups refer to the text to discuss how the author uses words and pictures to tell about the characters, setting, and events. **SL.K.2, SL.1.2**
2. Have children choose a character, a setting such as the sky or the village, or one particular event to draw and write about. Ask them to include in their work at least one thing they learned from the text and one thing they learned from a picture. **W.K.2, W.1.2**
3. Children return to their groups to share their writing and drawings with each other and edit their work. **W.K.5, W.1.5**
4. Individual children present their final work to classmates. Remind children to speak in a loud, clear voice and in full sentences. **SL.K.6, SL.1.6**

*See Copying Masters, pp. 242–245.*

### STUDENT CHECKLIST

#### Writing

- ✔ Write a paragraph that explains why Ananse's actions were important and helpful to people.
- ✔ Draw pictures that illustrate the paragraph.
- ✔ Use correct language conventions.

#### Speaking & Listening

- ✔ Engage effectively in collaborative conversations.
- ✔ Ask and answer questions about text details.
- ✔ Demonstrate a connection between information in the text and one's own writing and drawing.

## OBJECTIVES

- Use information from text and illustrations to demonstrate understanding
- Identify sensory words that suggest feeling
- Analyze text using text evidence

***The Paper Crane* is broken into three instructional segments.**

**SEGMENTS**

SEGMENT 1.........pp. 4–13
SEGMENT 2.........pp. 14–21
SEGMENT 3.........pp. 22–32

### Options for Reading

*Display the book's pictures, and read with expression to model fluent reading.*

**Uninterrupted** Focus on the flow of the story by reading aloud without stopping for comments or questions.

**Interactive** Stop at appropriate places while reading to make comments and ask children questions. Also, invite children to share their own comments and questions.

### Common Core Connection

**RL.K.7** describe the relationship between illustrations and the story; **SL.K.2** confirm understanding of a text read aloud, information presented orally, or through other media by asking/answering questions and requesting clarification

**RL.1.4** identify words and phrases that suggest feelings or appeal to senses; **RL.1.7** use illustrations and details to describe characters, settings, or events; **SL.1.2** ask and answer questions about details in a text read aloud, information presented orally, or through other media

# The Paper Crane

by Molly Bang

**SUMMARY** This version of a Chinese folktale tells the story of a poor restaurant owner who is kind to a stranger who cannot pay for a meal. The stranger gives him a paper crane that comes alive and dances. The crane attracts customers, and the restaurant is once again full and busy.

**ABOUT THE AUTHOR** **Molly Bang** has been writing and illustrating children's books for more than thirty years. Many are retellings of folktales. She also writes science books. Two of her books are Caldecott Honor Books and one is an ALA Notable book.

## Discuss Genre and Set Purpose

**FOLKTALE** Tell children you will be reading them a folktale. Discuss that folktales are old stories that have been passed down. Briefly page through the book to show children the text and accompanying illustrations.

**SET PURPOSE** Help children set a purpose for listening, such as to find out what happens in this story.

### TEXT COMPLEXITY RUBRIC

| Overall Text Complexity | | *The Paper Crane* FOLKTALE<br>ACCESSIBLE |
|---|---|---|
| Quantitative Measures | Lexile | N/A |
| | Guided Reading Level | N/A |
| Qualitative Measures | Text Structure | less familiar story concepts |
| | Language Conventionality and Clarity | longer descriptions |
| | Knowledge Demands | perspective includes unfamiliar aspects |
| | Purpose/Levels of Meaning | single level of complex meaning |

### Academic Vocabulary

Read each word with children and discuss its meaning.

**travelers** (p. 6) • people who go from one place to another
**guests** (p. 6) • people who pay to eat at a restaurant
**gentle** (p. 9) • kind and calm
**perform** (p. 17) • entertain an audience
**company** (p. 19) • a group of visitors
**overjoyed** (p. 23) • very happy

FIRST READ

## Think Through the Text

Have children use text evidence to answer these questions.

**pp. 4–5** • *What kind of work does the man do? He cooks and serves food in his restaurant.* **SL.K.2, SL.1.2**

**pp. 6–7** • *What happens after the new highway is built? People do not stop at the restaurant. What happens to the man who owns the restaurant? He becomes poor.* **SL.K.2, SL.1.2**

**pp. 10–13** • *What does the stranger give the man in payment for his meal? The stranger gives the man a crane made from a folded paper napkin.* **SL.K.2, SL.1.2**

SECOND READ

## Analyze the Text

- Reread page 5. Ask: *What words in the text show how the man feels about his work?* Sample answer: *The text uses the words* loved *and* happy *to show how the man feels.* **SL.K.2, RL.1.4**
- Reread page 6, and show children the diagram. Ask: *What information can you find out about the restaurant from looking at this diagram?* Sample answer: *The diagram shows that the new highway is farther away from the restaurant than the older road. Cars can't easily get to the restaurant from the new highway.* **RL.K.7, RL.1.7**
- Reread pages 8–11. *What is the meaning of the following text:* He served him like a king? *It means the man brought the stranger everything he needed as if the stranger were a very important person. What does this show you about what kind of person the man is? It shows that he is kind and generous.* **SL.K.2, RL.1.4**

**Use Visuals**

Show children the pictures on page 4. Use the following sentence frames to help them tell what is happening in the pictures:

The man is cooking ______. *food*

The man is setting the ______. *table*

Ask children to suggest additional sentences to describe what they see on page 4.

**RESPOND TO SEGMENT 1**

**Classroom Collaboration**

Have small groups summarize what they have heard and ask questions about anything they still don't understand.

## ENGLISH LANGUAGE LEARNERS

**Act It Out**

Review the pictures on pages 14–19. Have children act out the scene in the restaurant by taking the roles of the restaurant guests, the owner, and the dancing crane.

### RESPOND TO SEGMENT 2

**Classroom Collaboration**

Have small groups work together to create and present a summary, as well as raise questions that might be answered in the next segment.

**Common Core Connection**

**RL.K.4** ask and answer questions about unknown words; **RL.K.7** describe the relationship between illustrations and the story; **RL.K.10** engage in group reading activities with purpose and understanding; **W.K.2** use drawing, dictating, and writing to compose informative/explanatory texts; **W.K.5** respond to questions/suggestions from peers and add details to strengthen writing; **SL.K.2** confirm understanding of a text read aloud, information presented orally, or through other media by asking/answering questions and requesting clarification; **SL.K.6** speak audibly and express thoughts, feelings, and ideas clearly

**RL.1.4** identify words and phrases that suggest feelings or appeal to senses; **RL.1.7** use illustrations and details to describe characters, settings, or events; **RL.1.10** read prose and poetry; **W.1.2** write informative/explanatory texts; **W.1.5** focus on a topic, respond to questions from peers, and add details to strengthen writing; **SL.1.2** ask and answer questions about details in a text read aloud, information presented orally, or through other media; **SL.1.6** produce complete sentences when appropriate to task and situation

## FIRST READ Think Through the Text

Have children use text evidence to answer these questions.

**pp. 14–15** • *What is the boy doing on page 15?* He is clapping his hands and making the crane dance. **RL.K.7, RL.1.7**

**pp. 16–17** • *What happens when people hear about the dancing crane?* They come to the restaurant to see it perform. *How does this help the restaurant and the man?* The people eat at the restaurant, so the man is no longer poor. **SL.K.2, SL.1.2**

**pp. 18–21** • *How does the man feel now? Why does he feel this way?* He is happy because the restaurant is full of people and he is cooking from morning until night. **SL.K.2, SL.1.2**

## SECOND READ Analyze the Text

- *What does the man do to make the paper crane come alive and dance?* He claps his hands. Ask: *How do you feel when you clap your hands?* Sample answer: excited and happy *Why is clapping a good way to make the paper bird come alive?* Sample answer: A clap is a happy sound and the bird makes the man happy. **SL.K.2, RL.1.4**
- Point to the picture on pages 18–19. Ask: *How do the people feel about watching the crane? How do you know?* Sample answer: They are interested and happy. They are smiling, looking at the crane, or dancing like the crane. **RL.K.7, RL.1.7**
- Reread pages 20–21. Ask: *Why does the author write that the weeks passed and the months? What is happening during this time?* Sample answer: People continued to come to the restaurant to see the crane for a long time, and the restaurant continued to be busy. **SL.K.2, SL.1.2**

## FIRST READD Think Through the Text

Have children use text evidence to answer these questions.

**pp. 22–23** • *Who comes to the restaurant?* *The stranger who gave the man the crane.* *How does the man feel when he sees the stranger?* *very, very happy* *How do you know?* *The text says he was overjoyed.* **RL.K.4, RL.1.4**

**pp. 24–27** • *What happens when the stranger comes into the restaurant?* *He plays his flute, and the crane dances.* *How does the man feel when the stranger plays his flute?* *happy* *How do you know?* *He is smiling in the picture.* **RL.K.7, RL.1.7**

**pp. 28–31** • *What happens when the stranger finishes playing the flute?* *He climbs on the crane's back, and they fly away.* **SL.K.2, SL.1.2**

## SECOND READ Analyze the Text

- Reread the text and show children the pictures on pages 22–23. Ask: *How does the picture help you to understand the meaning of the word* overjoyed? *The restaurant owner is smiling in the picture.* **RL.K.7, RL.1.7**
- Show children pages 26–27 and reread page 27. Ask: *What does it mean that the crane danced as it had never danced before? Why did the crane dance like this?* Sample answer: *The crane dances a new dance or danced longer. It is probably happy to see the stranger.* **SL.K.2, SL.1.2**
- Reread page 31. Ask: *How is the crane still helping the man and his restaurant?* *Guests still come to eat at the restaurant and to hear the story of the crane.* *What do you see in the picture on page 30 that shows that the man still remembers the crane?* *The restaurant is named The Paper Crane.* **RL.K.7, RL.1.7**
- Show children page 32. Say: *There isn't any text on this page.* Ask: *What would you write for the text on this page?* Sample answer: *The boy learned to play the flute in case the crane came back.* **RL.K.7, RL.1.7**

# Independent/Self-Selected Reading

If children have already demonstrated comprehension and analysis of *The Paper Crane,* have them practice the skills using an independent reading book. Model selecting a book from the classroom library. Help them read the title and the author's name and any information about the book on the back or inside cover. Suggested titles:

- *Rainbow Bird* retold by Eric Maddern
- *Iktomi and the Berries* retold by Paul Goble **RL.1.10**

### WRITE & PRESENT

1. Review with children sensory words from the text that suggest the feeling of happiness experienced by the man *(clapped, loved, played, overjoyed).* **RL.K.4, RL.1.4**
2. Individual children use one or more of the words in a paragraph that describes the restaurant owner. Children illustrate the paragraph. **W.K.2, W.1.2**
3. Children return to their groups to share their writing and drawings with each other and edit their work. **W.K.5, W.1.5**
4. Individual children present their final work to classmates. **SL.K.6, SL.1.6**

*See Copying Masters, pp. 242–245.*

### STUDENT CHECKLIST

**Writing**

- ✔ Write a paragraph that uses selected words from the text to describe the restaurant owner.
- ✔ Draw a picture that illustrates the paragraph.
- ✔ Use correct language conventions.

**Speaking & Listening**

- ✔ Engage effectively in collaborative conversations.
- ✔ Ask and answer questions about text details.
- ✔ Demonstrate a connection between information in the text and one's own writing and drawing.

## OBJECTIVES

- Ask and answer questions about characters and story events
- Retell familiar stories
- Identify and describe characters, setting, and major events
- Analyze text using text evidence

***Lon Po Po* is broken into three instructional segments.**

**SEGMENTS**



### Options for Reading

*Display the book's pictures, and read with expression to model fluent reading.*

**Uninterrupted** Focus on the flow of the story by reading aloud without stopping for comments or questions.

**Interactive** Stop at appropriate places while reading to make comments and ask children questions. Also, invite children to share their own comments and questions.

### Common Core Connection

**RL.K.2** retell familiar stories; **RL.K.3** identify characters, settings, and major events; **SL.K.2** confirm understanding of a text read aloud, information presented orally, or through other media by asking/answering questions and requesting clarification

**RL.1.2** retell stories and demonstrate understanding of the message or lesson; **RL.1.3** describe characters, settings, and major events; **SL.1.2** ask and answer questions about details in a text read aloud, information presented orally, or through other media

# *Lon Po Po*

***A Red Riding Hood Story from China***

by Ed Young

**SUMMARY** A mother leaves her three daughters at home while she pays a visit to their grandmother. A wolf, disguised as the grandmother, visits the girls. Shang, the eldest daughter, figures out the wolf's trick, and the girls outsmart him.

**ABOUT THE AUTHOR** **Ed Young** was born in China and finds inspiration for his work in the philosophy of Chinese painting. He came to the United States as a student to study architecture, but became an artist instead. Young has written seventeen books for children and illustrated more than 80. In 1990, he won the Caldecott Medal for *Lon Po Po*.

## Discuss Genre and Set Purpose

**FAIRY TALE** Read aloud the title, and show children the illustrations. Tell them that the story you are about to read is a Chinese version of *Little Red Riding Hood*. Explain that many countries tell different versions of the same story.

**SET PURPOSE** Help children set a purpose for listening, such as to find out what the girls do when the wolf arrives at their door.

### TEXT COMPLEXITY RUBRIC

| Overall Text Complexity | | *Lon Po Po* FAIRY TALE ACCESSIBLE |
|---|---|---|
| Quantitative Measures | Lexile | N/A |
| | Guided Reading Level | N/A |
| Qualitative Measures | Text Structure | simple, familiar story concepts |
| | Language Conventionality and Clarity | more complex sentence structure |
| | Knowledge Demands | some cultural and literary knowledge useful |
| | Purpose/Levels of Meaning | single level of complex meaning |

## SEGMENT 1 pp. 4–11

### Academic Vocabulary

Read each word with children and discuss its meaning.

**disguised** (p. 6) • dressed up as something else
**cunning** (p. 11) • able to trick people; clever
**embraced** (p. 12) • hugged
**furious** (p. 24) • very angry

## FIRST READ Think Through the Text

Have children use text evidence to answer these questions.

**p. 5** • *Where does the children's mother go? The children's mother goes to visit their grandmother.* **SL.K.2, SL.1.2**

**pp. 6–11** • *Who knocks on the door? an old wolf Who does the wolf pretend to be? the girls' Po Po, or grandmother How do you know? The wolf says, "My little jewels, this is your grandmother, your Po Po."* **RL.K.3, RL.1.3**

**p. 11** • *Who lets the wolf in? Tao and Paotze let the wolf in.* **SL.K.2, SL.1.2**

## SECOND READ Analyze the Text

- Reread page 6. Ask: *How do you know that the wolf plans to harm the girls? What does he do and say that shows he is up to no good? The wolf waits until it is dark and the girls' mother has left. He dresses up as an old woman and tries to convince the girls he is their Po Po.* **SL.K.2, SL.1.2**
- Reread pages 8–11. Have children listen to the questions Shang asks the wolf. Ask: *Is Shang sure that the wolf is her Po Po? How do you know? No, she is surprised because her mother has gone to visit their Po Po. She wonders why Po Po is there so late and why her voice is so low.* **SL.K.2, SL.1.2**
- Ask children to recall the story of *Little Red Riding Hood*. Then ask them to tell one way this story is like *Little Red Riding Hood* and one way that it is different. Sample answer: *One way in which both stories are alike is that in both, the wolf pretends to be the grandmother. But in* Lon Po Po, *the wolf comes to the girl's house instead of waiting in grandmother's house as in* Little Red Riding Hood. **RL.K.2, RL.1.2**

### ENGLISH LANGUAGE LEARNERS

**Use Gestures**

Use gestures and motions to clarify story events. Mimic knocking, and say: *The wolf is knocking.* Have children repeat the gestures after you. Repeat the procedure for other story actions, such as unlatching the door, opening the door, and blowing out the candle. Then have children complete sentence frames, such as *The wolf is* _____. *knocking*

### RESPOND TO SEGMENT 1

**Classroom Collaboration**

Have partners summarize what they have read so far and then ask and answer questions about anything they still don't understand. Then invite children to predict what will happen next.

## ENGLISH LANGUAGE LEARNERS

**Use Comprehensible Input**

On page 17, restate *clever* as *smart* as you tap the side of your head. Say "Shang is clever" and have children repeat. Ask children to tell how they know Shang is clever.

## RESPOND TO SEGMENT 2

**Classroom Collaboration**

Have small groups work together to summarize what they have heard so far. Have them make ask questions about things they don't understand.

**Common Core Connection**

**RL.K.2** retell familiar stories; **RL.K.3** identify characters, settings, and major events; **RL.K.7** describe the relationship between illustrations and the story; **W.K.2** use drawing, dictating, and writing to compose informative/explanatory texts; **SL.K.1b** continue a conversation through multiple exchanges; **SL.K.2** confirm understanding of a text read aloud, information presented orally, or through other media by asking/answering questions and requesting clarification; **SL.K.3** ask and answer questions to seek help, get information, or clarify something not understood

**RL.1.2** retell stories and demonstrate understanding of the message or lesson; **RL.1.3** describe characters, settings, and major events; **RL.1.7** use illustrations and details to describe characters, settings, or events; **RL.1.10** read prose and poetry; **W.1.2** write informative/explanatory texts; **SL.1.1b** build on other's talk in conversations by responding to others' comments; **SL.1.1c** ask questions to clear up confusion about topics and texts under discussion; **SL.1.2** ask and answer questions about details in a text read aloud, information presented orally, or through other media

## FIRST READ Think Through the Text

Have children use text evidence to answer these questions.

**p. 12** • ***What does the wolf say about Tao and Paotze?*** *The wolf says Tao is plump and Paotze is sweet.* ***What do you think the wolf wants to do to the girls?*** *Eat them.* **SL.K.2, SL.1.2**

**pp. 12–15** • ***What does Shang see when she turns on the light?*** *She sees the wolf's hairy face.* **SL.K.2, SL.1.2**

**pp. 16–17** • ***What does Shang offer to do for the wolf?*** *She tells him that she and her sisters will pick gingko nuts for him.* **SL.K.2, SL.1.2**

**pp. 18–21** • ***What does Shang tell her sisters after they get to the gingko tree?*** *She tells them about the wolf.* **SL.K.2, SL.1.2**

## SECOND READ Analyze the Text

- Reread pages 12–14. Guide children to listen for all the unusual things Shang notices about Po Po. Ask: ***Why do you think Shang turns on the light?*** *She touches the wolf's tail and claws. She wants to see if it is really her grandmother.* **SL.K.2, SL.1.2**
- Reread page 17. Say: ***Shang tells the wolf that the magical gingko nuts are just outside the door. Why does she do this?*** *She is trying to trick the wolf. She wants to get herself and her sisters out of the house.* **SL.K.2, SL.1.2**
- Show children pages 18–19. Ask: ***Where are the children now? How has the setting of the story changed?*** *They are out in the tree.* ***What is a text or picture clue that helped you figure this out?*** *The text says the sisters go to the gingko tree. The picture shows them up high in the tree branches.* **RL.K.7, RL.1.7**
- Remind children that the text says that Shang is the most clever of the girls. Ask: ***Do you think that Shang is the most clever? Use what you heard in the story to tell why you agree or disagree.*** Sample answer: *She is the most clever because she was the one who thought of tricking the wolf as a way to get her sisters up in the tree and away from danger.* **SL.K.2, SL.1.2**
- Ask children to discuss what questions they had about the story after the first time they heard it and which ones they can now answer during the second reading. Encourage children to ask additional questions to help themselves clear up confusion about anything they still do not understand. **SL.K.3, SL.1.1c**

**SEGMENT 3** pp. 22–31

## FIRST READ Think Through the Text

Have children use text evidence to answer these questions.

**pp. 22–25** • *What happens to the wolf the first time he climbs into the basket?* Shang lets go of the rope, and the wolf falls. *Why does he get back into the basket?* He wants to taste a gingko nut. **SL.K.2, SL.1.2**

**pp. 26–29** • *What happens to the wolf?* He falls and dies. *Which sentences tell you this?* the last sentence on page 27 and the fifth sentence on page 28 **RL.K.3, RL.1.3**

**p. 31** • *What do the children tell their mother when she gets home?* They tell her about the wolf. **SL.K.2, SL.1.2**

## SECOND READ Analyze the Text

- Reread pages 22–27. Ask: *How can you tell that Shang wants to hurt or kill the wolf? Find examples of things she does.* She drops the wolf two times before dropping him from the top of the tree with her sisters' help. **SL.K.2, SL.1.2**
- Reread page 28. Say: *At the beginning of the story, the children had a problem—there was a wolf in their house. How do you know this problem is solved?* The wolf is dead. The children go back to their home and fall asleep. **SL.K.2, SL.1.2**
- Have children retell the ending of *Little Red Riding Hood*. Ask: *How is the ending the same in* Lon Po Po? *How is it different?* In both stories, the wolf dies. In Little Red Riding Hood, Red Riding Hood had to be rescued. In Lon Po Po, Shang figures out how to save the girls. **RL.K.2, RL.1.2**

## Independent/Self-Selected Reading

If children have already demonstrated comprehension of *Lon Po Po*, have them practice and apply reading comprehension skills using another book. Model selecting a book from the classroom library. Help children read the title of the book and the author's name and any information about the book on the back or inside cover. Suggested titles:

- *The Three Bears* by Byron Barton
- *The Enormous Turnip* by Alexei Tolstoy **RL.1.10**

### WRITE & PRESENT

1. Have partners work together to identify an important event that happens at the beginning, in the middle, and at the end of the story. **RL.K.3, RL.1.3**
2. Ask children to draw a picture of each event they identified. Then have children write about what happens in each pictured event. **W.K.2, W.1.2**
3. Have children return to their partners to share their writing and drawings with each other and edit their work. **SL.K.1b, SL.1.1b**
4. Have children present their final work to the class. **SL.K.2, SL.1.2**

*See Copying Masters, pp. 242–245.*

### STUDENT CHECKLIST

#### Writing

- ✓ Write about the important events that happen at the beginning, middle, and end of the story.
- ✓ Draw a picture of each event.
- ✓ Use correct language conventions.

#### Speaking & Listening

- ✓ Participate effectively in a collaborative discussion.
- ✓ Identify important story details
- ✓ Describe the events in their writing and drawings to demonstrate an understanding of the text.

## OBJECTIVES

- Ask and answer questions about key details
- Explain the role that traditions play in families
- Describe the relationship between illustrations and the story
- Analyze text using text evidence

***Family Pictures* is broken into three instructional segments**

**SEGMENTS**



### Options for Reading

*Display the book's pictures, and read with expression to model fluent reading.*

**Uninterrupted** Focus on the flow of the story by reading aloud without stopping for comments or questions.

**Interactive** Stop during your reading to make comments and ask questions. Invite children to share their own comments and questions.

### Common Core Connection

**RL.K.1** ask and answer questions about key details; **RL.K.6** name the author and illustrator and define the role of each; **RL.K.7** describe the relationship between illustrations and the story; **SL.K.2** confirm understanding of a text read aloud, information presented orally, or through other media by asking/answering questions and requesting clarification; **SL.K.4** describe familiar people, places, things, and events/provide detail

**RL.1.1** ask and answer questions about key details; **RL.1.6** identify who is telling the story; **RL.1.7** use illustrations and details to describe characters, settings, or events; **SL.1.2** ask and answer questions about details in a text read aloud, information presented orally, or through other media; **SL.1.4** describe people, places, things, and events with details/express ideas and feelings clearly

# Family Pictures

by Carmen Lomas Garza

**SUMMARY** Mexican-American artist Carmen Lomas Garza tells the story of her childhood in Kingsville, Texas, through paintings and descriptive narratives.

**ABOUT THE AUTHOR** Carmen Lomas Garza is a Mexican-American artist. Her stories and artwork reflect her memories of her childhood in South Texas.

## Discuss Genre and Set Purpose

**PERSONAL NARRATIVE** Display the book and read the title together. Show children the illustrations. Explain that the pictures and text tell about events from the author's childhood.

**SET PURPOSE** Help children set a purpose for listening, such as to find out about Carmen Lomas Garza's childhood and family.

**TEXT COMPLEXITY RUBRIC**

| Overall Text Complexity | | *Family Pictures* PERSONAL NARRATIVE<br>COMPLEX |
|---|---|---|
| Quantitative Measures | Lexile | N/A |
| | Guided Reading Level | N/A |
| Qualitative Measures | Text Structure | some unconventional story structure elements |
| | Language Conventionality and Clarity | increased unfamiliar or academic words |
| | Knowledge Demands | somewhat unfamiliar experience |
| | Purpose/Levels of Meaning | single level of complex meaning |

SEGMENT 1 pp. 3–9

**Academic Vocabulary**

Read each word with children and discuss its meaning.

**border** (p. 4) • the line that divides two countries, such as Mexico and the United States

**scene** (p. 8) • a view of a person or place

**shelter** (p. 20) • a place that gives protection from weather or danger

**future** (p. 30) • a time that is still to come

## FIRST READ Think Through the Text

Have children use text evidence to answer these questions.

**p. 3** • *Who is the author and illustrator of this story?* Carmen Lomas Garza *What does an author/illustrator do?* She both writes the words and draws the pictures. RL.K.6, RL.1.1

**pp. 4–5** • *Who is telling the story?* the author *How do you know?* She uses the words I and my. RL.K.1, RL.1.6

**pp. 4–5** • *What do people do at the fair in Reynosa?* They buy food and crafts from booths and watch entertainers. *Use the text and the picture to tell how you know.* The text talks about artisans, entertainers, and food and craft booths. In the picture, people go to the food and craft booths and watch an entertainer play a violin. RL.K.7, RL.1.7

**pp. 6–7** • *Why does the grandmother make a basket out of her apron?* The children have picked too many oranges for her to hold in her hands. SL.K.2, SL.1.2

## SECOND READ Analyze the Text

- Reread the author's introduction on page 3. *Why did Carmen Lomas Garza write and illustrate this book?* She wanted to share childhood memories and show her love for her family. *How do you know?* She says that the pictures are painted from her memories of growing up. SL.K.4, SL.1.4
- Display pages 4–5. Point out that the text gives additional information about the girl in the picture. *What do we know about the girl from reading the text that we wouldn't know from only looking at the picture?* The author says that the little girl is her father's favorite. SL.K.2, SL.1.2
- Show children pages 6–9. *What do the children see and do at their grandparents' house?* The children pick oranges and see their grandparents doing chores like hanging laundry or catching chickens. *How does the text help you understand the pictures?* The text explains what is happening in the pictures. RL.K.7, RL.1.7

**ENGLISH LANGUAGE LEARNERS**

**Use Visuals and Sentence Frames**

Discuss the things the author does with her family. Have children point to and name things she does, using the pictures in the story. Then help them complete sentence frames, such as:
The girl goes to a _____. *fair*
She picks_____. *oranges*

**RESPOND TO SEGMENT 1**

**Classroom Collaboration**

Have partners summarize what they have heard so far. Tell them to ask questions about anything they don't understand.

## ENGLISH LANGUAGE LEARNERS

**Use Comprehensible Input**

To ensure that children understand the vocabulary in the story, ask questions that can be answered using story words and picture support, such as: *What animal do you see on page 17?* a shark *What room is the family in on page 19?* the kitchen Then have children use these words in sentences as they point them out in the pictures.

**RESPOND TO SEGMENT 2**

**Classroom Collaboration**

Have small groups work together to summarize what they have heard so far. Have them ask questions about what they don't understand.

**Common Core Connection**

**W.K.2** use drawing, dictating, and writing to compose informative/explanatory texts; **W.K.5** respond to questions/suggestions from peers and add details to strengthen writing; **SL.K.2** confirm understanding of a text read aloud, information presented orally, or through other media by asking/answering questions and requesting clarification; **SL.K.4** describe familiar people, places, things, and events/ provide detail; **SL.K.6** speak audibly and express thoughts, feelings, and ideas clearly **RL.1.10** read prose and poetry; **W.1.2** write informative/explanatory texts; **W.1.5** focus on a topic, respond to questions/suggestions from peers, and add details to strengthen writing; **SL.1.2** ask and answer questions about details in a text read aloud, information presented orally, or through other media; **SL.1.4** describe people, places, things, and events with details/express ideas and feelings clearly; **SL.1.6** produce complete sentences when appropriate to task and situation

## FIRST READ Think Through the Text

Have children use text evidence to answer these questions.

**pp. 10–11** • *What is the girl in the picture doing?* hitting a piñata *What is she celebrating?* her sixth birthday *Which sentence in the text tells you the answer to these questions?* That's me hitting the piñata at my sixth birthday party. **RL.K.7, RL.1.7**

**pp. 12–13** • *What is the purpose of a cakewalk?* A cakewalk raises money to send Mexican Americans to the university. *Is the author playing the cakewalk?* no *How do you know?* The text says that she is sitting in front of the store scribbling on the sidewalk with a twig. **SL.K.2, SL.1.2**

**pp. 16–17** • *What does the family see at the beach?* a hammerhead shark *Why does the author say it was scary?* She says it was big enough to swallow a little kid whole. **SL.K.4, SL.1.4**

**pp. 14–19** • *What are some of the foods the family prepares and eats?* nopal cactus with eggs, chicken, rabbit, and tortillas **SL.K.2, SL.1.2**

**pp. 20–21** • *What is the Mexican custom of "Las Posadas"?* On each of the nine nights before Christmas, people act out the story of Mary and Joseph seeking shelter at the inn. *How does the picture show you that this event takes place during the winter?* The people are dressed in coats and long pants. There are no leaves on the tree. **SL.K.4, SL.1.4**

## SECOND READ Analyze the Text

- Show children pages 10–11. Say: *The text says that this picture shows the girl at her sixth birthday party. What details in the picture tell you that this is a birthday party?* There are cakes, presents, and a piñata. **RL.K.7, RL.1.7**
- Reread page 12 and then have children look at the picture on page 13. Ask: *How do the text and pictures work together to help you understand how cakewalk is played?* The text explains the rules, and the picture shows how the numbers are arranged and how people play. *If you only read the text, would you be able to play cakewalk? Why or why not?* Sample answer: I could not play because the text does not tell you that the game needs a big circle with numbers for people to stand on. Only the picture gives that information. **RL.K.7, RL.1.7**
- Reread pages 14–15 and 18–19. Ask: *Do you think the family buys most of its food already made from the grocery store? How do you know?* No, the text says that the family gathers and raises a lot of the food they eat. They pick nopal cactus, they raise chickens and rabbits, and the grandmother makes tortillas. **SL.K.2, SL.1.2**
- Show children pages 16–17. Ask: *Where is the family?* at the beach on Padre Island *What kind of shark do they see?* a hammerhead shark *What do you learn from the text that you cannot find out from looking at the picture?* the name of the beach and where it is; the name of the shark; how the author felt about seeing the shark **RL.K.7, RL.1.7**

**SEGMENT 3** pp. 22–31

## FIRST READ Think Through the Text

Have children use text evidence to answer these questions.

**pp. 22–25 •** *What are some of the things the family prepares and eats together? tamales and watermelon* **SL.K.2, SL.1.2**

**pp. 26–27 •** *Where are the people on pages 26–27? at church What is the woman doing? praying* **SL.K.2, SL.1.2**

**pp. 28–29 •** *What is wrong with the lady in the bed? She has the flu. Who is there to help her? A healer, or curandera, is there to help her get better.* **SL.K.2, SL.1.2**

**pp. 30–31 •** *What does the girl want to be when she grows up? an artist* **SL.K.2, SL.1.2**

## SECOND READ Analyze the Text

- Show children pages 22–25. Ask: *What do these pages tell about? the family making and eating food together* **Why has the author included so many stories about the family making and eating food? What message is she trying to give you?** Sample answer: *Making and eating food is a way for the family to come together. The message is that spending time together is important to the author and her family, and that the members of the family enjoy each other's company.* **SL.K.4, SL.1.4**
- Reread page 30 and show the illustration on page 31. Say: *The girl dreams of becoming an artist. Do her dreams come true? How do you know? Yes, she says that all those things that she dreamed of doing, she is finally doing now. She wrote this story and painted the pictures.* **SL.K.2, SL.1.2**

# Independent/Self-Selected Reading

If children have already demonstrated listening comprehension of *Family Pictures*, have them practice and apply comprehension skills using another book. Model selecting a book from the classroom library. Help them read the title of the book, the author's name, and any information about the book on the back or inside cover. Suggested titles:

- *In My Family* by Carmen Lomas Garza
- *I Love Saturdays y domingos* by Alma Flor Ada **RL.1.10**

### WRITE & PRESENT

1. Have pairs of children refer to the story to talk about ways the author uses words and pictures to show special events in her childhood. Guide them to ask and answer questions they have about the story. **SL.K.2, SL.1.2**
2. Ask children to each choose the family event they liked best from the book. Have them draw a picture of it. Then ask them to write sentences that answer these questions. *Who is in the picture? What are they doing? Where did the event take place? Why was the event special?* **W.K.2, W.1.2**
3. Have children share their drawing and writing with a partner. Ask them to add details to their writing based on their partner's suggestions. **W.K.5, W.1.5**
4. Individual children speak in audible, complete sentences to present their work. **SL.K.6, SL.1.6**

*See Copying Masters, pp. 242–245.*

### STUDENT CHECKLIST

#### Writing

- ✔ Draw a picture of a favorite event from the story.
- ✔ Write sentences about the event that answer who, what, where, and why.
- ✔ Add details based on peer feedback.

#### Speaking & Listening

- ✔ Participate effectively in a collaborative discussion.
- ✔ Ask and answer questions about text details.
- ✔ Describe details in their writing and drawing.

## OBJECTIVES

- Ask and answer questions about key details
- Identify characters, settings, and major events
- Use illustrations to comprehend text

***Tomás and the Library Lady* is broken into three instructional segments.**

**SEGMENTS**

**SEGMENT 1** . . . . . . . . . pp. 4–11
**SEGMENT 2** . . . . . . . . pp. 12–21
**SEGMENT 3** . . . . . . . . pp. 22–31

### Options for Reading

*Be sure to display the book's pictures and read with expression to model fluent reading.*

**Uninterrupted** Focus on the flow of the story by reading aloud without stopping for questions.

**Interactive** Stop at appropriate places while reading to make comments and ask questions. Also, invite children to share their own comments and questions.

### Common Core Connection

**RL.K.7** describe the relationship between illustrations and the story; **SL.K.2** confirm understanding of a text read aloud, information presented orally, or through other media by asking/answering questions and requesting clarification

**RL.1.7** use illustrations and details to describe characters, settings, or events; **SL.1.2** ask and answer questions about details in a text read aloud, information presented orally, or through other media; **SL.1.4** describe people, places, things, and events with details/express ideas and feelings clearly

# *Tomás and the Library Lady*

by Pat Mora

**SUMMARY** In this story Tomás and his family are migrant farmworkers in Iowa for the summer. One morning, Tomás visits the town library, befriends its librarian, and discovers the world of books. This story is based on a real experience in the childhood of Tomás Rivera, who went on to become a well-known author and educator.

**ABOUT THE AUTHOR Pat Mora** has written more than 30 books for children, many in both Spanish and English. Her grandparents came to the U.S. from Mexico, and she herself is bilingual. In a growing list of poetry, prose, and fiction, Mora celebrates her family's heritage.

## Discuss Genre and Set Purpose

**FICTION** Look at the selection with children, flipping through the pages and viewing the illustrations. Read the title and the names of the author and illustrator. Ask children to tell how they know this book tells a story, rather than gives information and facts.

**SET PURPOSE** Have children set a purpose for listening, such as to find out who Tomás is and what happens with the Library Lady.

**TEXT COMPLEXITY RUBRIC**

| Overall Text Complexity | | *Tomás and the Library Lady* FICTION |
|---|---|---|
| | | COMPLEX |
| Quantitative Measures | Lexile | N/A |
| | Guided Reading Level | N/A |
| Qualitative Measures | Text Structure | less familiar story structure |
| | Language Conventionality and Clarity | some unfamiliar language |
| | Knowledge Demands | somewhat unfamiliar experience |
| | Purpose/Levels of Meaning | multiple levels of meaning |

**SEGMENT 1** pp. 4–11

### Academic Vocabulary

Read each word with children and discuss its meaning.

**cot** (p. 7) • a small bed
**chattered** (p. 11) • made a series of clicking sounds by knocking together
**thorny** (p. 11) • full of thorns, prickly
**eager** (p. 19) • wanting to do something
**dump** (p. 21) • a place where people can bring garbage

## FIRST READ Think Through the Text

Have children use text evidence to answer these questions.

**pp. 4–7** • *Where are Tomás and his family from?* They are from Texas. *Why are they in Iowa?* They come to Iowa in the summer to pick fruit and vegetables. **SL.K.2, SL.1.4**

**pp. 8–9** • *What do the boys do while their parents are working?* They take water out to the field for their parents. Then they play with a ball that their mother made for them. **SL.K.2, SL.1.2**

**pp. 10–11** • *Look closely at the picture. What do you see in the leaves of the tree?* You can see a man riding a horse in the leaves of the tree. It's like a "picture within a picture." *How does the picture help you better understand the text?* It shows the story that Papá Grande is telling in the text. **RL.K.7, RL.1.7**

## SECOND READ Analyze the Text

- Reread and display the picture on page 7 and ask: *What do you know about Tomás and his family? Use clues from the text and pictures to describe their way of life.* They move back and forth from Texas to Iowa. They don't have very much money and live a simple life. You can tell because they have to live in a house with other workers. **SL.K.2, SL.1.2**
- Help children recall details from pages 8–9. *What other clues can you find that the family has to save money and live a simple way of life?* The mother and father don't bring bottled drinks to the field. Tomás and his brother bring them water. They don't buy new toys or games, either. Instead, their mom makes a soccer ball for them from an old teddy bear. **SL.K.2, SL.1.2**
- Look at the words and pictures on pages 10–11. *How can you tell that Papá Grande is a good storyteller?* He uses words that help the story come to life. The kids are listening to him very closely. The picture shows that the kids are actually starting to see things from the story in their "mind's eye." **RL.K.7, RL.1.7**

### Domain Specific Vocabulary

**storyteller** (p. 11) • a person who is very good at telling stories
**borrow** (p. 19) • to take a book from a library for a short period of time

### ELL ENGLISH LANGUAGE LEARNERS

**Use Formulaic Language**

Point out the phrase *Once upon a time* on page 11. Explain to children that this is a set phrase we use to begin folktales and other traditional stories. Use this phrase to tell the beginning of a traditional story that children are familiar with, such as *Once upon a time there were three bears that lived in a house in the woods.* Then invite more proficient language learners to take turns using this phrase in retelling the beginning of a story that they know.

### RESPOND TO SEGMENT 1

**Classroom Collaboration**

Have partners work together to ask and answer questions about the story so far and to make predictions about the next segment.

## ENGLISH LANGUAGE LEARNERS

**Use Illustrations, Comprehensible Input**

Point to the illustrations at key points and rephrase the text based on what's shown: *This picture shows Tomás peeking through the glass into the library. I can tell he wants to go in, but he's afraid.* Invite children to connect each illustration to the text in a similar way.

**RESPOND TO SEGMENT 2**

**Classroom Collaboration**

Have small groups work together to summarize what they have heard so far. Have them ask questions about what they don't understand.

**Common Core Connection**

**RL.K.7** describe the relationship between illustrations and the story; **W.K.2** use drawing, dictating, and writing to compose informative/explanatory texts; **W.K.5** respond to questions/suggestions from peers and add details to strengthen writing; **SL.K.2** confirm understanding of a text read aloud, information presented orally, or through other media by asking/answering questions and requesting clarification

**RL.1.7** use illustrations and details to describe characters, settings, or events; **RL.1.10** read prose and poetry; **W.1.2** write informative/explanatory texts; **W.1.5** focus on a topic, respond to questions/suggestions from peers, and add details to strengthen writing; **SL.1.1c** ask questions to clear up confusion about topics and texts under discussion; **SL.1.2** ask and answer questions about details in a text read aloud, information presented orally, or through other media; **SL.1.4** describe people, places, things, and events with details/express ideas and feelings clearly

## FIRST READ Think Through the Text

Have children use text evidence to answer these questions.

**pp. 12–13 •** *The text says that the library windows looked like glaring eyes. It also says that Tomás walked around the building several times before going into the library. What do those details tell you about Tomás? He feels small. He's probably afraid to go into the library. He's never been to a library before, so it's a new experience for him. He's probably a little nervous, especially because he's alone.* **SL.K.2, SL.1.2**

**pp. 14–15 •** *Now that Tomás is in the library, I have a question: What will the librarian say to him? What questions do you have about the text?* Sample answer: *Will Tomás be able to check out any books? At some libraries you need an address and telephone number to get a library card. But if Tomás doesn't have a phone number or a house with an address, how will he check out the books?* **SL.K.3, SL.1.1c**

**pp. 16–21 •** *What answers did you find to your questions? What other questions do you have?* Sample answer: *I was wondering how Tomás would check out books, and I found out that the librarian checks out books for him. Now I'm wondering what his family will say when he brings the books home.* **SL.K.3, SL.1.1c**

## SECOND READ Analyze the Text

- Have children look at the illustration on pages 16-17. Ask: *What does this picture show? What part is really happening in the story and what part is in Tomás's imagination? The part that shows Tomás sitting and reading is really happening. I know from the text that he is in the library, reading a book. But the part with him riding on the dinosaur is in his imagination. He's reading about dinosaurs, and the picture shows that he's imagining scenes from the book while he reads.* **RL.K.7, RL.1.7**
- Review the main events in this segment. Then say: *Tomás doesn't seem to be the same person he was at the beginning. How is he changing? He's more interested in books than before. When the family goes to the dump, his brother looks for toys, but Tomás looks for books. That shows he's getting more interested in things that older children like.* **SL.K.2, SL.1.4**

SEGMENT 3 pp. 22–31

## FIRST READ Think Through the Text

Have children use text evidence to answer these questions.

**pp. 22–25** • *How does Tomás spend the summer? He spends the summer reading books in the library. Sometimes he would read to the library lady, and sometimes he would read to himself. He also taught the library lady some words in Spanish.* **SL.K.2, SL.1.2**

**pp. 26–31** • *Why does Tomás have to say good-bye to the library lady? It's time for his family to go back to Texas. How does he feel about leaving? He's going to miss the library lady and he's sad to say good-bye, but now he has a new hobby, thanks to her. He will probably see her next year when he comes back to Iowa.* **SL.K.2, SL.1.4**

## SECOND READ Analyze the Text

- After finishing the story, ask: *What kind of person is the library lady? She is kind and likes to help other people. How can you tell? She always helps Tomás find good books to read. She even checks out some books for him. When he goes back to Texas, she gives him a new book for the trip home.* **SL.K.2, SL.1.4**
- Ask: *How do the illustrations in this book help tell the story? They show all the important events and what's going on in stories within the story. They help to show what an active imagination Tomás has.* **RL.K.7, RL.1.7**

# Independent/Self-Selected Reading

If children have already demonstrated listening comprehension of *Tomás and the Library Lady*, have them practice and apply reading comprehension skills using another book. Model selecting a book from the classroom library. Help them read the title of the book and the author's name and any information about the book on the back or inside cover. Suggested titles:

- *Pablo's Tree* by Pat Mora
- *Abuela* by Arthur Dorros **RL.1.10**

### WRITE & PRESENT

1. Have partners discuss the characters, setting, and major events of the story. Guide them to ask and answer questions they have about text details. **SL.K.2, SL.1.4**
2. Then guide children to each write a summary that includes the story's characters, setting, and major events. **W.K.2, W.1.2**
3. Have children share their writing with a partner. Ask them to add details to their writing based on their partner's suggestions. **W.K.5, W.1.5**
4. Invite children to take turns sharing their summaries with the class. **SL.K.6, SL.1.4**

*See Copying Masters, pp. 242–245.*

### STUDENT CHECKLIST

**Writing**

- ✓ Write a story summary.
- ✓ Include details about the characters, setting, and major events of the story.
- ✓ Use correct language conventions.

**Speaking & Listening**

- ✓ Participate effectively in collaborative discussion.
- ✓ Listen while others speak.
- ✓ Speak audibly and express ideas clearly.
- ✓ Demonstrate a connection between elements from the story and their own writing.

## OBJECTIVES

- Ask and answer questions about key details
- Describe characters, settings, and major events
- Use illustrations to comprehend text

***Kitten's First Full Moon* is broken into three instructional segments.**

**SEGMENTS**

**SEGMENT 1**. . . . . . . . .pp. 4–11
**SEGMENT 2**. . . . . . . . .pp. 12–21
**SEGMENT 3**. . . . . . . . .pp. 22–31

### Options for Reading

*Display the book's pictures and read with expression to model fluent reading.*

**Uninterrupted** Focus on the flow of the story by reading aloud without stopping for questions.

**Interactive** Stop at appropriate places while reading to make comments and ask questions. Also, invite children to share their own comments and questions.

### Common Core Connection

**RL.K.7** describe the relationship between illustrations and the story; **SL.K.2** confirm understanding of a text read aloud, information presented orally, or through other media by asking/answering questions and requesting clarification; **SL.K.4** describe familiar people, places, things, and events/provide detail

**RL.1.7** use illustrations and details to describe characters, settings, or events; **SL.1.2** ask and answer questions about details in a text read aloud, information presented orally, or through other media; **SL.1.4** describe people, places, things, and events with details/express ideas and feelings clearly

# *Kitten's First Full Moon*

by Kevin Henkes

**SUMMARY** When Kitten sees the full moon for the first time, she thinks it's a bowl of milk. But no matter how much she stretches and chases it, she never seems to get closer. Tired and hungry, she finally goes back home. There on the porch she finds a big bowl of milk, just waiting for her.

**ABOUT THE AUTHOR** **Kevin Henkes** is a prolific author and illustrator, having written over 30 picture books and a dozen novels. A recipient of the Caldecott Medal and Newbery Honor, Henkes has been recognized by the American Library Association for his "significant contributions to the field of children's literature."

## Discuss Genre and Set Purpose

**FICTION** Flip through the book, and view the illustrations with children. Read the title and the name of the author/illustrator. Ask children to tell how they know this book tells a story, rather than gives information and facts.

**SET PURPOSE** Help children set a purpose for reading, such as to find out what Kitten is like and what happens when she goes outside to see the full moon.

**TEXT COMPLEXITY RUBRIC**

| Overall Text Complexity | | *Kitten's First Full Moon* FICTION / ACCESSIBLE |
|---|---|---|
| Quantitative Measures | Lexile | N/AL |
| | Guided Reading Level | N/A |
| Qualitative Measures | Text Structure | conventional story structure |
| | Language Conventionality and Clarity | some figurative language |
| | Knowledge Demands | experience includes unfamiliar aspects |
| | Purpose/Levels of Meaning | single level of complex meaning |

**SEGMENT 1** pp. 4–11

### Academic Vocabulary

Read each word with children and discuss its meaning.

**full moon** (p. 4) • the phase of the moon in which it appears as a full circle

**porch** (p. 10) • a covered area in front of a door to a house

**tumbled** (p. 11) • fell and rolled

## FIRST READ Think Through the Text

Have children use text evidence to answer these questions.

**pp. 4–5** • *How does Kitten look? She is a small, white kitten. How do you know? The pictures show this. Where is Kitten? She is on the porch in front of her house. Is it daytime or nighttime? It's nighttime. How can you tell? The picture shows that it is dark and the moon is up in the sky.* **SL.K.2, SL.1.2**

**pp. 6–7** • *How did Kitten get a bug on the end of her tongue? She wanted to lick the moon, and so she stuck out her tongue. There were some bugs flying around and one of them got stuck on her tongue.* **SL.K.2, SL.1.2**

**pp. 8–11** • Point to the illustrations as you ask: *How does Kitten try to get the moon? She jumps off the porch, thinking that the moon is close enough for her to catch. What happens? She falls and tumbles down the steps.* **RL.K.7, RL.1.7**

## SECOND READ Analyze the Text

- *How old is Kitten? How can you figure this out? She is less than a month old. I can figure it out because the text says that it is her first full moon. There is a full moon every month, so if this is her first, she must be less than one month old.* **SL.K.4, SL.1.4**
- *Why does Kitten think that the moon is a bowl of a milk? She is less than a month old, so everything is new to her. The moon looks like a bowl of milk, and so she thinks it is a bowl of milk.* **SL.K.4, SL.1.4**
- *Look at the picture of Kitten on page 7. How does she feel about getting a bug on her tongue? She feels surprised and possibly disgusted. How do you know? The picture shows Kitten's eyes very wide which means that she is surprised.* **RL.K.7, RL.1.7**

### ENGLISH LANGUAGE LEARNERS

**Discuss Idioms**

Point out the phrase *ended up* on page 7. Explain to children that a sentence with this phrase means "In the end, what happened is that . . ." Rephrase: *So, this sentence means "In the end, what happened is that Kitten got a bug on her tongue."* Then guide children to explain that the expression *pulled herself together* on page 10 means "calmed down."

### RESPOND TO SEGMENT 1

**Classroom Collaboration**

Have partners work together to tell what Kitten is thinking. For visual support, they can draw a picture of Kitten with a thought balloon. Help children as necessary to fill in the thought balloon.

## ENGLISH LANGUAGE LEARNERS

**Use Illustrations**

Point to different elements of the illustrations as you read aloud corresponding parts of the text. Point to the appropriate strip on page 13, for example, as you read about the sidewalk, garden, field, and pond. Ask volunteers to name these objects in the picture.

### RESPOND TO SEGMENT 2

**Classroom Collaboration**

Have partners work together to confirm or modify their predictions so far, and to make predictions about the next segment.

**Common Core Connection**

**W.K.2** use drawing, dictating, and writing to compose informative/explanatory texts; **W.K.5** respond to questions/suggestions from peers and add details to strengthen writing; **SL.K.2** confirm understanding of a text read aloud, information presented orally, or through other media by asking answering questions and requesting clarification; **SL.K.3** ask and answer questions to seek help, get information, or clarify something not understood; **SL.K.4** describe familiar people, places, things, and events/provide detail; **SL.K.6** speak audibly and express thoughts, feelings, and ideas clearly

**RL.1.10** read prose and poetry; **W.1.2** write informative/explanatory texts; **W.1.5** focus on a topic, respond to questions/suggestions from peers, and add details to strengthen writing; **SL.1.1c** ask questions to clear up confusion about topics and texts under discussion; **SL.1.2** ask and answer questions about details in a text read aloud, information presented orally, or through other media; **SL.1.4** describe people, places, things, and events with details/express ideas and feelings clearly; **SL.1.6** produce complete sentences when appropriate to task and situation

## FIRST READ Think Through the Text

Have children use text evidence to answer these questions.

**pp. 12–17** • *In trying to reach the moon, where does Kitten go? She goes down the sidewalk, through the garden, past the field, by the pond, and up a tree.* **SL.K.2, SL.1.2**

**pp. 18–19** • Point to the illustration and say: *Kitten thinks she sees another bowl of milk in the pond. What does she really see? The pond is like a big mirror reflecting the moon. Kitten sees the moon reflected in the water and thinks that it's a bowl of milk.* **RL.K.7, RL.1.7**

**pp. 20–21** • *What does Kitten do when she sees the moon in the pond? She runs down the trunk of the tree and jumps into the pond as fast as she can.* **SL.K.2, SL.1.2**

## SECOND READ Analyze the Text

- *Why does Kitten jump from the tree and pounce on the pond so quickly? She thinks that the moon is playing a trick on her. She thinks that it's running away, so she needs to be really quick if she wants to catch it.* **SL.K.4, SL.1.4**
- *Kitten never seems to get closer to the moon. Why is that? The moon is too far away. No matter how far she goes, she won't really be that much closer.* **SL.K.4, SL.1.4**
- Reread the sentence on page 21 to children. *What does it mean to leap with all your might? It means to leap as hard as you can using all your strength and energy.* **SL.K.2, SL.1.2**
- *What is Kitten like? She is very young and inexperienced; she doesn't know a lot about the world. She also tries very hard to get the bowl of milk, even though she has a lot of difficulty.* **How do you know?** *Kitten is so young that she mistakes the moon for a bowl of milk; she keeps trying different ways to get the milk and doesn't give up.* **SL.K.4, SL.1.4**

## FIRST READ Think Through the Text

Have children use text evidence to answer these questions.

**pp. 22–23 •** *How does Kitten feel? She is sad and tired and hungry. Why is she so sad and tired? She's run all over the place, but she still isn't any closer to the moon. She's starting to realize that she will probably never actually reach the moon.* **SL.K.2, SL.1.2**

**pp. 24–25 •** *What's happening in these pictures? Tell me about all these places. Kitten is going back home the way she came. From the pond, she goes past the field, through the garden, and up the sidewalk. In the last picture she's going up the steps to her porch.* **RL.K.7, RL.1.7**

**pp. 26–29 •** *What does she find when she gets back home? She finds a bowl of milk waiting for her.* **SL.K.2, SL.1.2**

## SECOND READ Analyze the Text

- *Who do you think put the bowl of milk on the porch? Kitten's owners probably put it there. Why did they do that? They must have noticed she was gone, so they put the milk on the porch to let her know that this is her home.* **SL.K.2, SL.1.2**
- *What do you think Kitten learns? She discovers a lot of places in her neighborhood. More importantly, she learns that the moon isn't a bowl of milk. She probably won't try to catch the moon the next time she sees it. She also learns that she can always get a bowl of milk by going back to the house where she lives.* **SL.K.2, SL.1.2**

## Independent/Self-Selected Reading

If children have already demonstrated listening comprehension of *Kitten's First Full Moon,* have them practice and apply reading comprehension skills using another book. Model selecting a book from the classroom library. Help them read the title of the book and the author's name and any information about the book on the back or inside cover. Suggested titles:

- *Goodnight Moon* by Margaret Wise Brown
- *Corduroy* by Don Freeman **RL.1.10**

### WRITE & PRESENT

1. Have partners discuss the character of Kitten. Guide them to ask and answer questions they have about text details that help them understand Kitten's character. **SL.K.3, SL.1.1c**
2. Then guide children to each write sentences that tell what Kitten was like and how the story text and pictures helped them figure this out. Ask them to draw a picture to show what Kitten looked like. **W.K.2, W.1.2**
3. Have children share their drawings and writing with a partner. Ask them to add details to their writing based on their partner's suggestions. **W.K.5, W.1.5**
4. Invite children to take turns sharing their character descriptions with the class. **SL.K.6, SL.1.6**

*See Copying Masters, pp. 242–245.*

### STUDENT CHECKLIST

**Writing**

- ✔ Write a description of a story character.
- ✔ Include details that tell what the character was like and how the story text and pictures give clues.
- ✔ Use correct language conventions.

**Speaking & Listening**

- ✔ Participate effectively in collaborative discussion.
- ✔ Listen while others speak.
- ✔ Speak audibly and express ideas clearly.
- ✔ Demonstrate a connection between information in the text and their own writing.

### OBJECTIVES

- Understand that poetry is a type of writing
- Explore how a poem uses repetition
- Analyze text using text evidence

### Options for Reading

*Be sure to read with expression and a rhythm to model fluent reading.*

**Uninterrupted** Focus on the flow of the poem by reading without stopping for comments or questions.

**Interactive** Stop at the end of each stanza to make comments and ask children questions. Also, invite children to share their own comments and questions.

# "The Fox's Foray"

**SUMMARY** In this traditional ballad, a fox takes a goose from a farm to feed his family. The goose's cries wake the farmer's wife, but the fox escapes back to his den and enjoys a goose dinner with his family.

## Discuss Genre and Set Purpose

**POETRY** Recall with children that some traditional songs, such as "Found a Peanut," tell stories. Explain that songs are mostly poems that have been paired with music. Display "The Fox's Foray" and compare it to the sample song. Discuss how the lines of text are divided into sections called stanzas. Point out that "The Fox's Foray" also tells a story.

**TEXT FOCUS: Repetition** Tell children that poets often repeat words, phrases, and sentences. Sometimes a poet uses repetition because the idea is important to the poet's message. In other poems, the repeated words signal the end of a stanza.

**SET PURPOSE** Tell children that the poem they will listen to is actually a song that people sang long ago. Then help them set a purpose for listening to the poem, such as to listen for repeated words, phrases, and sentences or to find out what the title of the poem means.

### Common Core Connection

**RL.K.3** identify characters, settings, and major events; **W.K.2** use drawing, dictating, and writing to compose informative/explanatory texts; **W.K.5** respond to questions/suggestions from peers and add details to strengthen writing; **SL.K.2** confirm understanding of a text read aloud, information presented orally, or through other media by asking/answering questions and requesting clarification; **SL.K.3** ask and answer questions to seek help, get information, or clarify something not understood

**RL.1.3** describe characters, settings, and major events; **RL.1.10** read prose and poetry; **RF.1.4b** read on-level text orally with accuracy, appropriate rate, and expression; **W.1.2** write informative/explanatory texts; **W.1.5** focus on a topic, respond to questions/suggestions from peers, and add details to strengthen writing; **SL.1.2** ask and answer questions about details in a text read aloud, information presented orally, or through other media; **SL.1.3** ask and answer questions about what a speaker says

### TEXT COMPLEXITY RUBRIC

| Overall Text Complexity | | "The Fox's Foray" READ-ALOUD POETRY<br>COMPLEX |
|---|---|---|
| Quantitative Measures | Lexile | N/A |
| | Guided Reading Level | N/A |
| Qualitative Measures | Text Structure | simple, familiar poetic structure |
| | Language Conventionality and Clarity | some unfamiliar or academic words |
| | Knowledge Demands | situation includes unfamiliar aspects |
| | Purpose/Levels of Meaning | single level of simple meaning |

**Academic Vocabulary**

Read each word with children and discuss its meaning.

**foray** (title) • a trip into an enemy's area to get something
**declared** (line 9) • stated
**marred** (line 10) • spoiled or damaged
**shrill** (line 30) • high-pitched
**strife** (line 43) • argument; disagreement

## FIRST READ Think Through the Text

Have children use text evidence to answer these questions.

- *What is this poem mostly about? A fox goes to a farm and kills a goose to bring home to feed his family.* **RL.K.3, RL.1.3**
- *What are some words and phrases that are repeated?* Sample answer: Den O; Do Bones O; *the last sentences in each stanza* **SL.K.2, SL.1.2**

## SECOND READ Analyze the Text

- Reread the fourth stanza. Then ask: *Who is Mother Slipper Slopper? the woman who owns the goose What wakes her up? the goose's quack Why do you think Mother Slipper Slopper wakes John?* Sample answer: *She wants him to stop the fox.* **RL.K.3, RL.1.3**
- Reread the poem to children. Ask them to identify the repeated words, phrases, and sentences. Guide children to discuss the repetition: It makes the poem fun to read and listen to and it helps maintain the poem's rhythm. Help them note that sentence repetition signals the ending of a stanza. **SL.K.2, SL.1.2**

## Practice Fluency

**EMPHASIZE RATE** Remind children that rate is how fast or slow someone reads the words of a text. Then remind them that poems need to be read at regular speed to maintain a steady rhythm, or beat. Model reading the poem aloud. Then read the poem chorally with children, maintaining a steady rate and beat. **RF.1.4b**

## Independent/Self-Selected Reading

If children have demonstrated comprehension of "The Fox's Foray," have them use another poem to practice skills. Suggested titles:

- *Poetry for Young People: Animal Poems* selected by John Hollander
- *Poetry Speaks to Children* selected by Elise Paschen and Dominique Raccah **RL.1.10**

### WRITE & PRESENT

1. Have small groups summarize the events in "The Fox's Foray." Then have them discuss why a poet uses repeated words and phrases in a poem. Tell them to ask and answer questions if they do not understand a speaker's remarks. **SL.K.3, SL.1.3**
2. Individual children write or dictate sentences that explain why a poet repeats words. Tell children to include examples from "The Fox's Foray" in their writing. **W.K.2, W.1.2**
3. Have children type their sentences into the computer and print a copy. Encourage them to share their sentences with the group and discuss ways to edit their writing. Suggest that children incorporate the group's suggestions and correct their sentences on the computer. **W.K.5, W.1.5**
4. Invite children to take turns sharing their sentences with the class.

*See Copying Masters, pp. 242–245.*

### STUDENT CHECKLIST

**Writing**

- ✔ Write sentences telling why poets repeat words.
- ✔ Include examples from "The Fox's Foray" in their writing.
- ✔ Use correct language conventions.

**Speaking & Listening**

- ✔ Participate effectively in collaborative discussion.
- ✔ Ask questions to clarify comments.
- ✔ Demonstrate a connection between features in the poem and their own writing.

## OBJECTIVES

- Understand that poetry is a type of writing
- Examine repetition and rhyme in poetry
- Analyze text using text evidence

### Options for Reading

*Display the book's pictures, and read aloud with expression to model fluent reading.*

**Uninterrupted** Focus on the flow of the poem by reading aloud without stopping for comments or questions.

**Interactive** Stop at appropriate places to make comments and ask children questions. Also, invite children to share their own comments and questions.

**RF.K.2a** recognize and produce rhyming words; **W.K.2** use drawing, dictating, and writing to compose informative/explanatory texts; **W.K.5** respond to questions/suggestions from peers and add details to strengthen writing; **SL.K.2** confirm understanding of a text read aloud, information presented orally, or through other media by asking/answering questions and requesting clarification; **SL.K.3** ask and answer questions to seek help, get information, or clarify something not understood; **SL.K.6** speak audibly and express thoughts, feelings, and ideas clearly

**RL.1.10** read prose and poetry; **RF.1.4b** read on-level text orally with accuracy, appropriate rate, and expression; **W.1.2** write informative/explanatory texts; **W.1.5** focus on a topic, respond to questions/suggestions from peers, and add details to strengthen writing; **SL.1.2** ask and answer questions about details in a text read aloud, information presented orally, or through other media; **SL.1.4** describe people, places, things, and events with details/express ideas and feelings clearly

# Over in the Meadow

by John Langstaff

**SUMMARY** This book is an illustrated version of a traditional counting song that describes a variety of animals in a country meadow.

**ABOUT THE AUTHOR** John Langstaff was a musician, singer, and music educator. He wrote 25 books for children including *Frog Went a-Courtin'*, which won a Caldecott Medal, and two collections of African-American spirituals, one of which was a Coretta Scott King honor book.

## Discuss Genre and Set Purpose

**POETRY** Look at the poem. Guide children to identify characteristics of a poem. Discuss the regular beats, repetition, and rhymes at the ends of the lines. Tell children that this poem is based on a song.

**TEXT FOCUS: Repetition** Explain to children that many poems use repetition of words, sentence patterns, beginning sounds, and ending sounds. Poets may use repetition to create and emphasize rhythm and to make poems fun to read aloud.

**SET PURPOSE** Help children set a purpose for listening, such as to enjoy all the ways that repetition is used in this poem.

### TEXT COMPLEXITY RUBRIC

| Overall Text Complexity | | *Over in the Meadow* POETRY — ACCESSIBLE |
|---|---|---|
| Quantitative Measures | Lexile | N/A |
| | Guided Reading Level | N/A |
| Qualitative Measures | Text Structure | simple, familiar poetic structure |
| | Language Conventionality and Clarity | literal, accessible language |
| | Knowledge Demands | situation includes unfamiliar aspects |
| | Purpose/Levels of Meaning | single level of simple meaning (single theme) |

## FIRST READD Think Through the Text

Have children use text evidence to answer these questions.

**pp. 8–9** • *What is this rhyme mostly about?* *what different animals do in a meadow* SL.K.2, SL.1.2

**pp. 10–11** • *What is the first animal that the poet describes?* *turtles* *What words tell where they are?* *the words* sand in the sun *What word is repeated in the lines about the turtles?* one SL.K.2, SL.1.2

## SECOND READ Analyze the Text

- Point out that *Over in the Meadow* is a counting rhyme. Reread pages 12–13. *How many baby foxes are there?* two *What word rhymes with two?* grew Guide children to identify the rhyming pairs for the other number words. three/tree; four/sycamore; five/hive; six/sticks; eight/late, nine/pine, ten/den Then ask: *Which number does not follow this pattern?* *seven* RF.K.2a, SL.1.2
- Reread pages 16–17. Then ask: *What words are repeated?* chipmunk, play *Why does the rhyme repeat words?* Sample answer: *to make it sound fun to sing or read aloud* SL.K.2, SL.1.2
- Reread pages 18–21, and discuss the repeated pattern. Ask: *How does each number rhyme begin?* *with the words* over in the meadow Guide children to identify the remaining elements that are repeated in each rhyme. *Why does the rhyme have repeated sentence patterns?* Sample answers: *to make it sound fun; to make the rhyme easy to remember* SL.K.2, SL.1.2

## Practice Fluency

**EMPHASIZE RATE** Explain to children that a poem with many details should be read slowly enough so the listener can understand the details, but quickly enough to make the poem sound like a song. Read aloud *Over in the Meadow* at different rates. Ask children which reading allowed them to understand the details and hear the repetition. RF.1.4b

## Independent/Self-Selected Reading

If children have already demonstrated comprehension of *Over in the Meadow,* have them use another counting rhyme to practice recognizing repetition. Suggested titles:

- *Over in the Jungle: A Rainforest Rhyme* by Marianne Berkes
- *Count Me a Rhyme: Animal Poems by the Number* by Jane Yolen RL.1.10

### WRITE & PRESENT

1. Have partners refer to the text to discuss its use of repetition. Encourage children to ask and answer questions about details in the rhyme. SL.K.3, SL.1.2
2. Individual children write about how the rhyme uses repetition and include at least one example. W.K.2, W.1.2
3. Have children share their writing with their partner. Ask them to add details and edit their writing based on the partner's suggestions. W.K.5, W.1.5
4. Invite children to take turns sharing their writing with the class. SL.K.6, SL.1.4

*See Copying Masters, pp. 242–245.*

### STUDENT CHECKLIST

#### Writing

- ✔ Write about how the rhyme uses repetition.
- ✔ Include at least one example.
- ✔ Use correct language conventions.

#### Speaking & Listening

- ✔ Participate effectively in a collaborative discussion.
- ✔ Ask and answer questions about a rhyme's use of repetition.
- ✔ Demonstrate a connection between features in the rhyme and their own writing.

## OBJECTIVES

- Understand that narrative poetry is a type of poetry that tells a story
- Examine the use of rhythm and rhyme in poetry
- Analyze text using text evidence

### Options for Reading

*Be sure to read aloud with expression to model fluent reading.*

**Uninterrupted** Focus on the flow of the poem by reading aloud without stopping for comments or questions.

**Interactive** Stop at appropriate places to make comments and ask children questions. Also, invite children to share their own comments and questions.

### Common Core Connection

**RL.K.5** recognize common types of texts; **RL.K.9** compare and contrast adventures and experiences of characters; **W.K.2** use drawing, dictating, and writing to compose informative/explanatory texts; **W.K.5** respond to questions/suggestions from peers and add details to strengthen writing; **SL.K.2** confirm understanding of a text read aloud, information presented orally, or through other media by asking/answering questions and requesting clarification; **SL.K.6** speak audibly and express thoughts, feelings, and ideas clearly

**RL.1.5** explain major differences between story books and informational books; **RL.1.9** compare and contrast adventures and experiences of characters; **RL.1.10** read prose and poetry; **RF.1.4b** read on-level text orally with accuracy, appropriate rate, and expression; **W.1.2** write informative/explanatory texts; **W.1.5** focus on a topic, respond to questions/suggestions from peers, and add details to strengthen writing; **SL.1.2** ask and answer questions about details in a text read aloud, information presented orally, or through other media; **SL.1.4** describe people, places, things, and events with details/express ideas and feelings clearly

# "The Owl and the Pussy-Cat"

by Edward Lear

**SUMMARY** This classic nonsense poem is about a romance between an owl and a cat.

**ABOUT THE AUTHOR** Edward Lear was a British artist and poet, best known today for his children's limericks. His first book of poems, *A Book of Nonsense*, was published in 1846. Lear wrote "The Owl and the Pussy-Cat" for the children of a friend. It was published in 1871.

## Discuss Genre and Set Purpose

**POETRY** Ask children to look at the poem, and explain how they can tell it is a poem and not a story book or an informational text. Remind them that poetry often has rhyme, rhythm, and repetition that make it fun to listen to. As you read "The Owl and the Pussy-Cat," discuss what makes this poem fun to listen to. **RL.K.5, RL.1.5**

**TEXT FOCUS: Narrative Poetry** Explain to children that some poems tell stories. A poem that tells a story is called a narrative poem and has characters, a setting, and story events.

**SET PURPOSE** Help children set a purpose for listening to the poem, such as to find out its characters, setting, and events.

### TEXT COMPLEXITY RUBRIC

| Overall Text Complexity | | "The Owl and the Pussy-Cat" POETRY<br>COMPLEX |
|---|---|---|
| Quantitative Measures | Lexile | N/A |
| | Guided Reading Level | N/A |
| Qualitative Measures | Text Structure | somewhat complex poetic structure |
| | Language Conventionality and Clarity | increased unfamiliar or academic words |
| | Knowledge Demands | somewhat unfamiliar perspective |
| | Purpose/Levels of Meaning | single level of complex meaning |

## FIRST READD Think Through the Text

Have children use text evidence to answer these questions.

- *Who is the poem about?* an owl and a pussycat SL.K.2, SL.1.2
- *Where does the beginning of the story take place?* at sea SL.K.2, SL.1.2
- *What is the owl doing in the beginning of the poem?* singing to the cat *How does the owl feel about the cat?* He loves her. SL.K.2, SL.1.2
- *What do the owl and the pussy-cat decide to do next?* get married SL.K.2, SL.1.2
- *What happens at the end of the poem?* They are married and dance by the light of the moon. SL.K.2, SL.1.2

## SECOND READ Analyze the Text

- Help children recall the events in the poem. Then ask: *Could this happen in real life? How do you know?* It could not happen in real life. A real owl and cat could never go to sea, get married, or dance. SL.K.2, SL.1.2
- Help children recall the adventures and experiences of Owl in *Owl at Home* by Arnold Lobel, or another animal character. Guide children to compare and contrast the two. Ask: *How are the characters alike? How are they different?* Sample answer: Both owls do things that real owls couldn't do, for example, talk and have adventures. They are different because one owl is at home, but the other is on a boat. RL.K.9, RL.1.9

## Practice Fluency

**EMPHASIZE RHYTHM** Remind children that when they read poetry aloud, they can feel the rhythm when they emphasize its beat. Read the first two lines of the poem, ignoring its rhythm. Then reread the lines, emphasizing the beats. Ask children which reading they preferred and why. Then read the poem together with the class. RF.1.4b

## Independent/Self-Selected Reading

If children have already demonstrated comprehension of "The Owl and the Pussy-Cat," have them read another narrative poem or a poem by Edward Lear. Suggested titles:

- *Poetry for Young People: Edward Lear* edited by Edward Mendelson
- *The Complete Nonsense of Edward Lear* edited by Holbrook Jackson

RL.K.10, RL.1.10

### WRITE & PRESENT

1. Make a T-chart. Head one side "The Owl and the Pussy-Cat" and the other *Owl at Home*, or the title of another book children have read recently. Have children recall elements of each such as characters, setting, and events. Record their ideas in the appropriate spaces of the chart. RL.K.9, RL.1.9
2. Have each child use the chart to notice similarities and differences between the two pieces of literature. Have them draw and write about how the experiences and adventures of the two owls are the same and different. W.K.2, W.1.2
3. Have children share their drawing and writing with partners to get ideas for editing. W.K.5, W.1.5
4. Have children present their work to the class. SL.K.6, SL.1.4
5. Individual children turn in their final work to the teacher.

*See Copying Masters, pp. 242–245.*

### STUDENT CHECKLIST

**Writing**

- ✔ Draw and write about the owls in *Owl at Home* and "The Owl and the Pussy-Cat."
- ✔ Include at least one way the owls' adventures are the same and one way they are different.
- ✔ Use correct language conventions.

**Speaking & Listening**

- ✔ Describe events including details.
- ✔ Ask and answer questions to clarify what a speaker says.
- ✔ Express ideas and opinions clearly.

## OBJECTIVES

- Understand that poetry is a type of writing
- Examine word choice that appeals to the senses
- Analyze text using text evidence

### Options for Reading

*Be sure to read aloud with expression to model fluent reading.*

**Uninterrupted** Focus on the flow of the poem by reading aloud without stopping for comments or questions.

**Interactive** Stop at appropriate places to make comments and ask children questions. Also, invite children to share their own comments and questions.

### Common Core Connection

**RL.K.5** recognize common types of texts; **W.K.2** use drawing, dictating, and writing to compose informative/explanatory texts; **W.K.5** respond to questions/suggestions from peers and add details to strengthen writing; **SL.K.2** confirm understanding of a text read aloud, information presented orally, or through other media by asking/answering questions and requesting clarification; **SL.K.4** describe familiar people, places, things, and events/provide detail; **SL.K.6** speak audibly and express thoughts, feelings, and ideas clearly

**RL.1.4** identify words and phrases that suggest feelings or appeal to senses; **RL.1.6** identify who is telling the story; **RL.1.10** read prose and poetry; **RF.1.4b** read on-level text orally with accuracy, appropriate rate, and expression; **W.1.5** focus on a topic, respond to questions/suggestions from peers, and add details to strengthen writing; **SL.1.2** ask and answer questions about details in a text read aloud, information presented orally, or through other media; **SL.1.4** describe people, places, things, and events with details/express ideas and feelings clearly

# "April Rain Song"

by Langston Hughes

**SUMMARY** This poem describes what rain looks, feels, and sounds like. The poem includes vivid images and language patterns. It uses simple words to evoke feelings about experiencing rain.

**ABOUT THE AUTHOR** **Langston Hughes** was the author of more than fifty books of poetry, plays, and essays. Many of his poems are based on the experiences of African Americans and blues music. During the 1920s, he was an important part of a cultural movement called the Harlem Renaissance. He is considered one of America's most important poets.

## Discuss Genre and Set Purpose

**POETRY** Ask children to look at the poem and explain how they can tell it is a poem and not another kind of text. Help children note the way the poem is organized: many of the lines are long, one is short; there are no rhyming words; there is repetition of the word *rain*.

**TEXT FOCUS: Sensory Language** Explain that poems often use words that appeal to the reader's senses. The sensory language creates word pictures in the reader's mind. It helps a reader hear, see, taste, touch, and smell what the poet describes. RL.K.5

**SET PURPOSE** Help children set a purpose for listening to the poem, such as to enjoy the word pictures that the sensory language creates.

### TEXT COMPLEXITY RUBRIC

| Overall Text Complexity | | "April Rain Song" POETRY<br>ACCESSIBLE |
|---|---|---|
| Quantitative Measures | Lexile | N/A |
| | Guided Reading Level | N/A |
| Qualitative Measures | Text Structure | less familiar poetic structure |
| | Language Conventionality and Clarity | some figurative language |
| | Knowledge Demands | common everyday experience |
| | Purpose/Levels of Meaning | single level of simple meaning |

**Academic Vocabulary**

Read each word with children and discuss its meaning.

**lullaby** (line 3) • a peaceful and quiet song to put a child to sleep

**gutter** (line 5) • an area beside a road that is used to catch water

## FIRST READ Think Through the Text

Have children use text evidence to answer these questions.

- *What is the poem mostly about?* *the rain* *How do you know?* *The poem is titled "April Rain Song."* **SL.K.2, SL.1.2**
- *Who is the speaker in the poem?* Sample answer: *the poet* *How do you know?* *The poem uses the word* I. **SL.K.2, RL.1.6**
- *Where is the rain falling?* *in a city or town* *How do you know?* *The poem mentions a sidewalk and a gutter.* **SL.K.2, SL.1.2**

## SECOND READ Analyze the Text

- Remind children that sensory language helps them create pictures in their minds. Reread the first line. Then ask: *What does the rain feel like to the poet?* *Rain feels like a kiss.* **SL.K.2, RL.1.4**
- *What other words does the poet use to help you see, touch, and hear the rain?* Sample answer: *sight:* silver liquid drops, running pools in the gutter; *touch:* rain beat upon your head; *sound:* sing you a lullaby, plays a little sleep-song **SL.K.2, RL.1.4**
- Reread the first and last lines of the poem. Ask: *How does the poet feel about the rain?* *He loves the rain.* *What words does he use to describe how he feels?* kiss *and* love **SL.K.2, RL.1.4**

## Practice Fluency

**EMPHASIZE EXPRESSION** Remind children that they should read poetry with expression to make listening to it more enjoyable. Read aloud the first two lines of the poem to model expressive reading. Then chorally read the remaining lines, focusing on expression. **RL.K.10, RF.1.4b**

## Independent/Self-Selected Reading

If children have demonstrated comprehension of "April Rain Song," have them use another poem to practice recognizing sensory images. Model selecting a book and choosing a poem. Suggested titles:

- *Hip Hop Speaks to Children* compiled by Nikki Giovanni
- *The 20th Century Children's Poetry Treasury* compiled by Jack Prelutsky **RL.1.10**

### WRITE & PRESENT

1. Have small groups discuss how the poem describes rain. Encourage children to ask and answer questions about text details and sensory images. **SL.K.4, SL.1.4**
2. Individual children use sensory language to write about rain. Encourage them to describe what it looks, feels, sounds, tastes, and smells like. Suggest that children draw pictures to illustrate their writing. **W.K.2, W.1.2**
3. Children within each group share their writing and drawing with each other and edit their work. **W.K.5, W.1.5**
4. Groups present their final ideas and drawings with classmates. **SL.K.6, SL.1.4**

*See Copying Masters, pp. 242–245.*

### STUDENT CHECKLIST

**Writing**

- ✔ Write about and draw a scene with rain.
- ✔ Include one or more details using sensory language.
- ✔ Use correct language conventions.

**Speaking & Listening**

- ✔ Participate effectively in a collaborative discussion.
- ✔ Ask and answer questions about details in a poem.
- ✔ Demonstrate a connection between features in the poem and their own writing.

## OBJECTIVES

- Understand that poetry is a type of writing
- Examine word choices that appeal to the senses
- Analyze text using text evidence

***Zin! Zin! Zin! A Violin!*** **is broken into three instructional segments.**

**SEGMENTS**



### Options for Read Aloud

*Display the book's pictures, and read aloud with expression to model fluent reading.*

**Uninterrupted** Focus on the flow of the poem by reading aloud without stopping for comments or questions.

**Interactive** Stop at appropriate places to make comments and ask children questions. Also, invite children to share their own comments and questions.

### Common Core Connection

**RL.K.10** Engage in group reading activities with purpose and understanding; **RF.K.2a** recognize and produce rhyming words; **SL.K.2** confirm understanding of a text read aloud, information presented orally, or through other media by asking/answering questions and requesting clarification

**RL1.4** identify words and phrases that suggest feelings or appeal to senses; **RL.1.10** read prose and poetry; **SL.1.2** ask and answer questions about details in a text read aloud, information presented orally, or through other media

# Zin! Zin! Zin! A Violin

by Lloyd Moss

**SUMMARY** This picture book-length poem describes a variety of classical musicians gathering in a great hall. Rhymes and sensory images convey sounds of brass, woodwind, and string instruments.

**ABOUT THE AUTHOR Lloyd Moss** hosted a weekday radio program on a classical music station for more than 50 years. His first children's book was *Zin! Zin! Zin! A Violin*, which won the Caldecott Award in 1996.

## Discuss Genre and Set Purpose

**POETRY** Look at the poem. Guide children to identify characteristics of poetry including rhyming words, rhythm, repetition, and sensory images. Help them understand the differences between this long poem in picture book format and a picture book with a story written in prose.

**TEXT FOCUS: Sensory Language** Explain that the poet uses sensory words to create word pictures. As children listen to the poem, discuss how the sensory language helps them to see and hear each instrument.

**SET PURPOSE** Help children set a purpose for listening, such as to enjoy the poem's rhymes, rhythms, and sensory images.

**TEXT COMPLEXITY RUBRIC**

| Overall Text Complexity | | *Zin! Zin! Zin! A Violin!* POETRY<br>COMPLEX |
|---|---|---|
| Quantitative Measures | Lexile | N/A |
| | Guided Reading Level | N/A |
| Qualitative Measures | Text Structure | somewhat complex poetic structure |
| | Language Conventionality and Clarity | increased unfamiliar or academic words |
| | Knowledge Demands | somewhat unfamiliar situation |
| | Purpose/Levels of Meaning | single level of complex meaning |

## SEGMENT 1 pp. 6–13

### Academic Vocabulary

Read each word with children and discuss its meaning.

**mournful** (p. 6) • sad; full of grief
**silken** (p. 6) • like silk; smooth and soft
**coiled** (p. 11) • wound or twisted in a spiral shape
**mellow** (p. 12) • soft and full; without a harsh sound

## FIRST READ Think Through the Text

Have children use text evidence to answer these questions.

**pp. 6–7** • *What instrument is the musician playing?* *a trombone* Ask: *What words rhyme on this page?* moan/tone/alone/trombone; low/solo **RF.K.2a, SL.1.2**

**pp. 8–9** • *What instrument is this musician playing?* *a trumpet* *Who does she join?* *the trombone player* *How many musicians are there now?* *two* *Which word in the text means a group of two musicians playing together?* duo **RL.K.4, SL.1.2**

**pp. 6–11** • *Let's look at the first six pages. Which kinds of words are printed in all capital letters?* Sample answer: *the names of the instruments, number words, and words that tell the number of musicians playing in a group* **RL.K.10, RL.1.10**

**pp. 12–13** • *How many musicians are there now?* *four* *What is a quartet? How do you know?* *A quartet is a group of four musicians playing together. The text says a quartet is four, and the picture shows four musicians.* **RL.K.4, SL.1.2**

## SECOND READ Analyze the Text

- Remind children that the poet uses sensory language to help the reader "hear" the sound of each instrument. Reread page 6. Then ask: *What words does the poet use to describe the sound of the trombone?* Sample answer: mournful moan; silken tone; gliding, sliding, high notes go low **SL.K.2, RL.1.4**
- Reread page 9. Then ask: *What does the poet use to describe the sound of the trumpet?* sings, stings, a swinging song *What is alike about the sounds and letters in these words?* *They all begin with the /s/ sound and end with the sound for* ng. **SL.K.2, RL.1.4**
- Reread page 10. *What words help you picture how the French horn looks?* Sample answer: oiled; bright and brassy; loops all coiled; golden yellow **SL.K.2, RL.1.4**

### Domain Specific Vocabulary

**trombone** (p. 6) • a large, brass wind instrument with a long tube that slides

**trumpet** (p. 9) • a brass wind instrument that is curved

**French horn** (p. 11) • a brass wind instrument with a large circular piece

**cello** (p. 12) • a string instrument that looks like a big violin

### ENGLISH LANGUAGE LEARNERS

**Use Visuals**

Discuss the illustrations of the instruments on each spread. Read each instrument name aloud as you point to its picture. Have children repeat after you. Then ask children to use each instrument name in an oral sentence.

### RESPOND TO SEGMENT 1

**Classroom Collaboration**

Have small groups summarize what they have learned and predict what they will learn about in the next segment.

### Domain Specific Vocabulary

**violin** (p. 14) • an instrument with four strings that is played with a bow

**quintet** (p. 14) • a group of five musicians

**flute** (p. 17) • a long instrument that is shaped like a pipe

**sextet** (p. 17) • a group of six musicians

**clarinet** (p. 18) • a long instrument with a flare at the end

**oboe** (p. 20) • an instrument that makes high tones

### RESPOND TO SEGMENT 2

**Classroom Collaboration**

Have small groups work together to summarize what they have learned. Have them ask questions about what they don't understand.

### Common Core Connection

**RL.K.4** ask and answer questions about unknown words; **RL.K.7** describe the relationship between the illustrations and the story; **W.K.2** use drawing, dictating, and writing to compose informative/explanatory texts; **W.K.5** respond to questions/suggestions from peers and add details to strengthen writing; **SL.K.4** describe familiar people, places, things, and events/provide detail; **SL.K.5** add drawings or visual displays to descriptions to provide detail; **SL.K.6** speak audibly and express thoughts, feelings, and ideas clearly

**RF.1.4b** read on-level text orally with accuracy, appropriate rate, and expression; **RL.1.7** use illustrations and details to describe characters, settings, or events; **W.1.5** focus on a topic, respond to questions/suggestions from peers, and add details to strengthen writing; **SL.1.4** describe people, places, things, and events with details/express ideas and feelings clearly; **SL.1.5** add drawings or visual displays to descriptions to clarify ideas, thoughts, and feelings

### Academic Vocabulary

Read each word with children and discuss its meaning.

**slender** (p. 17) • thin

**sliver** (p. 17) • a small, thin piece of something

**sleek** (p. 18) • smooth and glossy

**bleating** (p. 20) • a sound like the cry made by a goat or sheep

## FIRST READ Think Through the Text

Have children use text evidence to answer these questions.

**pp. 14–15** • *What is the fifth instrument to join the others?* violin SL.K.2, SL.1.2

**pp. 16–17** • *How many musicians are there now?* six *What is a sextet? How do you know?* A sextet is a group of six musicians playing together. The text says a sextet is six, and the picture shows six musicians. RL.K.4, SL.1.2

**pp. 18–19** • *Which words tell what a clarinet looks like?* sleek, black, woody SL.K.2, RL.1.4

**pp. 20–21** • *What is the eighth instrument to join the others?* oboe SL.K.2, SL.1.2

## SECOND READ Analyze the Text

- Reread page 14. Then ask: *What sound words are used to describe the violin?* zin, zin, zin *What do these words sound like when you say them out loud?* They sound like the sound a violin makes. SL.K.2, RL.1.4
- Reread the first two lines on page 17. Then ask: *What words does the poet use to describe the flute?* that sends our soul a-shiver; that slender, silver sliver *What is alike about the sounds and letters in most of these words?* They begin with the /s/ sound and end with the sound for er. SL.K.2, RL.1.4
- Reread the first line on page 20. *What sense words describe the sounds of the oboe?* gleeful, bleating, sobbing, pleading Explain that these words describe feelings. Ask: *How does it feel to be gleeful?* happy *When you are sobbing, how do you feel?* very sad *Why does the poet use these words?* to help the reader understand how the instruments sound and how they may make listeners feel SL.K.2, RL.1.4

## SEGMENT 3 pp. 22–32

### Academic Vocabulary

Read each word with children and discuss its meaning.

**descends** (p. 24) • comes down

**galore** (p. 29) • in a great amount; overflowing

## FIRST READ Think Through the Text

Have children use text evidence to answer these questions.

**pp. 22–23** • *Are the musicians playing music? How do you know? No, the illustrations show the musicians being silly with their instruments.* **RL.K.7, RL.1.7**

**pp. 24– 25** • *What is the last instrument? harp How many are there now? ten What is the name for the group of 10? chamber group of ten* **SL.K.2, SL.1.2**

**pp. 26–27** • *Where are the musicians going to play? in a music hall What are they all doing for the first time now? All ten are playing together.* **SL.K.2, SL.1.2**

## SECOND READ Analyze the Text

- Reread page 24 and display the picture. *What is happening? The harp and the harpist are being lowered onto the stage. What words create a picture in the reader's mind?* descends with angel's wings, a heaven's blend through magic strings **SL.K.2, RL.1.4**
- Display the illustration on pages 28–29. Ask: *Who have the musicians been playing for so far? How do you know? They have been playing for a dog and two cats; the animals are in each picture.* Display pages 30–31. Ask: *Who are the musicians playing for now? a large audience* **RL.K.7, RL.1.7**

## Practice Fluency

**EMPHASIZE RATE** Remind children that they should read poetry at a pace that is not too fast or too slow. Read aloud the first page of the poem very quickly, very slowly, and finally at a moderate speed. Ask children which reading they preferred and why. **RF.1.4b**

## Independent/Self-Selected Reading

If children have demonstrated comprehension of *Zin! Zin! Zin! A Violin*, have them practice the skills with other poems. Suggested titles:

- *The Carnival of the Animals* by Jack Prelutsky
- *Hip Hop Speaks to Children* compiled by Nikki Giovanni **RL.1.10**

### WRITE & PRESENT

1. Have small groups review the poem to discuss how the poet uses sensory language to describe the instruments. Encourage children to ask and answer questions about text details and how the instruments look and sound. **SL.K.4, SL.1.4**
2. Ask children to think about their experiences with music and instruments. Have each child write a short paragraph or poem and draw pictures to show a favorite instrument. Tell them to include at least one sensory image. **W.K.2, W.1.2**
3. Children return to their groups and share their writings and drawings with each other. Have children edit their work. **W.K.5, W.1.5**
4. Individual children present their final work to the class. **SL.K.6, SL.1.4**

*See Copying Masters, pp. 242–245.*

### STUDENT CHECKLIST

**Writing**

- ✔ Write a short paragraph or poem that describes an instrument.
- ✔ Include at least one sensory image.
- ✔ Use correct language conventions.

**Speaking & Listening**

- ✔ Participate effectively in a collaborative discussion.
- ✔ Ask and answer questions about details in a poem.
- ✔ Include details in their own writing and drawings that demonstrate an understanding of the text.

## OBJECTIVES

- Identify reasons to support points
- Identify key details
- Recognize sequence
- Use illustrations to clarify text

***A Tree Is A Plant*** **is broken into three instructional segments.**

**SEGMENTS**



### Options for Reading

**Independent** Children read the book independently and then answer questions posed by the teacher.

**Supported** Small groups read a segment and answer questions with teacher support.

### Common Core Connection

**RI.K.1** ask and answer questions about key details; **RI.K.3** describe the connection between individuals, events, ideas, or information in a text; **RI.K.7** describe relationships between illustrations and the text; **RI.K.8** identify the reasons the author gives to support points

**RI.1.1** ask and answer questions about key details; **RI.1.3** describe the connection between individuals, events, ideas, or information in a text; **RI.1.7** use illustrations and details to describe key ideas; **RI.1.8** identify the reasons the author gives to support points

# *A Tree Is a Plant*

by Clyde Robert Bulla

**SUMMARY** Trees can live for a very long time, but a tree's life begins when a seed is planted. This book tells how an apple seed grows into a tree. It also describes the life cycle of a tree from season to season.

**ABOUT THE AUTHOR** **Clyde Robert Bulla** wrote more than sixty books for children. His first book, *The Donkey Cart*, was published in 1946. His stories are known for their simple language and fast-moving plots, which usually have a historical background.

## Discuss Genre and Set Purpose

**INFORMATIONAL TEXT** Display the book and read the title aloud. Show children the illustrations. Ask them to tell how they know that the text and pictures give facts and details about the life cycle of a tree.

**SET PURPOSE** Help children set a purpose for reading, such as to learn about the life cycle of an apple tree.

### TEXT COMPLEXITY RUBRIC

| Overall Text Complexity | | *A Tree Is A Plant* INFORMATIONAL TEXT<br>ACCESSIBLE |
|---|---|---|
| Quantitative Measures | Lexile | 290L |
| | Guided Reading Level | I |
| Qualitative Measures | Text Structure | largely simple graphics, supplementary to understanding of the text |
| | Language Conventionality and Clarity | clear, direct language |
| | Knowledge Demands | some specialized knowledge required |
| | Purpose/Levels of Meaning | explicitly stated |

## SEGMENT 1 pp. 4–9

### Academic Vocabulary

Read each word with children and discuss its meaning.

**soil** (p. 8) • dirt

**stem** (p.10) • main part of a plant

**blossoms** (p. 10) • flowers that make seeds or fruit

**ripe** (p. 15) • ready to eat

**bark** (p. 16) • outer part of a tree

**bare** (p. 23) • without leaves

## FIRST READ Think Through the Text

Have children use text evidence to answer these questions.

**p. 5** • *What reason does the author give to support the fact that a tree is a plant?* *Trees grow from seeds the way most plants do.* **RI.K.8, RI.1.8**

**p. 8** • *What two ways do apple seeds get into the ground?* *Some seeds are planted. Others fall to the ground.* **RI.K.1, RI.1.1**

**p. 9** • *In which season does an apple seed begin to grow?* *spring* *What helps the seed grow?* *the rain and the sun* **RI.K.1, RI.1.1**

## SECOND READ Analyze the Text

- Reread page 7 with children. Then ask: *Have you ever seen the inside of an apple? Are there seeds inside an apple? Where?* *The seeds are in the center of an apple.* **RI.K.3, RI.1.3**
- Review page 9. Point to each illustration and ask: *What do the illustrations show?* Sample answer: *The seed lies under the snow during the winter; the seed begins to grow in the warm sun during the spring.* **RI.K.7, RI.1.7**
- Encourage children to use sequence words to answer the question: *What happens to the seed during the fall, the winter, and the spring?* Sample answer: *First, in the fall, the seed falls to the ground. Wind blows leaves and soil over it. Next, in the winter, it is pushed into the ground by snow. Then, in the spring, it begins to grow.* **RI.K.3, RI.1.3**

### ENGLISH LANGUAGE LEARNERS

**Use Comprehensible Input**

Display a sequence chart. Help children write steps of planting and growing a seed. Have children reread the chart as you point to illustrations. For example:

1. *Seeds fall.*
2. *Wind blows.*
3. *Snow pushes seeds.*
4. *Spring comes.*
5. *Seeds grow.*

### RESPOND TO SEGMENT 1

**Classroom Collaboration**

Have small groups talk about what they have learned so far. Tell children to ask questions about anything they still don't understand.

## ENGLISH LANGUAGE LEARNERS

**Use Visuals and Sentence Frames**

Point to illustrations in the book. Have children complete sentence frames to describe the tree in each season. For example, children point to the illustration on page 28 and complete the sentence frame: *In the spring, trees are covered with _____.* *blossoms*

## RESPOND TO SEGMENT 2

**Classroom Collaboration**

Have small groups work together to summarize what they have learned. Have them ask questions about what they hope to learn in the last segment of the book.

**Common Core Connection**

**RI.K.1** ask and answer questions about key details; **RI.K.3** describe the connection between individuals, events, ideas, or information in a text; **RI.K.7** describe relationships between illustrations and the text; **RI.K.8** identify the reasons the author gives to support points; **RI.K.10** engage in group reading activities with purpose and understanding; **W.K.1** use drawing, dictating, and writing to compose opinion pieces; **W.K.5** respond to questions/suggestions from peers and add details to strengthen writing; **SL.K.3** ask and answer questions to seek help, get information, or clarify something not understood

**RI.1.1** ask and answer questions about key details; **RI.1.3** describe the connection between individuals, events, ideas, or information in a text; **RI.1.7** use illustrations and details to describe key ideas; **RI.1.8** identify the reasons the author gives to support points **RI.1.10** read informational texts; **W.1.1** write opinion pieces; **W.1.5** focus on a topic, respond to questions/suggestions from peers, and add details to strengthen writing; **SL.1.1c** ask questions to clear up confusion about topics and texts under discussion

## FIRST READ Think Through the Text

Have children use text evidence to answer these questions.

**pp. 10–11** • *How does the illustration on page 11 help you understand the text on page 10?* *It shows what the blossoms on an apple tree look like in the spring.* **RI.K.7, RI.1.7**

**pp. 12–13** • *What happens after the blossoms fall off the tree?* *Tiny green apples appear where the blossoms had been.* **RI.K.1, RI.1.1**

**p. 20** • *Which part of the tree carries water from the ground to the branches?* *the trunk* *Which part of the tree carries water to the leaves?* *the branches* **RI.K.1, RI.1.1**

## SECOND READ Analyze the Text

- Reread page 18 with children. Then ask: *Why does the author say that the roots are like branches under the ground?* Sample answer: *Both spread out from the tree. The branches spread out above ground. The roots spread out under the ground.* **RI.K.3, RI.1.3**
- Review pages 18–20. *What reasons does the author give to support the point that a tree could not live without roots?* Sample answers: *Roots hold the trunk in the ground and keep the tree from falling in the wind. Roots carry water into the tree trunk.* **RI.K.8, RI.1.8**
- Have children look back at page 20. Then ask: *How does water move from the ground through the tree?* *Water moves from the ground to the roots to the trunk to the branches to the leaves.* *Why is this important?* *It is important because the tree needs water to live.* **RI.K.3, RI.1.3**

**SEGMENT 3** pp. 21–31

## FIRST READ Think Through the Text

Have children use text evidence to answer these questions.

**p. 21** • *How do leaves help the tree?* *The leaves make food for the tree.* **RI.K.1, RI.1.1**

**pp. 22–23** • *What does the apple tree look like in the fall and in the winter?* *In the fall the tree is covered with apples. The tree has yellow and brown leaves. In the winter the tree is bare.* **RI.K.1, RI.1.1**

**pp. 26–27** • *When do apple tree blossoms and apples grow?* *in the spring* *What helps them grow?* *the rain and the sun* **RI.K.1, RI.1.1**

## SECOND READ Analyze the Text

- Reread pages 23–26. Then ask: *What reasons does the author give to support the point that a tree that looks dead in winter is still alive?* Sample answer: *The tree is still alive under its bark. When spring comes again, blossoms and apples grow on the tree.* **RI.K.8, RI.1.8**
- Have children discuss the questions on pages 28–31. Encourage them to give reasons to support their answers. Sample answer: *I like trees best in the fall. I like them then because they are covered with apples. I can pick the apples and eat them.* **RI.K.10, RI.1.10**

# Independent/Self-Selected Reading

Have children reread *A Tree Is a Plant* independently to practice analyzing the text on their own, or have them practice the skills using another book. Suggested titles:

- *A Tree Is Nice* by Janet May Udry
- *Time for Kids: Plants!* by the Editors of *Time for Kids* with Brenda Iasevoli **RI.1.10**

### WRITE & PRESENT

1. Have small groups discuss why the roots are so important to a tree. Encourage children to use illustrations and ask questions about the text. **RI.K.8, RI.1.8**
2. Have children dictate or write sentences about the season during which they like the apple tree best. Ask them to draw pictures that support the reasons for their opinion. **W.K.1, W.1.1**
3. Have children show their illustrations and share their sentences in small groups. Guide them to add details to their writing. **W.K.5, W.1.5**
4. Have children present their final sentences and pictures to classmates. Encourage children to ask and answer questions about the presentations. **SL.K.3, SL.1.1c**
5. Have individual children turn in their final work to the teacher.

*See Copying Masters, pp. 242–245.*

### STUDENT CHECKLIST

**Writing**

- ✔ Write about opinions.
- ✔ Give reasons to support opinions.
- ✔ Use correct language conventions.

**Speaking & Listening**

- ✔ Engage effectively in collaborative conversations.
- ✔ Ask and answer questions to clarify details.

## OBJECTIVES

- Ask and answer questions about information in a text
- Explore the concept of using the five senses

***My Five Senses* is broken into three instructional segments.**

**SEGMENTS**

SEGMENT 1 . . . . . . . . . pp. 4–13
SEGMENT 2 . . . . . . . . pp. 14–19
SEGMENT 3 . . . . . . . . pp. 20–32

### Options for Reading

**Independent** Children read the selection independently or with a partner and then answer questions posed by the teacher.

**Supported** Children read a segment and answer questions with teacher support and then reread the segment with the teacher or a partner. Encourage children to read at least a few words on their own.

### Common Core Connection

**RI.K.1** ask and answer questions about key details; **RI.K.3** describe the connection between individuals, events, ideas, or information in a text; **RI.K.7** describe relationships between illustrations and the text

**RI.1.1** ask and answer questions about key details; **RI.1.3** describe the connection between individuals, events, ideas or information in a text; **RI.1.7** use illustrations and details to describe key ideas

# *My Five Senses*

by Aliki

**SUMMARY** This book explains that our senses give us information about the world. We can get information through our senses of sight, hearing, taste, touch, and smell.

**ABOUT THE AUTHOR** Aliki is both an author and illustrator of more than 50 children's books. She started drawing at an early age and knew she wanted to be an artist from the time she was in kindergarten.

## Discuss Genre and Set Purpose

**INFORMATIONAL TEXT** Tell children that they will be reading an informational book about the five senses. Explain that an informational book gives facts, or true information, about real people, places, or things.

**SET PURPOSE** Help children set a purpose for reading, such as to learn information about the five senses.

### TEXT COMPLEXITY RUBRIC

| Overall Text Complexity | | *My Five Senses* INFORMATIONAL TEXT<br>ACCESSIBLE |
|---|---|---|
| Quantitative Measures | Lexile | 300L |
| | Guided Reading Level | E |
| Qualitative Measures | Text Structure | largely simple graphics, supplementary to understanding of the text |
| | Language Conventionality and Clarity | some unfamiliar language |
| | Knowledge Demands | moderately complex theme |
| | Purpose/Levels of Meaning | implied, but easy to identify from context |

SEGMENT 1 pp. 4–13

**Academic Vocabulary**

Read each word with children and discuss its meaning.

**sight** (p. 12) • seeing

**senses** (p. 14) • sight, hearing, taste, touch, and smell

**touch** (p. 15) • feeling with a part of the body, such as the fingers

**aware** (p. 26) • knowing what is around you

## ENGLISH LANGUAGE LEARNERS

**Use Visuals and Gestures**

Point to your eyes and say: *I see with my eyes.* Have children repeat. Continue with the other senses. Have children tell about some of their favorite things they can taste, smell, hear, see, or touch.

**RESPOND TO SEGMENT 1**

**Classroom Collaboration**

Have small groups summarize what they have learned and ask questions about anything they still don't understand.

## FIRST READ Think Through the Text

Have children use text evidence to answer these questions.

**pp. 4–9** • *What part of your body do you see with? hear with? smell with? eyes, ears, nose* **RI.K.1, RI.1.1**

**pp. 8–9** • *What does the boy smell? flowers* **RI.K.1, RI.1.1**

**pp. 10–13** • *How are touch and taste different? You touch with your fingers. You taste with your tongue.* **RI.K.1, RI.1.1**

## SECOND READ Analyze the Text

- Reread pp. 4–13. Ask: *How do the senses of sight and hearing give us information about the world?* Using text evidence, model how to answer the question. *On pp. 5–7 it says, I can see. I see with my eyes. I can hear. I hear with my ears. We use certain body parts to see and hear. When we see, we use our eyes to get information about what things look like. When we hear, we use our ears to get information from the sounds around us, such as people talking, traffic, or music.* **RI.K.3, RI.1.3**
- Show children pages 5–6. Point out how the text and picture both help to give information. Say: *The text tells about seeing with my eyes. What does the picture show?* Sample answer: *The picture shows a boy whose eyes are wide open. He is seeing with his eyes.* **RI.K.7, RI.1.7**
- Show children pages 6–7. Say: *The text tells about hearing with my ears. What does the picture show?* Sample answer: *The picture shows a boy with his hands by his ears to show he hears with his ears.* **RI.K.7, RI.1.7**
- Show children pages 10–11. Say: *Let's read page 10. I can taste. I can taste with my tongue. What does the picture on the next page show?* *the boy using his tongue to lick ice cream* **RI.K.7, RI.1.7**

## ENGLISH LANGUAGE LEARNERS

**Comprehensible Input**

To ensure that children understand all the words in the text, ask questions that can be answered using key story words, such as: *What do we use to wash our hands?* *soap* *What musical instrument can we see on page 16?* *a drum* Encourage more advanced English Learners to answer in complete sentences.

**RESPOND TO SEGMENT 2**

**Classroom Collaboration**

Have small groups work together to summarize what they learned. Have them ask questions about what they don't understand.

**Common Core Connection**

**RI.K.1** ask and answer questions about key details; **RI.K.3** describe the connection between individuals, events, ideas, or information in a text; **RI.K.7** describe relationships between illustrations and the text; **W.K.2** use drawing, dictating, and writing to compose informative/explanatory texts; **SL.K.4** describe familiar people, places, things, and events/provide detail; **SL.K.6** speak audibly and express thoughts, feelings, and ideas clearly

**RI.1.1** ask and answer questions about key details; **RI.1.3** describe the connection between individuals, events, ideas or information in a text; **RI.1.7** use illustrations and details to describe key ideas; **RI.1.10** read informational texts; **W.1.2** write informative/explanatory texts; **SL.1.4** describe people, places, things, and events with details/express ideas and feelings clearly

## FIRST READ Think Through the Text

Have children use text evidence to answer these questions.

**p. 15** • *According to page 15, what kinds of things might you see?* *sun, frog, baby sister* **RI.K.1, RI.1.1**

**p. 17** • *According to page 17, what kinds of things might you smell?* *soap, pine tree, cookies* **RI.K.1, RI.1.1**

**p. 18** • *When would you use your sense of taste?* Sample answer: *when you want to drink milk or eat food* **RI.K.1, RI.1.1**

**pp. 14–19** • *What body part or parts are used for each sense?* *eyes to see, ears to hear, nose to smell, tongue to taste; fingers to touch* **RI.K.1, RI.1.1**

## SECOND READ Analyze the Text

- Ask children to imagine that they are eating with the boy shown on page 18. Have them name the different senses they would use. Then have them discuss two of these senses. Ask children to identify one thing they would see on their plates. Then ask them to use one word to describe how their food might taste. *Sample answers include spaghetti and salad, and descriptive words such as sweet, salty, sour, spicy, and so on.* **RI.K.1, RI.1.1**
- Show children pages 18–19. *When do you use your senses of taste and touch?* Sample answer: *I use my sense of taste when I drink or eat food. I use my sense of touch when I feel a kitten or a balloon with my fingers.* **RI.K.1, RI.1.1**
- Guide children to look back at pages 14–19. Have them tell about something that didn't make sense to them when they first read the selection. Then have them tell how they figured out what they read. **RI.K.3, RI.1.3**

**SEGMENT 3** pp. 20–32

## FIRST READ Think Through the Text

Have children use text evidence to answer these questions.

**pp. 20–21** • *What fact did you learn about the senses?* Sample answer: *that you can use all your senses at one time or only one sense at a time* RI.K.1, RI.1.1

**pp. 24–25** • *Look at and think about the picture of the boy bouncing the ball. What does he see?* *hand and ball* *What does he hear?* *bouncing* *What does he touch?* *ball* RI.K.7, RI.1.7

**pp. 26–27** • *What does it mean to be aware?* *to know what is all around you* RI.K.1, RI.1.1

**pp. 20–32** • *How are the senses all alike?* Sample answer: *They all make you aware of what is around you.* RI.K.3, RI.1.3

## SECOND READ Analyze the Text

- Reread pp. 22–23. Point to the picture and ask: *How can you see, hear, smell, and touch when you laugh and play with a puppy?* Sample answer: *I can see the puppy; I can hear the sound I make when I laugh and the sounds the puppy makes; I can smell the puppy; I can feel the puppy's fur with my hands.* RI.K.7, RI.1.7
- Reread p. 32. Point out all of the items in the picture. Ask: *How might the boy be aware of the things around him?* Sample answers: *He uses his senses: he tastes the apple, smells the flower, hears the dog, feels the bear, sees what's in the book.* RI.K.7, RI.1.7

# Independent/Self-Selected Reading

If children have already demonstrated comprehension of *My Five Senses*, have them practice the skills using another independent reading book. Model selecting a book from the classroom library. Help children read the title of the book, the author's name, and any information about the book on the back or inside cover. Suggested titles:

- *The Listening Walk* by Paul Showers
- *My Five Senses* by Margaret Miller RI.1.10

### WRITE & PRESENT

1. Have small groups refer to the text to discuss ways the author explains and illustrates the five senses. Encourage children to ask and answer questions they have about text details. RI.K.1, RI.1.1
2. Individual children draw and write about a real or imagined scene where one or more senses are used. W.K.2, W.1.2
3. Children within each group share their writing and drawing with each other and edit their work. SL.K.4, SL.1.4
4. Groups present their final ideas and examples to classmates. SL.K.6

*See Copying Masters, pp. 242–245.*

### STUDENT CHECKLIST

**Writing**

- ✔ Write about and draw a scene where one or more senses are used.
- ✔ Include one or more details about the senses.
- ✔ Use correct language conventions.

**Speaking & Listening**

- ✔ Participate effectively in collaborative conversations.
- ✔ Ask and answer questions about text details.
- ✔ Demonstrate a connection between information in the text and their own writing and drawing.

## OBJECTIVES

- Define the role and materials the author and illustrator contribute to the text
- Identify main ideas and retell key details
- Interpret information presented visually
- Analyze text using text evidence

***Starfish* is broken into three instructional segments.**

**SEGMENTS**

**SEGMENT 1**. . . . . . . . . .pp. 4–15
**SEGMENT 2**. . . . . . . . .pp. 16–21
**SEGMENT 3**. . . . . . . . .pp. 22–33

### Options for Reading

**Independent** Children read the book independently and then answer questions posed by the teacher.

**Supported** Children read a segment with a partner and answer questions with teacher support.

### Common Core Connection

**RI.K.1** ask and answer questions about key details; **RI.K.2** identify the main topic and retell key details; **RI.K.3** describe the connection between individuals, events, ideas, or information in a text; **RI.K.6** name the author and illustrator and define the role of each

**RI.1.1** ask and answer questions about key details; **RI.1.2** identify the main topic and retell key details; **RI.1.3** describe the connection between individuals, events, ideas, or information in a text; **RI.1.6** distinguish between information provided by pictures and words

# *Starfish*

by Edith Thacher Hurd

**SUMMARY** This book describes a variety of starfish. It provides information about the physical characteristics of starfish and their habitats, as well as how they move, what they eat, and their life cycle.

**ABOUT THE AUTHOR** **Edith Thacher Hurd** worked together with her husband Clement Hurd on many picture books, including *Johnny Lion's Book* and *Wilson's World*. Their son Thacher, born in 1949, grew up to also become a children's book illustrator and author.

## Discuss Genre and Set Purpose

**INFORMATIONAL TEXT** Page through the selection with children, and help them discover characteristics of informational text, including facts and details as well as illustrations that show real-life starfish and their habitats.

**SET PURPOSE** Help children set a purpose for reading, such as to learn information about starfish including how they move, where they live, and what they eat.

### TEXT COMPLEXITY RUBRIC

| Overall Text Complexity | | *Starfish* INFORMATIONAL TEXT<br>ACCESSIBLE |
|---|---|---|
| Quantitative Measures | Lexile | 170L |
| | Guided Reading Level | I |
| Qualitative Measures | Text Structure | simple science |
| | Language Conventionality and Clarity | straightforward sentence structure |
| | Knowledge Demands | some specialized knowledge required |
| | Purpose/Levels of Meaning | explicitly stated |

**SEGMENT 1** pp. 4–15

### Academic Vocabulary

Read each word with children and discuss its meaning.

**glide** (p. 10) • move in a slow, smooth way
**underside** (p. 16) • the bottom
**float** (p. 22) • drift
**prickly** (p. 28) • spiny and spiky

## FIRST READ Think Through the Text

Have children use text evidence to answer these questions.

**pp. 4–7** • *These pages are mainly about where starfish live and what they look like. What details tell about these main topics? Starfish live deep down in the sea. Some are pink, and some are purple.* RI.K.2, RI.1.2

**pp. 8–11** • *How do starfish move? They glide on their tube feet.* RI.K.1, RI.1.1

**pp. 12–15** • *How is a basket star like a starfish? It has rays. How is it different? It does not have tube feet.* RI.K.3, RI.1.3

## SECOND READ Analyze the Text

- Guide children to look at the book cover. Ask: *Who is the author of this book? Edith Thacher Hurd Who is the illustrator? Robin Brickman* Then look at pages 4–5. Ask: *How is the information given by the author the same as the information from the illustrator? How is it different?* Sample answer: *Both the author and the illustrator give information about starfish. The author tells where the starfish live. The illustrator shows what starfish look like and what their habitat looks like.* RI.K.6, RI.1.6
- Help children make an inference about the size of a sunflower starfish. *Reread pages 8–9. What do the words* It is the biggest of all *mean?* Sample answer: *The sunflower starfish is the biggest of all the starfish.* RI.K.1, RI.1.1
- Have children look back at pages 12–15. *What are these pages mainly about? What details support this main idea? These pages are mainly about different kinds of starfish. The details tell about basket stars, brittle stars, and mud stars.* RI.K.2, RI.1.2

### Domain Specific Vocabulary

**rays** (p. 9) • the arms of a starfish

**snail** (p. 10) • a mollusk covered with a shell that moves very slowly

### ENGLISH LANGUAGE LEARNERS

**Use Visuals**

Have children point to the illustrations on different pages that show the key details of the text. For example, for pages 6–7, say *Point to a purple starfish. Point to a pink starfish.* After children point to each illustration, have them repeat the detail it shows.

### RESPOND TO SEGMENT 1

**Classroom Collaboration**

Have small groups talk about what they have read so far. Encourage children to ask questions to clarify information as needed before reading the next segment.

## ENGLISH LANGUAGE LEARNERS

**Use Peer-Supported Learning**

Organize children into mixed-proficiency groups to generate ideas to complete a web about starfish. Each group draws a web with the center labeled *starfish*. Children in the group support each other as they pass around the web adding details about starfish.

## RESPOND TO SEGMENT 2

**Classroom Collaboration**

Have small groups work together to summarize what they have learned. Have them ask questions about what they don't understand.

**Common Core Connection**

**RI.K.1** ask and answer questions about key details; **RI.K.3** describe the connection between individuals, events, ideas, or information in a text; **RI.K.6** name the author and illustrator and define the role of each; **RI.K.7** describe relationships between illustrations and the text; **W.K.2** use drawing, dictating, and writing to compose informative/explanatory texts; **SL.K.1b** continue a conversation through multiple exchanges; **SL.K.4** describe familiar people, places, things, and events/provide detail

**RI.1.1** ask and answer questions about key details; **RI.1.3** describe the connection between individuals, events, ideas, or information in a text; **RI.1.5** know and use text features to locate facts or information; **RI.1.6** distinguish between information provided by pictures and words; **RI.1.7** use illustrations and details to describe key ideas; **RI.1.10** read informational texts; **W.1.2** write informative/explanatory texts; **SL.1.1b** build on others' talk in conversations by responding to others' comments; **SL.1.4** describe people, places, things, and events with details/express ideas and feelings clearly

## FIRST READ Think Through the Text

Have children use text evidence to answer these questions.

**pp. 16–17** • *What do starfish eat?* mussels, oysters, clams **RI.K.1, RI.1.1**

**pp. 18–19** • *How do the illustrations help you understand what the text describes on pages 18 and 19?* *The illustrations show how a starfish wraps its rays around a clam and pulls the shell open to eat what is inside.* **RI.K.7, RI.1.7**

**pp. 20–21** • *What information do the author and illustrator share on these pages?* *The author uses words to explain that if a starfish loses a ray it grows another one. The illustrator shows what it looks like when a crab pulls off a ray and then the missing part of the ray grows back.* **RI.K.6, RI.1.6**

## SECOND READ Analyze the Text

- Guide children to reread pages 16–17. *What text evidence tells why the starfish feels for something to eat? How does the illustration support this evidence?* Sample answer: *The text says that the starfish has no eyes, ears, or nose. That means it cannot see, hear, or smell something to eat, so it must feel for it. The picture shows that the starfish does not have eyes, ears, or a nose. It also shows how it glides to feel for the food.* **RI.K.7, RI.1.7**
- Explain that sometimes a picture gives more information than the words do. Have children look through these pages and tell about a picture that shows more information than the words. Sample answer: *The picture on page 17 shows that a starfish can eat while upside down. The words do not say this.* **RI.K.7, RI.1.6**
- Point out that this book is mainly about interesting starfish facts. *What have you learned so far that is most interesting to you? Did you learn it from the text, the pictures, or both?* Sample answer: *The most interesting fact to me is that if a starfish loses a ray, the ray can grow back. I learned it in both the text and the pictures.* **RI.K.6, RI.1.6**

**SEGMENT 3** pp. 22–33

## FIRST READ Think Through the Text

Have children use text evidence to answer these questions.

**pp. 22–25** • *How do starfish eggs move differently than grown starfish? When they are eggs, starfish float. The waves move them up and down. When they are grown, starfish crawl on their tiny tube feet.* **RI.K.3, RI.1.3**

**pp. 26–27** • *What does the author mainly want the reader to know about baby starfish? How can you tell? Baby starfish eat a lot. The author repeated the word eat many times and wrote it in all capital letters to show that they eat a lot.* **RI.K.1, RI.1.1**

**pp. 28–29** • *How are starfish different from each other? They are different sizes, colors, and shapes.* **RI.K.1, RI.1.1**

**pp. 32–33** • *What are the four main topics you can learn about on these pages? how to make your own starfish, where to find starfish, how to help starfish, books to read about starfish* **RI.K.2, RI.1.2**

## SECOND READ Analyze the Text

- Guide children to review pages 22–27. Point out that these pages are mainly about how starfish change. Ask: *What information does the author contribute about how starfish change? The author tells about how starfish start out as eggs and grow into bigger starfish. She also tells how baby starfish eat tiny things but then eat mussels, oysters, and clams as they grow bigger. What information does the illustrator contribute about how starfish change? The illustrator shows what the eggs look like and how big they are compared to a fish. She also shows how they change as they grow from small starfish to big starfish.* **RI.K.6, RI.1.6**
- Guide children to look at pages 32–33. Say: *If you want to learn more about how to help other animals that live in the ocean, which section on pages 32–33 would you read? Help starfish How can you tell? This section tells about Greenpeace, which is an organization that helps all kinds of ocean life.* **RI.K.1, RI.1.5**

## Independent/Self-Selected Reading

If children have already demonstrated comprehension of *Starfish*, have them practice the skills using another independent reading book. Model selecting a book from the classroom library. Help children read the title of the book, the author's name, and any information about the book on the back or inside cover. Suggested titles:

- *What Lives in a Shell?* by Kathleen Weidner Zoehfeld
- *Under the Sea* by Anna Milbourne **RI.1.10**

### WRITE & PRESENT

1. Have small groups refer to the text to discuss what information the author contributes about starfish and what the illustrator contributes. Encourage children to label a piece of paper with two headings, *Author* and *Illustrator*, and then take notes about what they learned. **RI.K.6, RI.1.6**
2. Have children choose one of the following topics: many different kinds of starfish; the life cycle of a starfish; or how starfish eat and move. Guide children to write one or two informative sentences telling what they learned from the author and illustrator and draw a picture that adds to the details. **W.K.2, W.1.2**
3. Small groups reconvene to share their sentences with each other and edit their writing. **SL.K.1b, SL.1.1b**
4. Children present their final sentences and pictures to classmates. **SL.K.4, SL.1.4**
5. Individual children turn in their final work to the teacher.

*See Copying Masters, pp. 242–245.*

### STUDENT CHECKLIST

#### Writing

- ✔ Write informative sentences.
- ✔ Include details both in text and supportive illustrations.
- ✔ Use correct language conventions.

#### Speaking & Listening

- ✔ Engage effectively in collaborative conversations.
- ✔ Present visuals to support and add details.

## OBJECTIVES

- Identify sequence of events
- Describe connections between events and ideas
- Recognize cause and effect
- Analyze text using text evidence

***A Weed Is a Flower: The Life of George Washington Carver*** **is broken into three instructional segments.**

**SEGMENTS**



### Options for Reading

**Independent** Children read the book independently and then answer questions posed by the teacher.

**Supported** Small groups read a segment and answer questions with teacher support.

### Common Core Connection

**RI.K.1** ask and answer questions about key details; **RI.K.2** identify the main topic and retell key details; **RI.K.3** describe the connection between individuals, events, ideas, or information in a text; **RI.K.8** identify the reasons the author gives to support points

**RI.1.1** ask and answer questions about key details; **RI.1.2** identify the main topic and retell key details; **RI.1.3** describe the connection between individuals, events, ideas, or information in a text; **RI.1.8** identify the reasons the author gives to support points

# *A Weed Is a Flower: The Life of George Washington Carver*

by Aliki

**SUMMARY** This book is a biography of George Washington Carver. The author chronologically presents the major life events and contributions of Dr. Carver, from when he was an infant to his death.

**ABOUT THE AUTHOR/ILLUSTRATOR** Aliki has written and illustrated both fiction and nonfiction books read around the world. Many of her books are about nature, dinosaurs, folklore, and childhood.

## Discuss Genre and Set Purpose

**BIOGRAPHY** Page through the selection with children, and help them discover characteristics of a biography. Guide children to discover that this book is all about a real person: George Washington Carver.

**SET PURPOSE** Help children set a purpose for reading, such as to learn about major events in the life of George Washington Carver.

### TEXT COMPLEXITY RUBRIC

| Overall Text Complexity | | *A Weed Is a Flower: The Life of George Washington Carver* BIOGRAPHY<br>COMPLEX |
|---|---|---|
| Quantitative Measures | Lexile | 640L |
| | Guided Reading Level | P |
| Qualitative Measures | Text Structure | organization of main idea and details may be complex, but is clearly stated and generally sequential |
| | Language Conventionality and Clarity | more complex descriptions |
| | Knowledge Demands | some specialized knowledge required |
| | Purpose/Levels of Meaning | explicitly stated |

## SEGMENT 1 pp. 4–15

### Academic Vocabulary

Read each word with children and discuss its meaning.

**slaves** (p. 6) • people who were considered the property of others and forced to work for them

**advice** (p. 11) • opinion; suggestions

**college** (p. 16) • school after high school

**agriculture** (p. 19) • the study of farming

**crops** (p. 20) • plants usually grown for food

## FIRST READ Think Through the Text

Have children use text evidence to answer these questions.

**pp. 4–5** • *What is this book about? the life of George Washington Carver What helps you know this? The author says that this is Carver's story.* **RI.K.2, RI.1.2**

**pp. 6–9** • *What happens to George's mother? She is kidnapped and never found.* **RI.K.1, RI.1.1**

**pp. 10–15** • *What do the people who George lives with like about him? He is always willing to help.* **RI.K.1, RI.1.1**

## SECOND READ Analyze the Text

- Have children reread pages 4–9. Ask: *What do you know about George's life before he is kidnapped? Before he is kidnapped, he lives with his mother, who is a slave; he is a baby. What happens after he is kidnapped? After he is kidnapped, he is found and returned to his owners. He lives with them, but his mother is not found.* **RI.K.3, RI.1.3**
- *Why is George known as the Plant Doctor? He gives people advice about how to keep plants healthy.* **RI.K.1, RI.1.1**
- *Why does George move away from some places and stay in others? He wants to be in a place where he can go to school.* **RI.K.3, RI.1.3**
- *What are some words you can use to describe George Washington Carver? What information in the text supports your ideas?* Sample answer: *curious: He wanted to know about everything around him; responsible: George looked after each plant as though it was the only one in his garden; adventurous: When he was ten, George left the Carver farm and went off to find the answers to his questions.* **RI.K.8, RI.1.8**

### ENGLISH LANGUAGE LEARNERS

**Use Comprehension Input**

Point to each illustration on pages 4–15. Guide children to complete sentence frames such as the following to tell what is happening:

pp. 4–5 *George is a _____. baby*

pp. 10–11 *George has a _____. garden*

Then ask children to add details to tell about each illustration.

### RESPOND TO SEGMENT 1

**Classroom Collaboration**

Have small groups talk about what they have read so far. Encourage children to ask questions to clarify information as needed before reading the next segment.

## ENGLISH LANGUAGE LEARNERS

**Expand Language Production**

Help children expand on their answers to questions. For example, provide sentence frames and have children complete them: *Agriculture means to study* ______. *farming* Then encourage children to respond to additional questions in complete sentences and to give text evidence to support their answers.

## RESPOND TO SEGMENT 2

**Classroom Collaboration**

Have small groups work together to summarize what they have learned. Have them ask questions about what they don't understand or what they hope to learn in the last segment of the book.

**Common Core Connection**

**RI.K.4** ask and answer questions about unknown words; **RI.K.7** describe relationships between illustrations and the text; **W.K.2** use drawing, dictating, and writing to compose informative/explanatory texts; **SL.K.1b** continue a conversation through multiple exchanges; **SL.K.4** describe familiar people, places, things, and events/provide detail

**RI.1.4** ask and answer questions to determine or clarify the meaning of words and phrases; **RI.1.7** use illustrations and details to describe key ideas; **RI.1.10** read informational texts; **W.1.2** write informative/explanatory texts; **SL.1.1b** build on others' talk in conversations by responding to others' comments; **SL.1.4** describe people, places, things, and events with details/express ideas and feelings clearly

## FIRST READ Think Through the Text

Have children use text evidence to answer these questions.

**pp. 16–17 •** ***What part of George's life does the illustration show? How can you tell?*** *It shows George when he is in college enjoying painting. The words say that at college he continues to learn and thinks of becoming an artist.* **RI.K.7, RI.1.7**

**pp. 18–19 •** **Remind children that George decides to study agriculture. Ask:** ***What kinds of things does he study?*** *He learns about how plants and flowers grow; he learns the names of weeds.* **RI.K.4, RI.1.4**

**pp. 20–25 •** ***What does George discover about sweet potatoes?*** Sample answer: *He can make soap, coffee, and starch from them.* ***What does George discover about peanuts?*** Sample answer: *He can make many products from peanuts, including paper, ink, shaving cream, sauces, linoleum, shampoo, and milk.* **RI.K.1, RI.1.1**

## SECOND READ Analyze the Text

- **Guide children to reread this segment.** ***What major events do you learn about in this part of the book? Use the words*** **first, next,** ***and*** **then** ***to tell about them.*** Sample answer: *First, George goes to college to study agriculture. Next, he becomes a teacher at a college for African Americans. Then he shows farmers how important it is to grow sweet potatoes and peanuts.* **RI.K.3, RI.1.3**
- ***What do farmers think about George's advice to grow sweet potatoes and peanuts? What causes them to feel this way?*** Sample answer: *Farmers do not want to grow them because they are afraid people will not buy these crops.* **RI.K.1, RI.1.1**
- ***How does George try to convince farmers to grow sweet potatoes and peanuts?*** Sample answer: *He shows them that there are hundreds of things people can make from sweet potatoes and peanuts.* ***Do you think this will convince the farmers? Why or why not?*** Sample answer: *Yes, because it shows that people will buy the crops because they can make so many things from them.* **RI.K.3, RI.1.3**

**SEGMENT 3** pp. 26–32

## FIRST READ Think Through the Text

Have children use text evidence to answer these questions.

**pp. 26–27** • *What effect do George's experiments with peanuts and sweet potatoes have on Alabama?* *Farmers grow the crops, and the crops become two of the most important ones in Alabama.* **RI.K.3, RI.1.3**

**pp. 28–29** • *What does George do when people offer to pay him a lot of money for his knowledge?* *He turns down the money because money is not important to him.* **RI.K.1, RI.1.1**

**pp. 30–31** • *What does the illustration show on these pages?* *It shows George's light on at night while he is still working and the rest of the town is asleep.* **RI.K.7, RI.1.7**

## SECOND READ Analyze the Text

- Guide children to review pages 26–29. Ask: *What evidence from the text supports the idea that George is famous?* *The text says the whole country knows about Dr. Carver.* *What shows that he is a thoughtful and good person?* *The text says that throughout his life Carver asks nothing of others. He only seeks to help.* **RI.K.8, RI.1.8**
- Guide children to understand that Carver does not change his working practices even though he becomes famous. *What does George do before the world knows about him?* *He lives in Tuskegee and works with plants.* *What does he do after the world knows about him?* *He still stays in Tuskegee and works in his laboratory discovering more uses for plants.* **RI.K.3, RI.1.3**
- Guide children to summarize the end of the book. Ask: *What are the most important details in this segment?* *George Washington Carver becomes famous for his research but continues to live a simple life.* Ask: *Is this what you thought would happen when you started to read the book?* Sample answer: *Yes, because Dr. Carver worked hard his whole life and was very smart.* **RI.K.3, RI.1.3**

# Independent/Self-Selected Reading

If children have already demonstrated comprehension of *A Weed Is a Flower: The Life of George Washington Carver,* have them practice comprehension skills using another independent reading book. Model selecting a book from the classroom library. Help children read the title of the book, the author's name, and any information about the book on the back or inside cover. Suggested titles:

- *George Washington Carver* by Lynea Bowdish
- *The Story of Johnny Appleseed* by Aliki **RI.1.10**

### WRITE & PRESENT

1. Have partners look back at the text to discuss the most important events described in George Washington Carver's life. Help them to complete a flow chart showing the sequence of the events. **RI.K.3, RI.1.3**
2. Help children use their graphic organizer to write a paragraph that includes the sequence of events. **W.K.2, W.1.2**
3. Partners reconvene to share their paragraphs with each other and edit their writing. **SL.K.1b, SL.1.1b**
4. Children present their final paragraphs to classmates. **SL.K.4, SL.1.4**
5. Individual children turn in their final work to the teacher.

*See Copying Masters, pp. 242–245.*

### STUDENT CHECKLIST

**Writing**

- ✔ Write informative and sequential paragraphs.
- ✔ Identify and write about important events in correct order.
- ✔ Use correct language conventions.

**Speaking & Listening**

- ✔ Engage effectively in collaborative conversations.
- ✔ Ask and answer questions to clarify details.

## OBJECTIVES

- Use information from illustrations to demonstrate understanding
- Identify a sequence of events
- Analyze text using text evidence

### Options for Reading

**Independent** Children read the book independently or with a partner and then answer questions posed by the teacher.

**Supported** Children read a few pages and answer questions with teacher support.

### Common Core Connection

**RI.K.1** ask and answer questions about key details; **RI.K.2** identify the main topic and retell key details; **RI.K.3** describe the connection between individuals, events, ideas, or information in a text; **RI.K.7** describe relationships between illustrations and the text; **W.K.2** use drawing, dictating, and writing to compose informative/explanatory texts; **W.K.5** respond to questions/suggestions from peers and add details to strengthen writing; **SL.K.6** speak audibly and express thoughts, feelings, and ideas clearly

**RI.1.1** ask and answer questions about key details; **RI.1.2** identify the main topic and retell key details; **RI.1.3** describe the connection between individuals, events, ideas, or information in a text; **RI.1.7** use illustrations and details to describe key ideas; **RI.1.10** read informational texts; **W.1.2** write informative/explanatory texts; **W.1.5** focus on a topic, respond to questions/suggestions from peers, and add details to strengthen writing; **SL.1.4** describe people, places, things, and events with details/express ideas and feelings clearly

# Truck

by Donald Crews

**SUMMARY** This wordless book shows the journey of a big, red delivery truck. It is loaded with tricycles in New York and then makes its way across the country to deliver its load in California. Along the way, readers see road signs, traffic, and other typical highway sights.

**ABOUT THE AUTHOR** Donald Crews is a writer and illustrator who frequently creates books about transportation. Two of his books, *Truck* and *Freight Train*, won Caldecott Honor Awards.

## Discuss Genre and Set Purpose

**INFORMATIONAL TEXT** Page through the selection with children to notice pictures and words. Discuss with them how they can tell this book is informational.

**SET PURPOSE** Help children set a purpose for reading, such as to find information about how trucks deliver things.

### TEXT COMPLEXITY RUBRIC

| Overall Text Complexity | | *Truck* INFORMATIONAL TEXT<br>ACCESSIBLE |
|---|---|---|
| Quantitative Measures | Lexile | N/A |
| | Guided Reading Level | N/A |
| Qualitative Measures | Text Structure | simple, linear chronology |
| | Language Conventionality and Clarity | literal, accessible language |
| | Knowledge Demands | experience includes unfamiliar aspects |
| | Purpose/Levels of Meaning | single topic |

**Academic Vocabulary**

Read each word with children and discuss its meaning.

**tunnel** (pp. 10–11) • a covered path underground or underwater

**speed** (pp. 12–13) • how fast something goes

**limit** (pp. 12–13) • the most you can do

**diner** (pp. 18–19) • a small restaurant

## FIRST READ Think Through the Text

Have children use evidence from the illustrations to answer these questions.

**pp. 2–3** • *What is the truck carrying?* *tricycles* RI.K.7, RI.1.7

**pp. 4–5** • *What do the signs tell the truck to do?* *First, it must stop. Then it must turn right because the street is a one-way street.* RI.K.7, RI.1.7

**pp. 10–15** • *What do the pictures show?* *how the truck goes into and through the tunnel and then comes out of the tunnel* RI.K.7, RI.1.7

**pp.14–27** • *What does the truck driver see on his trip?* *a tunnel, a diner, a gas station, rain, a town, busy roads, and a bridge* RI.K.1, RI.1.1

## SECOND READ Analyze the Text

- *Is the trip short or long?* *long* *Why do you think that?* *The truck driver drives during the day and through the night. When the truck stops, it is day again.* RI.K.3, RI.1.3
- Ask children to think about the sequence of events in the book. Ask: *What happened first?* *The tricycles were put on the truck.* *What happened next?* *The truck driver drove the truck far away.* *What happened last?* *The tricycles were taken off the truck somewhere else.* RI.K.2, RI.1.2
- Revisit the last few pages of the book. Ask: *What do you think will happen next?* Sample answer: *After the truck is unloaded, other things will be put on it, and the driver will drive the truck back.* RI.K.3, RI.1.3

# Independent/Self-Selected Reading

If children have already demonstrated comprehension of *Truck*, have them practice comprehension skills using another book. Model selecting a book from the classroom library. Help them read the title of the book, the author's name, and any information about the book on the back or inside cover. Suggested titles:

- *Planes* by Byron Barton
- *Trains* by Gail Gibbons RI.1.10

### WRITE & PRESENT

1. Have small groups recall what happens first, next, and last in *Truck*. Encourage children to ask and answer questions about events in the story. RI.K.2, RI.1.2
2. Individual children write and illustrate sentences that tell what happens in *Truck* in order. Tell them to be sure to include time-order words, such as *first, next,* and *last*. W.K.2, W.1.2
3. Children reconvene to share their work with partners and edit their writing. W.K.5, W.1.5
4. Children present their final work to classmates. SL.K.6, SL.1.4
5. Individual children turn in their final work to the teacher.

*See Copying Masters, pp. 242–245.*

### STUDENT CHECKLIST

**Writing**

- ✔ Draw and write about what happens in *Truck*.
- ✔ Include time-order words, such as *first, next,* and *last*.
- ✔ Use correct language conventions.

**Speaking & Listening**

- ✔ Participate effectively in collaborative discussion.
- ✔ Ask and answer questions about story events.
- ✔ Demonstrate a connection between information in the text and their own writing.

### OBJECTIVES

- Use information from text and graphic features to demonstrate understanding
- Ask and answer questions about the photographs
- Analyze text using text evidence

### Options for Reading

**Independent** Children read the book independently or with a partner and then answer questions posed by the teacher.

**Supported** Children read the book and answer questions with teacher support and then reread the book with a teacher or partner.

### Common Core Connection

**RI.K.1** ask and answer questions about key details; **RI.K.2** identify the main topic and retell key details; **RI.K.7** describe relationships between illustrations and the text; **W.K.2** use drawing, dictating, and writing to compose informative/explanatory texts; **W.K.5** respond to questions/suggestions from peers and add details to strengthen writing; **SL.K.6** speak audibly and express thoughts, feelings, and ideas clearly

**RI.1.1** ask and answer questions about key details; **RL.1.2** identify the main topic and retell key details; **RI.1.7** use illustrations and details to describe key ideas; **RI.1.10** read informational texts; **W.1.2** write informative/explanatory texts; **W.1.5** focus on a topic, respond to questions/suggestions from peers, and add details to strengthen writing; **SL.1.6** produce complete sentences when appropriate to task and situation

# *I Read Signs*

by Tana Hoban

**SUMMARY** This informational book shows signs that people might see as they walk around their neighborhood or drive in a car on longer trips.

**ABOUT THE AUTHOR** **Tana Hoban** turned her love of photographing children into a career creating books for children with pictures of simple, everyday things. She was born in Philadelphia and attended the School of Design for Women. Hoban died in 2006, having produced more than 110 books.

## Discuss Genre and Set Purpose

**INFORMATIONAL TEXT** Page through the selection with children. Discuss how they can tell that *I Read Signs* is informational text and not a story. Guide them to understand that the photographs give factual information and that the book does not have characters or a plot.

**SET PURPOSE** Help children set a purpose for reading, such as to learn information from reading signs.

### TEXT COMPLEXITY RUBRIC

| Overall Text Complexity | | *I Read Signs* INFORMATIONAL TEXT<br>ACCESSIBLE |
|---|---|---|
| Quantitative Measures | Lexile | N/A |
| | Guided Reading Level | N/A |
| Qualitative Measures | Text Structure | simple social studies concepts |
| | Language Conventionality and Clarity | literal, accessible language |
| | Knowledge Demands | everyday knowledge required |
| | Purpose/Levels of Meaning | single purpose |

**Academic Vocabulary**

Read each word with children and discuss its meaning.

**beware** (p. 8) • be careful

**lane** (p. 10) • a narrow way or road

**express** (p. 19) • a vehicle that travels faster and makes fewer stops

**caution** (p. 24) • a warning to be careful

**detour** (p. 25) • a departure from the usual course

## FIRST READ Think Through the Photographs

Have children use evidence from the photographs to answer these questions.

**pp. 3–7** • *What do the signs say on these pages?* come in, we're open; walk; don't walk; school, speed limit 15; playground RI.K.1, RI.1.1

**p. 8** • *If you saw this sign next to a dog, would you pet the dog? Why or why not?* Sample answer: *I would not pet the dog because the sign tells me to beware of it. That means that the dog might hurt me.* *What is the reason for this sign?* Sample answer: *to keep people safe* RI.K.1, RI.1.1

**p. 13** • *What might you find near this sign?* a taxi *What is the reason for this sign?* to tell people where to find a taxi RI.K.1, RI.1.1

## SECOND READ Analyze the Photographs

- Page through the photographs. Ask: *What do you notice about the letters on most signs?* They are capital letters. *Why are capital letters used?* Sample answer: *They are easier to read.* RI.K.1, RI.1.1
- Point out the graphic features on the signs on page 19. Ask: *Why does the EXPRESS sign have a picture of a bus on it?* Sample answer: *to show that an express bus stops there* RI.K.7, RI.1.7
- Ask: *Why do you think the author created this book?* to give information about signs Ask: *Why are signs important?* Sample answer: *They help people stay safe.* RI.K.2, RI.1.2

## Independent/Self-Selected Reading

If children have already demonstrated comprehension of *I Read Signs*, have them practice the skills using another book. Model selecting a book. Read the title, the author's name, and any information on the back or inside cover. Suggested titles:

- *I Read Symbols* by Tana Hoban
- *City Signs* by Zoran Milich RI.1.10

### WRITE & PRESENT

1. Have small groups discuss what they learned about signs from the selection. Guide them to ask and answer questions they have about details. RI.K.2, RI.1.2
2. Individual children draw a sign from the selection and then write about what the sign says, its graphic features, and the reason for the sign. W.K.2, W.1.2
3. Have children within each group share their drawings and writing and edit their work. W.K.5, W.1.5
4. Ask children to take turns sharing their work with the class. Remind them to speak clearly and in complete sentences. SL.K.6, SL.1.6
5. Individual children turn in their final work to the teacher.

*See Copying Masters, pp. 242–245.*

### STUDENT CHECKLIST

**Writing**

- ✔ Draw a sign from the selection.
- ✔ Write about what the sign says, its graphic features, and the reason for the sign.
- ✔ Use correct language conventions.

**Speaking & Listening**

- ✔ Engage effectively in collaborative conversations.
- ✔ Ask and answer questions about text details.
- ✔ Demonstrate a connection between information in the text and their own writing and drawing.

## OBJECTIVES

- Ask and answer questions about information in a text
- Explore the process of making ice cream
- Identify sequence of events
- Analyze text using text evidence

**_Let's Find Out About Ice Cream_ is broken into three instructional segments.**

**SEGMENTS**

| | |
|---|---|
| SEGMENT 1 | pp. 3–9 |
| SEGMENT 2 | pp. 10–17 |
| SEGMENT 3 | pp. 18–24 |

### Options for Reading

**Independent** Children read the selection independently or with the teacher and then answer questions posed by the teacher.

**Supported** Children read a segment and answer questions with teacher support and then reread the segment independently or with a partner.

### Common Core Connection

**RI.K.1** ask and answer questions about key details; **RI.K.3** describe the connection between individuals, events, ideas, or information in a text; **RI.K.7** describe relationships between illustrations and the text

**RI.1.1** ask and answer questions about key details; **RI.1.3** describe the connection between individuals, events, ideas, or information in a text; **RI.1.7** use illustrations and details to describe key ideas

# *Let's Find Out About Ice Cream*

by Mary Ebeltoft Reid

**SUMMARY** This book explains the basic process of how ice cream is made. Photographs and a diagram give additional details about the process.

**ABOUT THE AUTHOR** **Mary Ebeltoft Reid** has written several nonfiction books for children. Her books include *Let's Find Out About Bicycles, Owls and Other Birds of Prey, Howlers and Other New World Monkeys,* and *Wolves and Other Wild Dogs.*

## Discuss Genre and Set Purpose

**INFORMATIONAL TEXT** Have children briefly page through the book to examine the text and accompanying photographs and diagram. Discuss with children how they can tell the book is an informational book that gives facts, or true information, about ice cream.

**SET PURPOSE** Help children set a purpose for reading, such as to learn information about ice cream.

### TEXT COMPLEXITY RUBRIC

| Overall Text Complexity | | *Let's Find Out About Ice Cream* INFORMATIONAL TEXT<br>ACCESSIBLE |
|---|---|---|
| Quantitative Measures | Lexile | AD500L |
| | Guided Reading Level | H |
| Qualitative Measures | Text Structure | clearly stated and sequential organization of main idea and details |
| | Language Conventionality and Clarity | clear, direct language |
| | Knowledge Demands | everyday knowledge required |
| | Purpose/Levels of Meaning | single topic |

SEGMENT 1 pp. 3–9

### Academic Vocabulary

Read each word with children and discuss its meaning.

**factory** (p. 8) • a building where something is made
**blends** (p. 8) • mixes together
**pumps** (p. 10) • machines that force liquids from one place to another
**tanks** (p. 10) • large containers for liquids
**spiral** (p. 15) • winding or curving
**warehouse** (p. 16) • a large building where things are stored

## FIRST READ Think Through the Text

Have children use text evidence to answer these questions.

**pp. 4–5** • *Where does ice cream come from?* *from cow's milk and cream* *How much milk and cream does it take to make ice cream?* *a lot* RI.K.1, RI.1.1

**p. 8** • *What does a mixologist do?* *blends everything together* RI.K.1, RI.1.1

**p. 9** • *Why does a scientist test the mix?* *to make sure it is healthy to eat* RI.K.3, RI.1.3

## SECOND READ Analyze the Text

- Show children the photographs on pages 4–5. Ask: *What can you learn from the photographs that you cannot learn from the text?* Sample answer: *The cows eat grass and live in fields. Someone has to milk the cows.* RI.K.7, RI.1.7
- Review the photographs on pages 6–7. Ask: *What can you learn from the photographs that you cannot learn from the text?* Sample answer: *The sugar cane plants are tall. The eggs are delivered in boxes.* RI.K.7, RI.1.7
- Reread pages 3–9 with children. Review the steps in the ice cream making process that they have learned so far. Ask: *What is the first step in making ice cream?* *Milk comes from cows.* *What is the first thing that happens at the factory?* *A mixologist blends everything together.* RI.K.3, RI.1.3

### ENGLISH LANGUAGE LEARNERS

**Use Comprehensible Input**

Rephrase more difficult sentences in the selection as necessary. To ensure comprehension, ask questions that can be answered using key story words, such as: *What comes from cows?* *milk* *What pushes the mix through pipes and into tanks?* *pumps*

### RESPOND TO SEGMENT 1

**Classroom Collaboration**

Have partners work together to summarize what they have learned as well as raise questions that might be answered in the next segment.

## ENGLISH LANGUAGE LEARNERS

**Use Cognates**

Point out the English/Spanish cognates to aid comprehension: cream/crema; plants/plantas; cane/caña; factory/factoría; scientist/científico; tanks/tanques; chocolate/chocolate.

**RESPOND TO SEGMENT 2**

**Classroom Collaboration**

Have small groups summarize what they have learned and ask questions about anything they still don't understand.

**Common Core Connection**

**RI.K.1** ask and answer questions about key details; **RI.K.3** describe the connection between individuals, events, ideas, or information in a text; **RI.K.7** describe relationships between illustrations and the text; **W.K.2** use drawing, dictating, and writing to compose informative/explanatory texts; **W.K.5** respond to questions/suggestions from peers and add details to strengthen writing; **SL.K.6** speak audibly and express thoughts, feelings, and ideas clearly

**RI.1.1** ask and answer questions about key details; **RI.1.3** describe the connection between individuals, events, ideas, or information in a text; **RI.1.7** use illustrations and details to describe key ideas; **RI.1.10** read informational texts; **W.1.2** write informative/explanatory texts; **W.1.5** focus on a topic, respond to questions from peers, and add details to strengthen writing; **SL.1.6** produce complete sentences when appropriate to task and situation

## FIRST READ Think Through the Text

Have children use text evidence to answer these questions.

**pp. 10–11** • *What do the pumps do? They push the mix through pipes and into tanks.* ***What happens next?*** *The flavoring is put in the mix.* **RI.K.1, RI.1.1**

**pp. 12–13** • *What does the mix go next? into the freezer* ***When are the chunks put in?*** *after the mix is hard* ***Why?*** *so they won't sink to the bottom* **RI.K.3, RI.1.3**

**pp. 14–15** • *Where do machines put the ice cream? into containers* **RI.K.1, RI.1.1**

**pp. 16–17** • *What happens to the ice cream while it is in the spiral freezer? It gets really hard.* **RI.K.1, RI.1.1**

## SECOND READ Analyze the Text

- Show children pages 10–11. Point out how the text and photographs both give information. Say: *The text tells about the next steps that go on at the factory. What do you learn from the photograph on page 10?* Sample answer: *The mix is still soft. The pipe is not very wide. The tank is big and shiny.* Ask: *What additional information do you get from the photographs on page 11? The worker uses a lot of the coffee flavoring. A machine stirs the mix after the coffee flavor is put in.* **RI.K.7, RI.1.7**
- Show children the photograph of the machine on page 15. Ask: *What do you learn about this machine from the photograph? It is very cold; it can hold a lot of ice cream. How do you know?* Sample answer: *It has frozen ice on it; there is plenty of room on the machine for more ice cream.* **RI.K.7, RI.1.7**
- Reread pages 10–17 with children. Review the steps in the ice cream making process that they have learned in this segment. Ask: *What happens after the pumps put the mix into tanks? The flavoring is added. What happens before the ice cream goes to the warehouse? It goes into a spiral freezer. Where does the ice cream go next? into trucks* **RI.K.3, RI.1.3**

## FIRST READ Think Through the Text

Have children use text evidence to answer these questions.

**p. 18** • *What kinds of trucks are used to take the ice cream to the stores?* *freezer trucks* RI.K.1, RI.1.1

**p. 19** • *What happens next at the factory?* *A worker cleans the machines, and then the workers start making a new batch of ice cream.* RI.K.3, RI.1.3

**pp. 20–21** • *What do flavorologists do?* *They invent new ice cream flavors.* *What do the testers do?* *They taste ice cream every hour.* RI.K.1, RI.1.1

**pp. 22–23** • *Where does making ice cream start?* *with the cows on the farm* *Where does the ice cream go after it leaves the hand truck?* *into the ice cream store* *What is the very last step in making ice cream?* *People buy it and eat it.* RI.K.3, RI.1.3

## SECOND READ Analyze the Text

- Show children page 18, and reread the text. Ask: *What does the text tell you?* *that freezer trucks take the ice cream to stores* *What additional information do you learn from the photographs?* Sample answer: *that someone dressed in special clothing loads the ice cream onto the truck using a special lift* RI.K.7, RI.1.7
- Display the diagram on pages 22–23, and reread the labels. Guide children to follow the red arrows from start to finish. Ask: *What information do you get from the diagram?* *You see what each machine looks like. You can follow each step in order.* RI.K.7, RI.1.7
- Review the text and photographs with children. Have partners tell each other something they learned from the text and photographs about making ice cream. RI.K.7, RI.1.7

# Independent/Self-Selected Reading

If children have already demonstrated comprehension and analysis of *Let's Find Out About Ice Cream*, have them practice the skills using an independent reading book. Help them read the title of the book, the author's name, and any information about the book on the back or inside cover. Suggested titles:

- *Ice Cream* by Jill Neimark
- *Ice Cream* by Elisha Cooper RI.1.10

### WRITE & PRESENT

1. Discuss with children the ways the author uses sequence to give information about how ice cream is made. Draw a sequence chart on the board and fill it out with children using information from both the text and photographs. RI.K.3, RI.1.3
2. Individual children use the chart to write and illustrate an explanation of how ice cream is made. W.K.2, W.1.2
3. Have children meet in pairs to share their writing and drawings and edit their work. W.K.5, W.1.5
4. Individual children present their final work to classmates. SL.K.6, SL.1.6

*See Copying Masters, pp. 242–245.*

### STUDENT CHECKLIST

#### Writing

- ✔ Use a graphic organizer as an aid to writing.
- ✔ Write a paragraph that uses information from the text to describe how ice cream is made.
- ✔ Draw pictures that illustrate the paragraph.
- ✔ Use correct language conventions.

#### Speaking & Listening

- ✔ Engage effectively in collaborative conversations.
- ✔ Ask and answer questions about text sequence.
- ✔ Demonstrate a connection between information in the text and one's own writing and drawing.

## OBJECTIVES

- Identify the main topic and key details
- Describe relationships between visual elements and the text
- Analyze text using text evidence

**"Garden Helpers" is broken into three instructional segments.**

### SEGMENTS

SEGMENT 1. . . . . . . . . . pp. 2–3
SEGMENT 2. . . . . . . . . . pp. 4–5
SEGMENT 3. . . . . . . . . . pp. 6–7

### Options for Reading

**Independent** Children read the selection independently or with a partner and then answer questions posed by the teacher.

**Supported** Children read a segment and answer questions with teacher support.

### Common Core Connection

**RI.K.1** ask and answer questions about key details; **RI.K.3** describe the connection between individuals, events, ideas, or information in a text; **RI.K.4** ask and answer questions about unknown words; **RI.K.7** describe relationships between illustrations and the text

**RI.1.1** ask and answer questions about key details; **RI.1.3** describe the connection between individuals, events, ideas, or information in a text; **RI.1.4** ask and answer questions to determine or clarify the meaning of words and phrases; **RI.1.5** know and use text features to locate facts or information; **RI.1.7** use illustrations and details to describe key ideas

# "Garden Helpers"

**SUMMARY** This article from *National Geographic Young Explorer!* describes how bugs and worms can be helpful in a garden. Worms can make soil richer. Ladybugs, praying mantids, and spiders can catch bugs that eat plants in a garden. Colorful photographs display the garden helpers.

## Discuss Genre and Set Purpose

**INFORMATIONAL TEXT** Ask children to recall that an informational text gives facts, or true information, about a topic. Then show children the photographs of garden helpers.

**SET PURPOSE** Help children set a purpose for reading, such as to learn about worms and bugs that are garden helpers.

### TEXT COMPLEXITY RUBRIC

| Overall Text Complexity | | "Garden Helpers" INFORMATIONAL TEXT<br>ACCESSIBLE |
|---|---|---|
| Quantitative Measures | Lexile | 550L |
| | Guided Reading Level | E |
| Qualitative Measures | Text Structure | clearly stated organization of main ideas and details |
| | Language Conventionality and Clarity | some unfamiliar or academic words |
| | Knowledge Demands | everyday knowledge required |
| | Purpose/Levels of Meaning | explicitly stated |

SEGMENT 1 pp. 2–3

### Academic Vocabulary

Read each word with children and discuss its meaning.

**pests** (p. 2) • something that annoys or bothers

**soil** (p. 4) • dirt

**web** (p. 7) • a thin net of threads made by a spider

## FIRST READ Think Through the Text

Have children use text evidence to answer these questions.

**p. 2** • *What do you think this article will be about?* garden helpers *How can you tell?* *The title tells me what the article is about.* RI.1.5

**p. 3** • *What can bugs and worms do in gardens?* *Some bugs and worms can help your garden grow.* RI.K.1, RI.1.1

## SECOND READ Analyze the Text

- Have children think about a garden they have seen. *What do you think a garden helper is?* Sample answer: *something that helps the plants grow in a garden; a bug or worm* RI.K.4, RI.1.4
- Point to the photograph on pages 2–3. Then ask: *What kind of bug is in the photo?* *a ladybug* *Do you think ladybugs help in a garden? Explain.* *Answers will vary.* RI.K.7, RI.1.7
- Reread pages 2–3. Ask children to think about bugs they have seen in gardens or on plants. Then ask: *How do you think some bugs and worms are garden helpers?* Sample answer: *I think bigger bugs eat smaller bugs that eat plants. I know bees can help carry pollen and seeds.* RI.K.3, RI.1.3

### ENGLISH LANGUAGE LEARNERS

**Use Visuals**

Have children look at the photograph of the ladybug. Ask them to describe what ladybugs look like. Then ensure that children understand the words in the text, by asking: *Do you think ladybugs are pests?*

### RESPOND TO SEGMENT 1

**Classroom Collaboration**

Have partners work together to talk about the title page. Ask them to raise questions that may be answered in the text.

## ENGLISH LANGUAGE LEARNERS

**Use Comprehensible Input**

Ensure children understand key details by using questions, such as the following.

- *What do earthworms do?* They make soil rich.
- *What do ladybugs eat?* Ladybugs eat small bugs.

## RESPOND TO SEGMENT 2

**Classroom Collaboration**

Have small groups work together to talk about what they have learned. Have them ask questions about what they don't understand.

## Common Core Connection

**RI.K.1** ask and answer questions about key details; **RI.K.2** identify the main topic and retell key details; **RI.K.3** describe the connection between individuals, events, ideas, or information in a text; **RI.K.4** ask and answer questions about unknown words; **RI.K.7** describe relationships between illustrations and the text; **W.K.2** use drawing, dictating, and writing to compose informative/explanatory texts; **W.K.5** respond to questions/suggestions from peers and add details to strengthen writing; **SL.K.6** speak audibly and express thoughts, feelings, and ideas clearly

**RI.1.1** ask and answer questions about key details; **RI.1.2** identify the main topic and retell key details; **RI.1.3** describe the connection between individuals, events, ideas, or information in a text; **RI.1.4** ask and answer questions to determine or clarify the meaning of words and phrases; **RI.1.5** know and use text features to locate facts or information; **RI.1.7** use illustrations and details to describe key ideas; **RI.1.10** read informational texts; **W.1.2** write informative/explanatory texts; **W.1.5** focus on a topic, respond to questions/suggestions from peers, and add details to strengthen writing; **SL.1.6** produce complete sentences when appropriate to task and situation

## FIRST READ Think Through the Text

Have children use text evidence to answer these questions.

**p. 4 •** *How can earthworms help plants grow strong?* Earthworms make the soil in a garden rich and healthy. **RI.K.1, RI.1.1**

**p. 5 •** *What do ladybugs do in a garden?* Ladybugs eat small bugs so the bugs can't eat the plants in the garden. **RI.K.1, RI.1.1**

## SECOND READ Analyze the Text

- Reread page 4 and point to the photograph of the earthworms. Then ask: *What information do you learn from looking at the photograph that you don't learn from the text?* Sample answer: The worms crawl around in the soil. Worms have long, thin bodies. **RI.K.7, RI.1.7**
- Point out that the text mentions rich soil. Then ask: *What does the word* rich *mean when it describes soil?* Sample answer: The word rich means that the soil is full of vitamins and other things that are good for plants and help them grow. **RI.K.4, RI.1.4**
- Reread page 5 with children. Then ask: *What is the main topic on this page?* Sample answer: Ladybugs are garden helpers. *What are key details that support the main topic?* Sample answers: Ladybugs eat small bugs that eat plants in the garden. Ladybugs keep the plants safe by eating the bugs. **RI.K.2, RI.1.2**
- Review pages 4–5. Then ask: *What is the difference between what earthworms do and what ladybugs do in a garden?* The earthworms make the soil healthy. The ladybugs eat garden pests. **RI.K.3, RI.1.3**

## FIRST READ Think Through the Text

Have children use text evidence to answer these questions.

**p. 6 •** ***What is the garden helper described in the text and shown in the photograph?*** *a praying mantid* ***What key details tell how the praying mantid is a garden helper?*** *A prayer mantid is a quick hunter. It eats any bug it can catch.* **RI.K.1, RI.1.1**

**p. 7 •** ***What is the main topic?*** *A spider is a garden helper.* ***What key details support the main topic?*** *A spider catches bugs in its web. It keeps bugs away from the garden.* **RI.K.2, RI.1.2**

## SECOND READ Analyze the Text

- Reread page 6. Ask: *How do you know the praying mantid eats many bugs? The text says not many bugs can get past the praying mantid.* **RI.K.3, RI.1.3**
- Show children the photograph on page 6. Then ask: *What does the photograph show you about the praying mantid?* Sample answer: *The praying mantid is long and thin. The body of a praying mantid looks like a stick.* **RI.K.7, RI.1.7**
- Ask children to think about a spiderweb they have seen. Ask: *What do you know about spiderwebs?* Sample answer: *The spider's web is bigger than the spider. The spider wraps its web around the bugs it catches. A spider eats the bugs it catches.* Then point to the photograph on page 7. *How does a spider's web help a garden? A spider catches bugs that might eat plants in the garden. It helps the garden grow.* **RI.K.7, RI.1.7**

# Independent/Self-Selected Reading

If children have demonstrated comprehension of "Garden Helpers," have them practice the skills by reading another book independently. Model selecting a book from the classroom library. Guide children to read the title of the book and to notice the illustrations on the cover. Suggested titles:

- *Earthworms* by Claire Llewellyn
- *Helpful Ladybugs* by Molly Smith **RI.1.10**

### WRITE & PRESENT

1. Have small groups discuss the ways bugs and worms help in a garden. Tell them to record information on a graphic organizer and include information from the text and photographs. **RI.K.1, RI.1.1**
2. Have individual children draw a picture of one of the garden helpers. Then tell children to write a short paragraph about how that worm or bug helps in a garden. Remind them to use the graphic organizer for ideas. **W.K.2, W.1.2**
3. Have children share their writing and drawings in small groups, and then edit their work. **W.K.5, W.1.5**
4. Have individual children present their final work to classmates. **SL.K.6, SL.1.6**

*See Copying Masters, pp. 242–245.*

### STUDENT CHECKLIST

**Writing**

- ✔ Use a graphic organizer.
- ✔ Write a paragraph using details from the text.
- ✔ Draw a picture that illustrates the main idea of the paragraph.
- ✔ Use correct language conventions.

**Speaking & Listening**

- ✔ Ask and answer questions about text details.
- ✔ Describe a connection between text and photographs.
- ✔ Engage effectively in collaborative conversations.

## OBJECTIVES

- Identify the main topic and key details
- Use context to determine the meaning of words
- Use text features to find information
- Use illustrations and photos to clarify text

**"Wind Power" is broken into three instructional segments.**

**SEGMENTS**



### Options for Reading

**Independent** Children read the article independently and then answer questions posed by the teacher.

**Supported** Children read a segment and answer questions with teacher support.

### Common Core Connection

**RI.K.1** ask and answer questions about key details; **RI.K.3** describe the connection between individuals, events, ideas, or information in a text; **RI.K.7** describe relationships between illustrations and the text

**RI.1.1** ask and answer questions about key details; **RI.1.3** describe the connection between individuals, events, ideas, or information in a text; **RI.1.5** know and use text features to locate facts or information; **RI.1.7** use illustrations and details to describe key ideas

# "Wind Power"

**SUMMARY** This article from *National Geographic Young Explorer!* explains what wind is and describes what wind power can do. It can push a sailboat and can help create electricity through a windmill. A diagram of the movement of wind and colorful photographs supplement the text.

## Discuss Genre and Set Purpose

**INFORMATIONAL TEXT** Have children look through the article to determine that it is informational text that gives facts, or true information, about wind power. Discuss with children how the photographs and captions also convey important information about the topic.

**SET PURPOSE** Help children set a purpose for reading, such as to learn what wind power is and what it can do.

### TEXT COMPLEXITY RUBRIC

| Overall Text Complexity | | "Wind Power" INFORMATIONAL TEXT<br>ACCESSIBLE |
|---|---|---|
| Quantitative Measures | Lexile | 180L |
| | Guided Reading Level | H |
| Qualitative Measures | Text Structure | largely simple graphics, supplementary to understanding of the text |
| | Language Conventionality and Clarity | some unfamiliar or academic words |
| | Knowledge Demands | everyday knowledge required |
| | Purpose/Levels of Meaning | explicitly stated |

SEGMENT 1 pp. 10–11

### Academic Vocabulary

Read each word with children and discuss its meaning.

**whip up** (p. 12) • create; get started

**rises** (p. 13) • moves upward

**energy** (p. 14) • power; the ability to make things move

**windmill** (p. 15) • machine that uses energy from the wind to turn a large wheel

**electricity** (p. 15) • a kind of energy that is used for making things work

FIRST READ
## Think Through the Text

Have children use text evidence to answer these questions.

**p. 10** • *What do you think this article will be about?* wind power *How can you tell?* The title tells me what the article is about. RI.1.5

**p. 11** • *How does wind affect the dog shown in the photograph?* Wind blows the dog's fur. RI.K.7, RI.1.7

SECOND READ
## Analyze the Text

- *How are all of the photos on page 11 alike?* They all show something wind can do. *How are they different?* They show different things wind can do. RI.K.3, RI.1.3
- Point to each photo. For each photo, ask: *What is the wind doing in this photo?* Sample answer: *blowing the umbrella; keeping the hang glider in the air or moving the hang glider through the air; spinning the wheel; blowing the dog's fur* RI.K.7, RI.1.7
- *What are other examples of things wind can move?* Answers will vary. *What would you like to find out about wind power?* Sample answer: *I would like to find out how wind gets its power.* RI.K.1, RI.1.1

**Use Visuals and Sentence Frames**

Point to each photo on page 11. Guide children to complete and repeat sentence frames, such as the following.

- The wind makes the umbrella _____. *move, blow away*
- The wind keeps the hang glider _____. *up in the air*
- The wind makes the wheel _____. *spin*
- The wind make the dog's fur _____. *blow back, move around*

**RESPOND TO SEGMENT 1**

**Classroom Collaboration**

Have small groups talk about what they have learned so far. Encourage children to ask questions that may be answered in the next segment.

## ENGLISH LANGUAGE LEARNERS

**Use Comprehensible Input**

Ensure that children understand key concepts by asking questions, such as:

- *Is wind moving air or air that stays still?* moving air
- *What does warm air do?* *It rises.*

**RESPOND TO SEGMENT 2**

**Classroom Collaboration**

Have small groups work together to talk about what they have learned. Have them ask questions about what they don't understand.

**Common Core Connection**

**RI.K.1** ask and answer questions about key details; **RI.K.2** identify the main topic and retell key details; **RI.K.3** describe the connection between individuals, events, ideas, or information in a text; **RI.K.4** ask and answer questions about unknown words; **RI.K.7** describe relationships between illustrations and the text; **W.K.2** use drawing, dictating, and writing to compose informative/explanatory texts; **W.K.5** respond to questions/suggestions from peers and add details to strengthen writing; **SL.K.6** speak audibly and express thoughts, feelings, and ideas clearly

**RI.1.1** ask and answer questions about key details; **RI.1.2** identify the main topic and retell key details; **RI.1.3** describe the connection between individuals, events, ideas, or information in a text; **RI.1.4** ask and answer questions to determine or clarify the meaning of words and phrases; **RI.1.5** know and use text features to locate facts or information; **RI.1.7** use illustrations and details to describe key ideas; **RI.1.10** read informational texts; **W.1.2** write informative/explanatory texts; **W.1.5** focus on a topic, respond to questions/suggestions from peers, and add details to strengthen writing; **SL.1.6** produce complete sentences when appropriate to task and situation

## FIRST READ Think Through the Text

Have children use text evidence to answer these questions.

**p. 12** • *How does the photo give information about wind?* It shows that wind can make all kinds of kites fly. **RI.K.7, RI.1.7**

**p. 13** • *What key details tell us about wind?* The key details tell us that the sun warms the land and water. Warm air rises and cooler air rushes in. That moving air is wind. **RI.K.2, RI.1.2**

**p. 13** • *What are the labels on the diagram?* sun; water; land; warm air rises; cool air rushes in **RI.K.7, RI.1.5**

## SECOND READ Analyze the Text

- Have children look at the photograph on page 12. Then ask: *What do you think would happen to the kites if there were no wind?* The kites would fall down. *Why do you think this would happen?* Sample answer: The wind blows the kites and keeps them up in the air. **RI.K.3, RI.1.3**
- Have children look at the diagram on page 13. Then ask: *What is the title of the diagram?* What Is Wind? *Based on the title, what do you think you will learn from this diagram?* Sample answer: what wind is, what causes the wind to blow **RI.K.7, RI.1.5**
- Have children look at the diagram more closely. Say: *Find the arrow that points up. What does it show?* The arrow pointing up shows what warm air does. *How can you tell?* Sample answer: The label says that warm air rises. *Find the arrow that points sideways. What does it show?* The arrow that points sideways shows what cool air does. *How can you tell?* Sample answer: The label says that cool air rushes in. **RI.K.7, RI.1.5**
- Ask children to think about what they learned from the diagram. Ask: *How does this diagram help you understand that wind is moving air?* Sample answer: The diagram shows how air moves and what causes it to move. **RI.K.7, RI.1.5**

## FIRST READ Think Through the Text

Have children use text evidence to answer these questions.

**pp. 14–15 •** *What is the main topic of these pages?* The main topic is that wind is energy. *What key details tell about the main topic?* Wind can push a sailboat. Wind can make windmills spin. Wind energy can make electricity. **RI.K.2, RI.1.2**

**p. 15 •** *What does the photograph show?* windmills *How does the photograph help you understand the details in the text?* It shows how the windmills spin to make electricity. **RI.K.7, RI.1.7**

## SECOND READ Analyze the Text

- Remind children that energy is power. Ask: *What are some things you do that show you have energy?* Sample answer: run, jump, push things, pull things **RI.K.4, RI.1.4**
- Review page 14 and point to the photograph. Then ask: *What information do the text and the photograph tell you about wind power?* The text says that wind is energy. The photograph shows how wind power pushes a sailboat across the water. **RI.K.7, RI.1.7**
- *What else can wind do?* Sample answer: It blows my hair in front of my face. It blows leaves all over my yard. **RI.K.1, RI.1.1**

## Independent/Self-Selected Reading

Have children reread "Wind Power" to practice analyzing the text on their own or have them practice the skills using another book. Model selecting a book from the classroom library. Suggested titles:

- *Clouds* (Ready-to-Read Series) by Marion Dane Bauer
- *Wind* (Ready-to-Read Series) by Marion Dane Bauer **RI.1.10**

### WRITE & PRESENT

1. Have partners discuss the main topic of the article. Point out that the title of an article often tells the main topic. Then help children retell key details they learned about wind power. **RI.K.2, RI.1.2**
2. Have individual children copy the title of the article onto a sheet of paper. Have them draw two pictures that show how wind has power. Ask them to write sentences that tell about each picture. **W.K.2, W.1.2**
3. Have partners share their pictures and sentences with each other. Then ask children to make suggestions and edit their sentences. **W.K.5, W.1.5**
4. Have children present their final pictures and sentences to classmates. Encourage children to ask and answer questions about the presentations. **SL.K.6, SL.1.6**
5. Have individual children turn in their final pictures and writing to the teacher.

*See Copying Masters, pp. 242–245.*

### STUDENT CHECKLIST

#### Writing

- ✔ Write about main topics.
- ✔ Use pictures and sentences to tell key details about main topics.
- ✔ Use correct language conventions.

#### Speaking & Listening

- ✔ Engage effectively in collaborative conversations.
- ✔ Ask and answer questions to clarify details.

## OBJECTIVES

- Identify the main topic and retell key details
- Identify causes and effects
- Analyze text using text evidence

***The Year at Maple Hill Farm*** **is broken into three instructional segments.**

**SEGMENTS**

**SEGMENT 1** .......... pp. 3–11
**SEGMENT 2** .......... pp. 12–21
**SEGMENT 3** .......... pp. 22–32

### Options for Read Aloud

*Be sure to display the book's pictures and read with expression to model fluent reading.*

**Uninterrupted** Focus on the flow of the story by reading aloud without stopping for comments or questions.

**Interactive** Stop at appropriate places while reading to make comments and ask children questions. Also, invite children to share their own comments and questions.

### Common Core Connection

**RI.K.2** identify the main topic and retell key details; **RI.K.3** describe the connection between individuals, events, ideas, or information in a text; **RI.K.7** describe relationships between illustrations and the text; **SL.K.2** confirm understanding of a text read aloud, information presented orally, or through other media by asking/answering questions and requesting clarification

**RI.1.2** identify the main topic and retell key details; **RL.1.3** describe the connection between individuals, events, ideas or information in a text; **RI.1.7** use illustrations and details to describe key ideas; **SL.1.2** ask and answer questions about details in a text read aloud, information presented orally, or through other media

# The Year at Maple Hill Farm

by Alice and Martin Provensen

**SUMMARY** This informational picture book describes the changes that animals on a farm experience during each season over the course of a year.

**ABOUT THE AUTHOR** **Alice and Martin Provensen** were a husband and wife team that collaborated on many award-winning picture books. Martin died in 1987, but Alice continues to live in upstate New York on Maple Hill Farm.

## Discuss Genre and Set Purpose

**INFORMATIONAL TEXT** Tell children that they will be listening to an informational text about what happens on a farm throughout the year. Display the cover, and discuss the illustrations and the information in the captions. Then page through the book with children. Guide them to identify elements that show that *The Year at Maple Hill Farm* is an informational text, not a story or poem.

**SET PURPOSE** Help children set a purpose for listening, such as to find out how the changing seasons affect people and animals on a farm during each month of the year.

**TEXT COMPLEXITY RUBRIC**

| Overall Text Complexity | | *The Year at Maple Hill Farm* INFORMATIONAL TEXT<br>ACCESSIBLE |
|---|---|---|
| Quantitative Measures | Lexile | N/A |
| | Guided Reading Level | N/A |
| Qualitative Measures | Text Structure | genre traits less common to informational text |
| | Language Conventionality and Clarity | some unfamiliar or academic words |
| | Knowledge Demands | some specialized knowledge required |
| | Purpose/Levels of Meaning | explicitly stated |

## SEGMENT 1 pp. 3–11

### Academic Vocabulary

Read each word with children and discuss its meaning.

**divided** (p. 3) • separated into two or more parts

**windfall** (p. 5) • something blown down by wind

**marshy** (p. 7) • containing soft, wet land with long grass

**eaves** (p. 11) • the lower edge of a roof that sticks out past the wall

## FIRST READ Think Through the Text

Have children use text evidence to answer the following questions.

**pp. 4–5** • *What month is described on these pages?* January *In what season is January?* winter SL.K.2, SL.1.2

**pp. 6–7** • *What do some children do in February? How do you know?* The text says they go ice skating and sit by the fire. The illustrations show children skating and a fire burning. RI.K.7, RI.1.7

**pp. 8–9** • *Look at the animal mothers on page 8. How are they all alike?* They are all with their young. RI.K.3, RI.1.3

**pp. 10–11** • *How can you tell that spring has come?* Many birds lay eggs. SL.K.2, SL.1.2

## SECOND READ Analyze the Text

- Reread the sentences at the top of pages 4–5. *What are some details from the text that tell what the weather is like in January?* The ground is covered with snow. It is a cold, gray time of year. RI.K.2, RI.1.2
- Guide children to look back at pages 4–7. *What do people and animals do in cold weather that is the same?* Both people and animals try to stay warm. Animals keep close to the barn; people build fires. RI.K.3, RI.1.3
- Review pages 8–9 with children. *What is the main idea on these pages?* In March, signs of spring are everywhere. *What are some details that tell more about this main idea?* Sample answer: The sun shines more brightly. The robins are back, and the meadow mice are out. RI.K.2, RI.1.2

### ENGLISH LANGUAGE LEARNERS

**Use Visuals**

Point out and name the animals in the pictures on pages 4–5, and have children repeat after you. Then ask them to name and describe other farm animals that they know. Repeat the activity for subsequent pages.

### RESPOND TO SEGMENT 1

**Classroom Collaboration**

Have small groups summarize what they have learned and ask questions about anything they still don't understand.

**ENGLISH LANGUAGE LEARNERS**

**Use Visuals and Sentence Frames**

Show children the illustrations on pages 18 and 19 to help them understand the details in the text. Ask yes/no questions to build understanding, such as: *Are the people sleeping?* no *Are the men working in the barn?* yes Then have children orally complete sentences frames such as:

*The _____ are hooting to each other.* owls

*In the field are _____.* cows, horses

**RESPOND TO SEGMENT 2**

**Classroom Collaboration**

Have small groups work together to summarize what they have learned. Have them ask questions about what they don't understand.

**Common Core Connection**

**W.K.2** use drawing, dictating, and writing to compose informative/explanatory texts; **W.K.5** respond to questions/suggestions from peers and add details to strengthen writing; **SL.K.3** ask and answer questions to seek help, get information, or clarify something not understood; **SL.K.6** speak audibly and express thoughts, feelings, and ideas clearly

**RI.1.6** distinguish between information provided by pictures and words; **RI.1.10** read informational texts; **W.1.2** write informative/explanatory texts; **W.1.5** focus on a topic, respond to questions/suggestions from peers, and add details to strengthen writing; **SL.1.1c** ask questions to clear up confusion about topics and texts under discussion; **SL.1.4** describe people, places, things, and events with details/express ideas and feelings clearly

**Academic Vocabulary**

Read each word with children and discuss its meaning.

**shorn** (p. 12) • to have cut the hair or the wool of an animal

**molt** (p. 13) • to shed feathers or hair

**conveyor** (p. 19) • a mechanical device that carries large things from one place to another

## FIRST READ Think Through the Text

Have children use text evidence to answer the following questions.

**pp. 12–13** • *Which animals get haircuts?* the sheep and the dog *Which animals lose their feathers or hair?* the chickens and the cats **SL.K.2, SL.1.2**

**pp. 14–15** • *Why are the chickens out in the pasture?* They are chasing and eating insects that the horses have stirred up with their feet. *How does the illustration help you understand this?* The illustration shows the chickens catching and eating insects near the horses. **RI.K.7, RI.1.6**

**pp. 18–19** • *What animals make noise on the farm on a July night?* frogs, crickets, cows, mother geese, horses *What are some noises that are caused in some way by people?* the people chatting; the conveyor clanking; the men laughing **RI.K.3, RI.1.3**

**pp. 20–21** • *Why is late summer called a drowsy time of year?* Sample answer: The days are hot; the animals lie around and sleep more. **SL.K.2, SL.1.2**

## SECOND READ Analyze the Text

- *What month do pages 12–13 describe?* May *What month was described on pages 10–11?* April *What month do you think will be described on pages 14–15?* June *Why do you think so?* So far, the months are described in order from the beginning of the year. **SL.K.2, SL.1.2**
- Remind children that the animals are fed grain in the winter. Then ask: *How is the food for some animals different in summer than in winter? Why?* In summer they eat the new green grass in the pasture. In winter the ground is covered with snow so the animals must be fed. **RI.K.3, RI.1.3**
- Reread pages 20–21. *What is the main idea?* August is hot and lazy. *Which captions give details that tell more about this main idea?* Sample answer: the captions for the cows, the flowers, the sleeping dog, the geese, the pig, and the cat Point out that the captions for the sheep and the dog with the rabbits do not tell more about the main idea. Ask: *How do you know this?* Sample answer: The information about sheep grazing, lambs growing, and someone stealing the lettuce do not have anything to do with August being hot and lazy. **RI.K.2, RI.1.2**

### Academic Vocabulary

Read each word with children and discuss its meaning.

**temperamental** (p. 23) • likely to get upset
**suspicious** (p. 25) • uncertain, without trust
**harvest** (p. 26) • the ripe crops that are gathered
**migrant** (p. 27) • moving from place to place

## FIRST READ Think Through the Text

Have children use text evidence to answer the following questions.

**pp. 22–23** • *How does the weather change in September? The wind begins to pick up, the air begins to cool down, and it gets rainy.* **SL.K.2, SL.1.2**

**pp. 26–27** • *In October the harvest is in. Which details from the text tell more about this idea? The hay is in the barn. The corn is in the crib.* **SL.K.2, SL.1.2**

**pp. 30–31** • *Where are the farm animals in December? in the barn* **SL.K.2, SL.1.2**

**p. 32** • *What event is described on this page? New Year's Eve* **SL.K.2, SL.1.2**

## SECOND READ Analyze the Text

- Ask children to think about what happens every month on the farm. Ask: *Do you think that what happens is about the same year after year? Why do you think this?* Sample answer: *I think it is about the same because the author describes what the animals and people do as the seasons change. The seasons happen over and over in the same order year after year.* **RI.K.3, RI.1.3**
- Guide children to look back over the selection. Have them tell about something that didn't make sense to them when they first listened to the selection being read. Then have them tell how they figured out what was being read. **SL.K.3, SL.1.1c**

## Independent/Self-Selected Reading

If children have demonstrated listening comprehension of *The Year at Maple Hill Farm,* have them practice and apply reading comprehension skills using another book. Model selecting a book from the classroom library. Help children read the title of the book, the author's name, and any information about the book on the back or inside cover. Suggested titles:

- *Our Animal Friends at Maple Hill Farm* by Alice and Martin Provensen
- *Animals Grow and Change* by Bobbie Kalman **RI.1.10**

### WRITE & PRESENT

1. Have partners find and discuss examples of how the information on each spread included a main idea and details. **SL.K.2, SL.1.2**
2. Have individual children write and draw about one month or one season at Maple Hill Farm. Tell them to include a main idea and at least two details. **W.K.2, W.1.2**
3. Partners reconvene to share and edit their work. **W.K.5, W.1.5**
4. Partners present their writing and pictures to their classmates. **SL.K.6, SL.1.4**
5. Individual children turn in their final writing to the teacher.

*See Copying Masters, pp. 242–245.*

### STUDENT CHECKLIST

#### Writing

- ✔ Write and draw about a month or a season on Maple Hill Farm.
- ✔ Include a main idea and at least two details.
- ✔ Use correct language conventions.

#### Speaking & Listening

- ✔ Participate effectively in collaborative conversations.
- ✔ Ask and answer questions about details in the text and illustrations.
- ✔ Demonstrate a connection between information in the text and their own writing and illustration.

## OBJECTIVES

- Ask questions about the text and answer using key details
- Use information from the text and graphic features to demonstrate understanding
- Describe the similarities and differences between how firefighters battle different kinds of fires

***Fire! Fire!* is broken into three instructional segments.**

**SEGMENTS**



### Options for Reading

*Be sure to display the book's pictures and read with expression to model fluent reading.*

**Uninterrupted** Focus on the flow of the selection by reading aloud without stopping for questions.

**Interactive** Stop at appropriate places while reading to make comments and ask questions. Also, invite children to share their own comments and questions.

### Common Core Connection

**RI.K.1** ask and answer questions about key details; **RI.K.7** describe relationships between illustrations and the text; **SL.K.2** confirm understanding of a text read aloud, information presented orally, or through other media by asking/answering questions and requesting clarification

**RI.1.1** ask and answer questions about key details; **RI.1.6** distinguish between information provided by pictures and words; **RI.1.7** use illustrations and details to describe key ideas; **SL.1.2** ask and answer questions about details in a text read aloud, information presented orally, or through other media

# *Fire! Fire!*

by Gail Gibbons

**SUMMARY** This book describes the ways firefighters battle fires in the city, in the country, in the forest, and on the waterfront. Labeled illustrations show the equipment firefighters use to put out blazes.

**ABOUT THE AUTHOR** **Gail Gibbons** enjoyed drawing and painting while growing up. One of her first jobs was doing artwork for a children's television show. After that she wrote her first book. Since then she has written more than 135 informational books.

## Discuss Genre and Set Purpose

**INFORMATIONAL TEXT** Discuss that you will read an informational text that gives facts about how firefighters put out fires. Page through the book and show children the graphics. Discuss that the illustrations are based on the real-life work of firefighters.

**SET PURPOSE** Have children set a purpose for listening, such as to learn information about the different ways firefighters put out fires.

### TEXT COMPLEXITY RUBRIC

| Overall Text Complexity | | *Fire! Fire!* INFORMATIONAL TEXT<br>ACCESSIBLE |
|---|---|---|
| Quantitative Measures | Lexile | N/A |
| | Guided Reading Level | N/A |
| Qualitative Measures | Text Structure | (2nd of 4 points) organization of main idea and details may be complex but is clearly stated and generally sequential |
| | Language Conventionality and Clarity | (2nd of 4 points) some unfamiliar language |
| | Knowledge Demands | (2nd of 4 points) some specialized knowledge required |
| | Purpose/Levels of Meaning | (1st of 4 points) single topic |

SEGMENT 1 pp. 3–16

### Academic Vocabulary

Read each word with children and discuss its meaning.

**blares** (p. 5) • makes a loud, harsh sound

**aerial** (p. 10) • happening in the air

**attach** (p. 10) • to connect one thing to another

**equipment** (p. 15) • the things a person needs to do a job

**report** (p. 15) • a written statement about something that has happened

## FIRST READ Think Through the Text

Have children use text evidence to answer these questions.

**p. 3** • *Where is the fire?* *in an apartment house* SL.K.2, SL.1.2

**p. 7** • *Who tells the firefighters what to do?* *the fire chief* SL.K.2, SL.1.2

**p. 11** • *Why do firefighters break holes in the roof and windows?* *They break holes to let out gases, heat, and smoke before these things cause an explosion.* SL.K.2, SL.1.2

**p. 15** • *What do the firefighters do when the fire is out?* *They clean up and make a report about what happened.* SL.K.2, SL.1.2

## SECOND READ Analyze the Text

- Reread pp. 8–13. Ask: *Once the firefighters arrive at the fire, how do they put it out?* *They use a ladder to get to a floor above the fire to spray water on the fire below. They break a hole in the roof and windows to let out gases. Firefighters on the ground spray water on the fire, too.* Have children point to the places in the book that show the answers. RI.K.7, RI.1.7
- Explain that many of the drawings in the book have labels. Point out that the labels tell the names of the firefighters' equipment. Turn to p. 10. Point to and read the labels. Say: *The words tell us firefighters attach a hose to the building's standpipe. What does the picture of the standpipe show?* *It is a pipe in a box where firefighters connect their hose.* Ask: *How does the picture help us understand what a standpipe is?* *The picture shows exactly what it looks like and how firefighters use it.* RI.K.7, RI.1.6
- Guide children in a discussion about how firefighters respond to a fire in the city. Encourage children to ask questions about things they don't understand and to answer questions using key details from the text. RI.K.1, RI.1.1

### Domain Specific Vocabulary

**dispatcher** (p. 4) • a person who quickly sends something, such as a message, to a particular place

**hydrants** (p. 12) • upright pipes with a spout (often found in the street) that firefighters draw water from

**doused** (p. 31) • soaked with water

**nozzles** (p. 34) • the ends of hoses where water comes out

### ENGLISH LANGUAGE LEARNERS

**Use Visuals**

Prompt children to point to the firefighters in a picture. Then have children repeat the word *firefighters*. Direct children to name some of the equipment firefighters use, including *truck*, *hose*, and *ladder*. Ask children to explain what each piece of equipment does.

### RESPOND TO SEGMENT 1

**Classroom Collaboration**

Have small groups work together to summarize what they have learned and to ask questions about anything they don't understand.

## ENGLISH LANGUAGE LEARNERS

**Use Sentence Frames**

Ask questions from the text that require children to complete a sentence with one-word answers. For example, say: *In the country, the firefighters put out a fire in a ______.* barn Rephrase questions for children to answer in complete sentences. For example, ask: *In the country, where do firefighters put out a fire?* *Firefighters put out a fire in a barn.*

**RESPOND TO SEGMENT 2**

**Classroom Collaboration**

Have partners work together to summarize what they have learned and ask questions about anything they don't understand.

**Common Core Connection**

**RI.K.3** describe the connection between individuals, events, ideas, or information in a text; **RI.K.4** ask and answer questions about unknown words; **W.K.2** use drawing, dictating, and writing to compose informative/explanatory texts; **W.K.5** respond to questions/suggestions from peers and add details to strengthen writing; **SL.K.6** speak audibly and express thoughts, feelings, and ideas clearly **RI.1.3** describe the connection between individuals, events, ideas, or information in a text; **RI.1.4** ask and answer questions to determine or clarify the meaning of words and phrases; **RI.1.5** know and use text features to locate facts and information; **RI.1.10** read informational texts; **W.1.2** write informative/explanatory texts; **W.1.5** focus on a topic, respond to questions/suggestions from peers, and add details to strengthen writing; **SL.1.4** describe people, places, things, and events with details/express ideas and feelings clearly

## FIRST READ Think Through the Text

Have children use text evidence to answer these questions.

**pp. 19–20 •** ***How do the volunteer firefighters get to the fire?*** *They leave their jobs or homes. Some drive in their own cars to the fire. Others go to the firehouse to get the fire trucks.* **SL.K.2, SL.1.2**

**pp. 21–24 •** ***How do the firefighters get water?*** *A pumper truck carries water. When it runs out, a tanker truck brings more. Water from a stream is sucked through a hose into a truck and then pumped to other trucks.* **SL.K.2, SL.1.2**

**p. 23 •** ***What happens if the firefighters need more help?*** *Firefighters from another town come with equipment.* ***Which sentences help you know this?*** *The fire chief calls the dispatch center for more equipment and firefighters. Another town is called for help.* **SL.K.2, SL.1.2**

## SECOND READ Analyze the Text

- Reread p. 17 and point to the word *ignited*. Ask: *What clues help you know what* ignited *means?* Sample answer: *The words* caught fire *are a clue. There is also a picture clue that shows a fire starting in the barn.* **RI.K.4, RI.1.4**
- Have children look at the pictures on page 19 and reread the second paragraph. Ask: *What are the firefighters doing when they get the message there's a fire?* *One firefighter is fixing a car; one is at home; another is working on a farm.* ***What do you think it means to be a volunteer firefighter?*** Sample answer: *Being a firefighter isn't the job they do all the time. They have other jobs, but they help out by being a firefighter and don't get paid.* **RI.K.7, RI.1.6**
- Have children look at the picture on p. 22. Say: *The text tells us that a tanker truck is standing by to help. What does the picture show?* *It shows that the tanker truck dumps water into a portable water tank. A hose from the pumper truck sucks up the water. Then a firefighter sprays out the water with a hose.* ***How do you know the names of the equipment?*** *from the labels* **RI.K.7, RI.1.6**
- Encourage children to ask questions about how firefighters respond to fires in the country. Then remind them of the discussion in the first segment and ask: *When firefighters put out fires in the city and in the country, what is the same?* *A call is made to a dispatch center, and firefighters respond. Firefighters spray water on the fire. After the fire, the fire chief writes an official report, and firefighters clean their equipment.* ***What is different?*** *In the country, firefighters are volunteers. They do not live in a firehouse; they come from their homes or jobs. There are no fire hydrants, so firefighters must pump water from a truck or nearby body of water.* **RI.K.1, RI.1.1**

SEGMENT 3 pp. 29–40

## FIRST READ Think Through the Text

Have children use text evidence to answer these questions.

**p. 29** • *What causes the fire to start in the forest?* Lightning strikes in a place where the ground and trees are dry. RI.K.3, RI.1.3

**p. 31** • *Name three things firefighters do to stop a forest fire from spreading.* cut down trees in front of the fire; spray water on the ground; spray chemicals from a plane SL.K.2, SL.1.2

**p. 33** • *What did you learn about fireboats?* They are floating fire companies. Firefighters use them when fire trucks can't get close to a fire on the waterfront. SL.K.2, SL.1.2

## SECOND READ Analyze the Text

- Display p. 30. Say: *The words tell us that planes drop off smoke jumpers and supplies. Why might smoke jumpers have to parachute to the fire?* Sample answer: There may not be roads for the firefighters to drive to the fire. It helps firefighters get to the fire faster. SL.K.2, SL.1.2
- *What is similar about how firefighters deal with fires in the forest and on the waterfront?* They require special equipment, such as helicopters and fireboats, to get to the fires. *What is different?* In the forest, firefighters drop chemicals. On the waterfront, they spray water. RI.K.3, RI.1.3
- Display the glossary of fire-fighting equipment on p. 38. Explain that a glossary is like a dictionary. It lists important words and includes definitions and sometimes pictures. Glossaries usually come at the end of books. Read about the different types of equipment. Ask: *Which equipment would be more important to firefighters in a city than in the country?* fire escapes, life nets, and helicopters *Why?* All of these things help firefighters rescue people from tall buildings. RI.1.5
- Show the list of ways to prevent a fire on p. 39. Have children classify the tips into two categories. Ask: *Which tips help prevent a fire in the forest?* the tips about matches, barbecue fire, and campfire *Which tips help prevent a fire in a building?* All the rest of the tips would help prevent a fire in a building, including the tip about matches. RI.K.3, RI.1.3

# Independent/Self-Selected Reading

If children have demonstrated listening comprehension of *Fire! Fire!*, have them practice and apply reading comprehension skills using another book. Model selecting a book from the classroom library. Help children read the title of the book, the author's name, and any information on the back or inside cover. Suggested titles:

- *Firefighter* by Dana Meachen Rau
- *The Fire Station* by Gail Saunders-Smith RI.1.10

### WRITE & PRESENT

1. Have small groups ask questions about how firefighters respond to a fire. Children should answer using key details from the text. SL.K.2, SL.K.2
2. Individual children draw and write how firefighters would respond to a fire in a city, on a farm, in the forest, or on the waterfront. W.K.2, W.1.2
3. Children share their drawings and writing with their groups and work together to edit their work. W.K.5, W.1.5
4. Children present their drawings and writing to classmates. SL.K.6, SL.1.4

*See Copying Masters, pp. 242–245.*

### STUDENT CHECKLIST

**Writing**

- ✔ Write and draw how firefighters put out fires in one of four settings.
- ✔ Add details to drawing and writing based on peers' questions.
- ✔ Use correct language conventions.

**Speaking & Listening**

- ✔ Confirm understanding of the text read aloud by asking and answering questions.
- ✔ Participate in conversations with small groups, partners, and whole class.
- ✔ Speak audibly to express ideas clearly.

## OBJECTIVES

- Identify the main topic and key details
- Ask and answer questions after listening to the text
- Ask and answer questions about unknown words in the text
- Analyze the text using text evidence

***Follow the Water from Brook to Ocean*** **is broken into three instructional segments.**

**SEGMENTS**



### Options for Reading

*Be sure to display the book's pictures and read with expression to model fluent reading.*

**Uninterrupted** Focus on the flow of the selection by reading aloud without stopping for questions.

**Interactive** Stop at appropriate places while reading to make comments and ask questions. Also, invite children to share their own comments and questions.

### Common Core Connection

**RI.K.2** identify the main topic and retell key details; **RI.K.4** ask and answer questions about unknown words; **RI.K.7** describe relationships between illustrations and the text; **SL.K.2** confirm understanding of a text read aloud, information presented orally, or through other media by asking/answering questions and requesting clarification

**RI.1.2** identify the main topic and retell key details; **RI.1.4** ask and answer questions to determine or clarify the meaning of words and phrases; **RI.1.7** use illustrations and details to describe key ideas; **SL.1.2** ask and answer questions about details in a text read aloud, information presented orally, or through other media

# Follow the Water from Brook to Ocean

by Arthur Dorros

**SUMMARY** This book describes how water travels from brooks to streams to rivers and finally to oceans. The author/illustrator uses visuals to explain water's journey.

**ABOUT THE AUTHOR** **Arthur Dorros** is both an author and illustrator. Before he started writing children's books at age 30, he had worked as a carpenter, photographer, and teacher—among other jobs. He has since published more than 30 books.

## Discuss Genre and Set Purpose

**INFORMATIONAL TEXT** Show children the front cover and read the title. Have children page through the book and predict what information the book might provide about water.

**SET PURPOSE** Help children set a purpose for reading, such as to learn information about how water travels to oceans.

**TEXT COMPLEXITY RUBRIC**

| Overall Text Complexity | | *Follow the Water from Brook to Ocean* INFORMATIONAL TEXT<br>COMPLEX |
|---|---|---|
| Quantitative Measures | Lexile | N/A |
| | Guided Reading Level | N/A |
| Qualitative Measures | Text Structure | organization of main idea and details may be complex, but is clearly stated and generally sequential |
| | Language Conventionality and Clarity | more complex sentence structure |
| | Knowledge Demands | some specialized knowledge required |
| | Purpose/Levels of Meaning | multiple topics |

## SEGMENT 1 pp. 4–13

### Academic Vocabulary

Read each word with children and discuss its meaning.

**gush** (p. 5) • to flow out with force

**erosion** (p. 16) • when water or wind wears away the surface of the earth

**polluted** (p. 26) • unclean

**journey** (p. 31) • a long trip

## FIRST READ Think Through the Text

Have children use text evidence to answer these questions.

**p. 8** • *Which way does water always flow?* *downhill* *What does the author compare this to?* *a skateboard going down a hill* **SL.K.2, SL.1.2**

**p. 9** • *When does water stop flowing?* *Water stops flowing when it reaches the lowest point and can't flow downhill anymore.* *Where are the lowest parts of the earth?* *The oceans are the lowest parts of the earth.* **SL.K.2, SL.1.2**

**p. 10** • *Name three things that happen to rain and melting snow.* *The water runs over ground, soaks into the ground, or is soaked up by trees and other plants.* **SL.K.2, SL.1.2**

## SECOND READ Analyze the Text

- Reread pages 5–13. Remind children that the main topic of a text is what it is mostly about. Ask: *From what we've read so far, what is the main topic of this book?* *Water travels downhill until it reaches the ocean.* **RI.K.2, RI.1.2**
- Look at pages 10–11 with children. Ask: *Where does water in a brook, stream, or river start?* *It starts as rain and melting snow.* Then ask: *How do the two pictures show where water comes from?* *The picture on the left shows water falling as rain. The picture on the right shows water that comes from melted snow.* **RI.K.7, RI.1.7**
- Reread page 12. Point out that the text and the picture help define the word *brook*. Ask: *What words give you a clue to what* brook *means?* flowing over the ground; isn't very deep or wide *Ask: What extra information does the picture give us about a brook?* *It is a body of water small enough for the boy to step over.* **RI.K.4, RI.1.4**

### Domain Specific Vocabulary

**spring** (p. 14) • a source of water coming from the ground

**bank** (p. 17) • the ground on the side of a river or lake that forms its edge

**canyons** (p. 19) • deep narrow valleys that often have rivers flowing through them

**delta** (p. 27) • a triangle of sand and soil deposited at the mouth of some large rivers

### ELL ENGLISH LANGUAGE LEARNERS

**Use Gestures**

Tell children: *Water flows downhill.* Then, with your arms starting above your head, make a gesture for downhill. Have children mimic the gesture. Ask: *What other things go downhill?* *a ball rolling down a hill, a skier, a skateboard*

### RESPOND TO SEGMENT 1

**Classroom Collaboration**

Have small groups work together to recount the main topic of the text and discuss questions that might be answered in the next segment.

## ENGLISH LANGUAGE LEARNERS

**Use Visuals**

Say *stream* and have children repeat the word. Prompt them to point to the picture of the stream. Repeat this activity with *river*. Then ask: *What are one or two words that describe a stream?* big, fast *a river?* deep, wide Have them find additional water words in the text and describe them.

**RESPOND TO SEGMENT 2**

**Classroom Collaboration**

Have partners work together to summarize what they have learned and ask questions about anything they don't understand.

**Common Core Connection**

**RI.K.8** identify the reasons an author gives to support points; **W.K.2** use drawing, dictating, and writing to compose informative/explanatory texts; **W.K.5** respond to questions/suggestions from peers and add details to strengthen writing; **SL.K.2** confirm understanding of a text read aloud, information presented orally, or through other media by asking/answering questions and requesting clarification; **SL.K.6** speak audibly and express thoughts, feelings, and ideas clearly

**RI.1.6** distinguish between information provided by pictures and words; **RI.1.8** identify the reasons an author gives to support points; **RI.1.10** read informational texts; **W.1.2** write informative/explanatory texts; **W.1.5** focus on a topic, respond to questions/suggestions from peers, and add details to strengthen writing; **SL.1.2** ask and answer questions about details in a text read aloud, information presented orally, or through other media; **SL.1.4** describe people, places, things, and events with details/express ideas and feelings clearly

## FIRST READ Think Through the Text

Have children use text evidence to answer these questions.

**p. 14 •** *What are two ways water ends up in streams?* The water comes from brooks or springs. *Point to the words that tell you the answer.* **SL.K.2, SL.1.2**

**p. 21 •** *What are meanders?* Meanders are bends in a river. *Which sentence tells you what* meanders *means?* the last sentence **RI.K.4, RI.1.4**

**p. 22 •** *Why do some rivers look muddy?* Rain and melting snow have carried soil into the river. **SL.K.2, SL.1.2**

**p. 24 •** *What does a dam do?* It holds back water so a river doesn't flood. *What happens when water is released from a dam?* Water rushing out of a dam is used to make electricity. **SL.K.2, SL.1.2**

**p. 25 •** *What is a reservoir?* A reservoir is a lake behind a dam. *How is water from a reservoir used?* Sample answer: It is used to water crops. People drink and bathe in it after it is piped to their homes. **RI.K.4, RI.1.4**

**p. 26 •** *What reasons does the author give about why polluting water is bad?* Polluted water can kill plants, fish, and other animals. It also can be dangerous to humans. **RI.K.8, RI.1.8**

## SECOND READ Analyze the Text

- Revisit pages 14–26. Ask: *What is the main topic of this part of the book?* rivers Say: *We learned many details about rivers. Which details are the most important?* Sample answer: Rivers are usually deep and wide enough for boats to use them. Rivers can carve out canyons. Some rivers flow fast over waterfalls, while others go slowly over flat land. Rivers can overflow and cause floods. People build dams to hold back rivers. **SL.K.2, SL.1.2**
- Focus on pages 16–17. *What sound words does the author include on these pages?* clunk, thunk, sploosh *Why do you think the author adds these words?* Sample answer: The sound words help the reader imagine what it's like to be near a stream. **SL.K.2, SL.1.2**
- Reread the following sentences on pages 19 and 21: *Fast-flowing rivers can carve deep canyons in the land. Where a river moves slowly it doesn't carve as deeply.* Ask: *What does carve mean in these sentences?* Carve means to cut or dig into the land. **RI.K.4, RI.1.4**

## FIRST READ Think Through the Text

Have children use text evidence to answer these questions.

**p. 27** • *Where would you find a delta?* at the mouth of a river where it meets the ocean *What are two things that make up a delta?* soil, rock SL.K.2, SL.1.2

**p. 28** • *How far might water travel before it reaches the ocean?* thousands of miles SL.K.2, SL.1.2

**p. 28** • *Where is most of the water on Earth?* in oceans Say: *The map gives us more information about the oceans. What are the names of the two oceans on the map?* Atlantic Ocean, Pacific Ocean RI.K.7, RI.1.6

## SECOND READ Analyze the Text

- *Look closely at the picture on p. 27. Why do you think this part of the river is called the mouth?* Sample answer: *It is an opening from the river to the ocean. It may look like a person's open mouth.* RI.K.7, RI.1.7
- *What is this section mainly about?* the ocean *What are some of the key details in the text that tell about the ocean?* Sample answer: *The ocean is the last place the water goes. It is filled with lots of fish, animals, and plants.* RI.K.2, RI.1.2
- Revisit predictions from Segment 1 about the main topic of the book. Ask children to revise their thoughts about what the book is mainly about. Sample answer: *Water takes a long journey from rain or snow on a mountain to the ocean.* RI.K.2, RI.1.2

# Independent/Self-Selected Reading

If children have demonstrated listening comprehension of *Follow the Water from Brook to Ocean,* have them practice and apply reading comprehension skills using another book. Model selecting a book from the classroom library. Help children read the title of the book, the author's name, and any information on the back or inside cover. Suggested titles:

- *Water's Way* by Lisa Westberg Peters
- *Water* by Frank Asch RI.1.10

### WRITE & PRESENT

1. Have partners refer to the text to retell the main topic of the book in their own words. Prompt them by asking: *What happens to water as it flows from high to low?* Have children share several key details that support the main idea. SL.K.2, SL.1.2
2. Ask children to each write a sentence that tells the main topic. Then have them write and draw additional details that tell more about what happens to water. W.K.2, W.1.2
3. Children share their drawings and writing with partners. Have them respond to questions and suggestions by editing and adding to their work. W.K.5, W.1.5
4. Children present their final work for classmates. SL.K.6, SL.1.4

*See Copying Masters, pp. 242–245.*

### STUDENT CHECKLIST

#### Writing

- ✔ Write and draw how water moves from brooks to oceans.
- ✔ Indicate correct sequence of water flow.
- ✔ Add details to drawing and writing based on partners' suggestions.

#### Speaking & Listening

- ✔ Confirm understanding of the main idea and key details of text read aloud.
- ✔ Follow rules in partner and whole-group discussions.
- ✔ Ask questions and provide suggestions to partner to clarify any confusion.

## OBJECTIVES

- Ask and answer questions about details in a text
- Use information from text and photographs to demonstrate understanding
- Explore the concept of the importance of water for all living things

***Water, Water Everywhere*** **is broken into three instructional segments.**

**SEGMENTS**

**SEGMENT 1** . . . . . . . . . pp. 6–15
**SEGMENT 2** . . . . . . . . pp. 16–23
**SEGMENT 3** . . . . . . . . pp. 24–32

**Options for Reading**

*Be sure to display the book's pictures and read with expression to model fluent reading.*

**Uninterrupted** Focus on the flow of the story by reading aloud without stopping for comments or questions.

**Interactive** Stop at appropriate places while reading to make comments and ask children questions. Invite children to share their own comments and questions.

**Common Core Connection**

**RI.K.3** describe the connection between individuals, events, ideas, or information in a text; **RI.K.7** describe relationships between illustrations and the text; **SL.K.2** confirm understanding of a text read aloud, information presented orally, or through other media by asking/answering questions and requesting clarification

**RI.1.3** describe the connection between individuals, events, ideas, or information in a text; **RI.1.7** use illustrations and details to describe key ideas; **SL.1.2** ask and answer questions about details in a text read aloud, information presented orally, or through other media

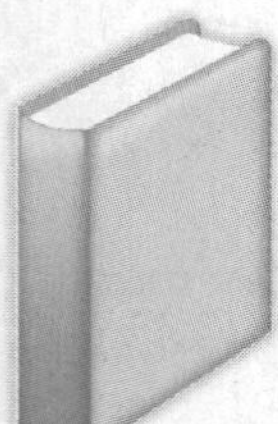

# *Water, Water Everywhere*

by Mark J. Rauzon and Cynthia Overbeck Bix

**SUMMARY** This book explains that water is everywhere on Earth. It gives examples of water as a solid, liquid, gas, and vapor and describes the water cycle. The authors use photographs to give additional information about water.

**ABOUT THE AUTHOR** **Mark J. Rauzon** is a geographer and a biologist. He has written over 20 science books for children. Writer and editor **Cynthia Overbeck Bix** has written more than 35 science books for children and adults.

## Discuss Genre and Set Purpose

**INFORMATIONAL TEXT** Tell children that you will read aloud an informational book about water. Briefly page through the book and have children identify features that show that the book gives facts, or true information, about water.

**SET PURPOSE** Help children set a purpose for listening, such as to learn information about water.

**TEXT COMPLEXITY RUBRIC**

| Overall Text Complexity | | *Water, Water Everywhere* INFORMATIONAL TEXT<br>COMPLEX |
|---|---|---|
| Quantitative Measures | Lexile | N/A |
| | Guided Reading Level | N/A |
| Qualitative Measures | Text Structure | somewhat complex science concepts |
| | Language Conventionality and Clarity | less straightforward sentence structure |
| | Knowledge Demands | specialized knowledge demands |
| | Purpose/Levels of Meaning | multiple topics |

## SEGMENT 1 pp. 6–15

### Academic Vocabulary

Read each word with children and discuss its meaning.

**planet** (p. 6) • a large heavenly body that orbits a star

**surface** (p. 14) • the outside of something

**cycle** (p. 14) • a series of events that repeat in the same order

**pollute** (p. 28) • to make dirty with waste products

## FIRST READ Think Through the Text

Have children use text evidence to answer these questions.

**pp. 6–7** • *What would Earth be like without water?* *It would be dusty, dry, and dead.* **SL.K.2, SL.1.2**

**pp. 8–9** • *Where can you find water?* Sample answer: *in rivers, waterfalls, dewdrops, plants, and in the bodies of humans and other animals* **SL.K.2, SL.1.2**

**pp. 10–11** • *What happens when water gets very cold?* *It freezes into solid ice.* **RI.K.3, RI.1.3**

**pp. 12–15** • *How does water change forms in the water cycle?* Sample answer: *It changes from a liquid to a vapor, back into water droplets that make rain or snow, and back to liquid water on the earth.* **RI.K.3, RI.1.3**

## SECOND READ Analyze the Text

- Reread pages 6–9. Ask: *How do the writers feel about water? How do you know?* Sample answer: *The writers think water is important. They say it brings life and color to the earth. They give examples of places to find water. They say it is part of every living thing.* **RI.K.3, RI.1.3**
- Show children pages 10–11. Point out how the text and photographs work together to give information. Say: *The text tells that hot water produces steam. What does the photograph on page 11 show?* *The photograph shows the steam erupting from a hot spring underground.* **RI.K.7, RI.1.7**
- Show children pages 12–13. Say: *The text explains the water cycle. What do the photographs show?* *The photograph on page 12 shows water vapor when it forms clouds. The photograph on page 13 shows water that changed to snow when the air got cold.* **RI.K.7, RI.1.7**

### Domain Specific Vocabulary

**form** (p. 10) • shape

**liquid** (p. 10) • a substance that flows and can be poured

**solid** (p. 10) • hard and firm; not a liquid or gas

**vapor** (p. 13) • a gas formed from a liquid

**gas** (p. 13) • a substance that spreads to fill any space that contains it

### ELL ENGLISH LANGUAGE LEARNERS

**Use Visuals and Key Words**

To ensure that children understand the text, use key words to ask questions such as: *Which photo shows water as a liquid?* *the one on p. 10* *Which photo shows water as steam?* *the photo on page 11*

### RESPOND TO SEGMENT 1

**Classroom Collaboration**

Have partners work together to summarize what they have learned as well as raise questions that might be answered in the next segment.

## ENGLISH LANGUAGE LEARNERS

**Use Cognates**

Point out English/Spanish cognates to aid comprehension: *animal/animal; form/forma, formar; garden/jardín; gas/gas; glacier/glaciar; liquid/líquido; mountain/montaña; solid/sólido; vapor/vapor; valley/valle.*

**RESPOND TO SEGMENT 2**

**Classroom Collaboration**

Have small groups summarize what they have learned and ask questions about anything they still don't understand.

**Common Core Connection**

**RI.K.3** describe the connection between individuals, events, ideas, or information in a text; **RI.K.7** describe relationships between illustrations and the text; **RI.K.8** identify the reason an author gives to support points; **W.K.2** use drawing, dictating, and writing to compose informative/explanatory texts; **W.K.5** respond to questions/suggestions from peers and add details to strengthen writing; **SL.K.2** confirm understanding of a text read aloud, information presented orally, or through other media by asking/answering questions and requesting clarification; **SL.K.6** speak audibly and express thoughts, feelings, and ideas clearly

**RI.1.3** describe the connection between individuals, events, ideas, or information in a text; **RI.1.7** use illustrations and details to describe key ideas; **RI.1.8** identify the reason an author gives to support points; **RI.1.10** read informational texts; **W.1.2** write informative explanatory texts; **W.1.5** focus on a topic, respond to questions from peers, and add details to strengthen writing; **SL.1.2** ask and answer questions about details in a text read aloud, information presented orally, or through other media; **SL.1.6** produce complete sentences when appropriate to task and situation

## FIRST READ Think Through the Text

Have children use text evidence to answer these questions.

**pp. 16–17** • *What are all the things that happen to water that bubbles out of a mountain stream?* Sample answer: *It rushes down a mountainside, splashes around rocks, and tumbles over waterfalls. It joins with other little streams to form a small river and then flows over the land until it meets the sea.* **SL.K.2, SL.1.2**

**pp. 18–19** • *What do you know about glaciers from listening to this text?* Sample answer: *Glaciers are made of ice. They slide downhill and make deep valleys.* **SL.K.2, SL.1.2**

**pp. 20–21** • *What are some ways that water brings life?* Sample answer: *Rain helps the trees and plants in forests and gardens to grow. Animals drink water. Some animals live in water.* **SL.K.2, SL.1.2**

**pp. 22–23** • *What are some ways that people use water?* Sample answer: *People use water for cooking, washing, bathing, and making electricity.* **SL.K.2, SL.1.2**

## SECOND READ Analyze the Text

- Point to the photographs on pages 16–17. Say: *The text tells how water moves. What do these photographs show?* *The photograph on page 16 shows a waterfall. The photograph on page 17 shows water splashing around rocks or flowing over the land.* **RI.K.7, RI.1.7**
- Show children pages 18–19. Ask: *How can you use the photographs to help you understand the text better?* Sample answer: *The photograph on page 18 shows the power of water because the canyon is so deep. The photograph on page 19 shows how the sand has been broken down by the waves.* **RI.K.7, RI.1.7**
- Reread pages 20–23. Have partners tell each other something they learned about water. Ask: *What do you think is the most important use of water?* Answers will vary. **RI.K.3, RI.1.3**

## FIRST READ Think Through the Text

Have children use text evidence to answer these questions.

**pp. 24–25 •** ***What did you learn about fresh water and salt water?*** Sample answer: *Most of the water on the earth is salt water. Only a little bit is fresh water, and most of that is frozen in glaciers.* **SL.K.2, SL.1.2**

**pp. 26–27 •** ***Why do we need to use fresh water wisely?*** Sample answer: *There is not a lot of fresh water, and more people are using it. Water can't recycle itself fast enough for all of the people who need to use it.* **RI.K.3, RI.1.3**

**pp. 28–29 •** ***What are some ways that our water supply gets polluted?*** Sample answer: *Cities dump waste into the ocean; factories empty chemicals into rivers; smoke gets into the air and falls as acid rain.* **RI.K.3, RI.1.3**

**pp. 30–32 •** ***The authors say that being near water keeps us in touch with the life of the earth. What are some examples they give of things we do near water?*** Sample answer: *We watch a clear lake, catch snowflakes on our tongues, and go skiing in the mountains.* **RI.K.8, RI.1.8**

## SECOND READ Analyze the Text

- Show children pages 24–25 and reread page 25. Ask: ***Do the photographs and the text work together to give information about fresh water? Explain.*** *Yes, the text explains about glaciers and the photograph on page 24 shows fresh water frozen in a glacier. The text also says that water supports plant and animal life and the photographs on page 25 show birds and a child using water.* **RI.K.7, RI.1.7**
- Show children pages 26–27 and reread page 27. Say: ***The text talks about using fresh water wisely. What does the photograph show?*** *It shows how dry the ground is when there is not enough water.* ***Why do you think this photograph is with this text?*** *to show what happens when water is not used wisely* **RI.K.7, RI.1.7**
- Reread pages 28–32. ***What message do the writers give you about water pollution?*** Sample answer: *Pollution harms our water by making it too dirty to drink or use. Pollution also spoils the beauty of water.* **SL.K.2, SL.1.2**

# Independent/Self-Selected Reading

If children have already demonstrated listening comprehension and analysis of *Water, Water Everywhere*, have them practice comprehension skills using an independent reading book. Suggested titles:

- *The Water Cycle* by Helen Frost
- *We Use Water* by Robin Nelson **RL.1.10**

### WRITE & PRESENT

1. Have small groups ask and answer questions they have about the details in the text. Encourage children to discuss ways the authors use text and photographs to give information about water. **SL.K.2, SL.1.2**
2. Have each child write sentences that use information in the text to explain the uses and the importance of water. Ask children to include illustrations that help explain their writing. **W.K.2, W.1.2**
3. Children return to their groups to share their writing and drawings with each other and edit their work. **W.K.5, W.1.5**
4. Individual children present their final work to classmates. Encourage children to speak audibly and to use complete sentences. **SL.K.6, SL.1.6**

*See Copying Masters, pp. 242–245.*

### STUDENT CHECKLIST

#### Writing

- ✔ Write sentences that use information from the text to describe the uses and importance of water.
- ✔ Draw pictures that illustrate the sentences.
- ✔ Use correct language conventions.

#### Speaking & Listening

- ✔ Engage effectively in collaborative conversations.
- ✔ Ask and answer questions about text details.
- ✔ Demonstrate a connection between information in the text and one's own writing and drawing.

## OBJECTIVES

- Explore the life of earthworms
- Identify main idea and details
- Analyze text using text evidence
- Use text features

*Earthworms* is broken into three instructional segments.

**SEGMENTS**

**SEGMENT 1**. . . . . . . . . pp. 6–13
**SEGMENT 2**. . . . . . . . pp. 14–21
**SEGMENT 3**. . . . . . . . pp. 22–29

### Options for Reading

*Be sure to display the book's pictures and read with expression to model fluent reading.*

**Uninterrupted** Focus on the flow of the story by reading aloud without stopping for comments or questions.

**Interactive** Stop at appropriate places while reading to make comments and ask children questions. Also, invite children to share their own comments and questions.

### Common Core Connection

**RI.K.5** identify the front cover, back cover, and title page of a book; **RI.K.7** describe relationships between illustrations and the text; **SL.K.2** confirm understanding of a text read aloud, information presented orally, or through other media by asking/answering questions and requesting clarification

**RI.1.5** know and use text features to locate facts or information; **RI.1.7** use illustrations and details to describe key ideas; **SL.1.2** ask and answer questions about details in a text read aloud, information presented orally, or through other media

# Earthworms

## by Claire Llewellyn and Barrie Watts

**SUMMARY** This book explains what earthworms are and how they live. The authors use photographs, illustrations, and diagrams to give additional information about earthworms.

**ABOUT THE AUTHOR** Claire Llewellyn was a children's book editor before becoming a writer. She has written more than 50 nonfiction books for children. **Barrie Watts** travels the world taking nature photographs. He has published his photographs in over 80 books for children.

## Discuss Genre and Set Purpose

**INFORMATIONAL TEXT** Tell children you will be reading them an informational book about earthworms. Briefly page through the book and have children identify text features such as photographs, illustrations, and diagrams. Discuss with them how they can tell the book is informational.

**SET PURPOSE** Help children set a purpose for listening, such as to learn information about earthworms.

**TEXT COMPLEXITY RUBRIC**

| Overall Text Complexity | | *Earthworms* INFORMATIONAL TEXT<br>ACCESSIBLE |
|---|---|---|
| Quantitative Measures | Lexile | N/A |
| | Guided Reading Level | N/A |
| Qualitative Measures | Text Structure | more difficult science concepts |
| | Language Conventionality and Clarity | longer descriptions |
| | Knowledge Demands | experience includes unfamiliar aspects |
| | Purpose/Levels of Meaning | single topic |

**SEGMENT 1** pp. 6–13

### Academic Vocabulary

Read each word with children and discuss its meaning.

**soil** (p. 6) • the top layer of earth in which plants grow
**tube** (p. 10) • a shape like a pipe or a drinking straw
**segment** (p. 10) • a section or part of something
**surface** (p. 11) • the outside or top layer of something
**crawl** (p. 13) • to move close to the ground
**tunnel** (p. 16) • something dug underground that things can travel through

### Domain Specific Vocabulary

**wriggly** (p. 6) • twisting and turning
**damp** (p. 8) • slightly wet
**skeleton** (p. 10) • the frame of bones that supports the body
**anchor** (p. 15) • to fasten or keep in place
**hatch** (p. 20) • to break out of an egg

## FIRST READ Think Through the Text

Have children use text evidence to answer these questions.

**Front Cover** • *What information do you find on the book's cover?* *the title of the book, the names of the author and photographer* RI.K.5, RI.1.5

**pp. 6–7** • *What did you learn about the size and color of worms?* *Some worms are small but others are gigantic. They come in many colors.* SL.K.2, SL.1.2

**pp. 8–9** • *Where do earthworms live?* *Earthworms live in damp soil in woods, meadows, gardens, and compost heaps.* SL.K.2, SL.1.2

**pp. 10–11** • *What does a worm's body look like?* *It is a tube with segments but without a skeleton, lungs, eyes, or ears.* SL.K.2, SL.1.2

## SECOND READ Analyze the Text

- Display and read the Contents page. Ask: *How can you tell from this page what kinds of information are in the book?* *The different topics are listed.* *What other information is on the Contents page?* *the page numbers for each topic.* *What topic is discussed on pages 12–13?* *feeding* *On which pages would you find information about enemies?* *pages 22–23* *What information would you expect to find in "Worm Wonders" on pages 26–27?* *interesting facts about worms* SL.K.2, RI.1.5
- Display pages 10–11. Point out how the text, illustration, and photographs give information. Say: *The text tells about a worm's body. What does the illustration on page 10 show?* *the worm's body parts* *What additional information do you get from the photographs on page 11?* *what the worm's skin looks like, how it moves in the soil* RI.K.7, RI.1.7
- Show children pages 12–13. and point out the title, "Feeding." Ask: *How is the information organized?* *First, the text tells what worms eat. Then it tells how and when they eat.* SL.K.2, RI.1.5

### Use Key Words

Guide children to answer questions with key words, such as: *Do worms crawl or walk?* *crawl* *Do worms eat soil to make tunnels?* *yes* Then have children ask and answer their own questions about the selection.

### RESPOND TO SEGMENT 1

**Classroom Collaboration**

Have partners work together to summarize what they have learned as well as raise questions that might be answered in the next segment.

## ENGLISH LANGUAGE LEARNERS

**Use Cognates**

Point out English/Spanish cognates to aid comprehension: *animal/animal; escape/escapar; garden/jardín; liquid/líquido; segment/segmento; tube/tubo; tunnel/túnel; vegetable/vegetal.*

## RESPOND TO SEGMENT 2

**Classroom Collaboration**

Have small groups summarize what they have learned and ask questions about anything they still don't understand.

## Common Core Connection

**RI.K.5** identify the front cover, back cover, and title page of a book; **RI.K.7** describe relationships between illustrations and the text; **W.K.2** use drawing, dictating, and writing to compose informative/explanatory texts; **W.K.5** respond to questions/suggestions from peers and add details to strengthen writing; **SL.K.2** confirm understanding of a text read aloud, information presented orally, or through other media by asking answering questions and requesting clarification; **SL.K.6** speak audibly and express thoughts, feelings, and ideas clearly

**RI.1.5** know and use text features to locate facts or information; **RI.1.7** use illustrations and details to describe key ideas; **RI.1.10** read informational texts; **W.1.2** write informative/explanatory texts; **W.1.5** focus on a topic, respond to questions from peers, and add details to strengthen writing; **SL.1.2** ask and answer questions about details in a text read aloud, information presented orally, or through other media; **SL.1.6** produce complete sentences when appropriate to task and situation

## FIRST READ Think Through the Text

Have children use text evidence to answer these questions.

**pp. 14–15, 28** • *Where in the book can you find the meaning of the word* muscle? *in the glossary* *What do an earthworm's muscles do?* *Ring-shaped muscles make the body shrink or spread out. Other muscles make the body grow long or short.* **SL.K.2, RI.1.5**

**pp. 16–17** • *How do some worms protect themselves in very cold or dry weather?* *They burrow deep underground.* **SL.K.2, SL.1.2**

**pp. 18–19** • *Why can any worm be a mate to any other worm?* *Every worm has both female and male parts.* **SL.K.2, SL.1.2**

**pp. 20–21** • Point out the section heading. *What do you learn about in this section?* *how a worm's eggs hatch* *How long does it take for a young worm to grow up and lay eggs of its own?* *eighteen months* **SL.K.2, RI.1.5**

## SECOND READ Analyze the Text

- Browse through the book. Point out that each section starts with a heading. Explain: *The first sentence in each section states a main idea. The rest of the section gives details about the main idea.* Then ask: *How is this organization helpful to you?* Sample answer: *The organization helps you to figure out what to listen for and read. It helps you remember the information.* **SL.K.2, RI.1.5**
- Point to the photograph on page 16 and the illustration on page 17. Say: *The text describes tunneling. What do the photograph and the illustration show?* *The photograph shows a worm tunneling in the soil. The illustration shows a worm sleeping after it burrowed underground.* **RI.K.7, RI.1.7**
- Reread pages 18–19. Ask: *Why is the belt on a worm's body so important during mating?* *The belt turns into a cocoon that protects the eggs.* **SL.K.2, SL.1.2**
- Show children pages 20–21. Ask: *How can you use the illustration and the photograph to help you understand the text better?* Sample answer: *The illustration shows what a cocoon looks like. The photograph shows how the young earthworms and their parents are alike and different.* **RI.K.7, RI.1.7**

**SEGMENT 3** pp. 22–29

## FIRST READ Think Through the Text

Have children use text evidence to answer these questions.

**pp. 22–23** • *Which animals are an earthworm's enemies?* hedgehogs, shrews, and moles *Why is a mole an earthworm's greatest enemy?* It eats as many as thirty earthworms in one day. **SL.K.2, SL.1.2**

**pp. 22, 28** • *Use the glossary to find the meaning of the word* shrew. *What is a shrew?* It is a small animal that looks like a mouse but has a longer nose. *Is the animal in the illustration a shrew?* no *What does the illustration show?* a hedgehog **RI.K.7, RI.1.5**

**pp. 24–25** • *How do birds find earthworms?* The birds look and listen for tiny movements of earthworms in the ground. *How does a bird get the worm out of the ground?* The bird pulls on the worm's tail until the worm comes out of the ground. **SL.K.2, SL.1.2**

**pp. 26–27** • *Why did Charles Darwin believe that the worm is the most important animal in the world?* It helps plants grow. **SL.K.2, SL.1.2**

**p. 29** • *Where would you look to find information about worm casts?* on pages 12 and 28 **SL.K.2, RI.1.5**

## SECOND READ Analyze the Text

- Show children page 23 and reread the text. Ask: *How does the illustration help you figure out the meaning of the word* pantry? Sample answer: The illustration shows what a mole's pantry looks like. **RI.K.7, RI.1.7**
- Show children pages 22–25 and reread the text. Ask: *How can you use the illustrations to help you compare the ways that different animals hunt for worms?* Sample answer: You can see that the mole tunnels underground while the bird stays above the ground. **RI.K.7, RI.1.7**
- Reread pages 26–27. Have partners tell each other something they learned about earthworms. **SL.K.2, SL.1.2**

# Independent/Self-Selected Reading

If children have already demonstrated listening comprehension of *Earthworms*, have them practice skills using an independent reading book. Model selecting a book from the classroom library. Help them read the title of the book, the author's name, and any information about the book on the back or inside cover. Suggested titles:

- *Lowdown on Earthworms* by Norma Dixon
- *Garden Wigglers: Earthworms in Your Backyard* by Nancy Loewen **RL.1.10**

### WRITE & PRESENT

1. Discuss with children how the author uses the Contents page, section headings, main ideas, and details to give information about earthworms. Then draw a web on the board. Using the content of one section of the book, guide children to complete the web with a main idea and details. Use both text and illustrations in the web. **SL.K.2, SL.1.2**
2. Have small groups choose a section of the book and create a main idea and details web for that topic. Then individuals use the charts to write and illustrate a summary of that section. **W.K.2, W.1.2**
3. Children return to their groups to share their writings and drawings and edit their work. **W.K.5, W.1.5**
4. Individual children present their final work to classmates. **SL.K.6, SL.1.6**

*See Copying Masters, pp. 242–245.*

### STUDENT CHECKLIST

#### Writing

- ✔ Use a graphic organizer as an aid to writing.
- ✔ Write a paragraph that uses information from the text to describe earthworms.
- ✔ Use correct language conventions.

#### Speaking & Listening

- ✔ Engage effectively in collaborative conversations.
- ✔ Ask and answer questions about text main ideas and details.
- ✔ Demonstrate a connection between information in the text and one's own writing and drawing.

## OBJECTIVES

- Use illustrations and text to describe key ideas
- Describe connections between pieces of information in a text
- Ask and answer questions about animals

***What Do You Do with a Tail Like This?*** **is broken into three instructional segments.**

**SEGMENTS**

**SEGMENT 1**. . . . . . . . . .pp. 2–15
**SEGMENT 2**. . . . . . . . .pp. 16–27
**SEGMENT 3**. . . . . . . . .pp. 28–31

### Options for Reading

*Display the book's pictures and read with expression to model fluent reading.*

**Uninterrupted** Focus on the flow of the selection by reading aloud without stopping for comments or questions.

**Interactive** Stop at appropriate places while reading to make comments and ask children questions. Invite children to share their own comments and questions.

### Common Core Connection

**RI.K.3** describe the connections between individuals, events, ideas, or information in a text; **RI.K.4** ask and answer questions about unknown words; **RI.K.7** describe relationships between illustrations and the text; **SL.K.2** confirm understanding of a text read aloud, information presented orally, or through other media by asking/answering questions and requesting clarification

**RI.1.3** describe the connection between individuals, events, ideas, or information in a text; **RI.1.4** ask and answer questions to determine or clarify the meaning of words and phrases; **RI.1.7** use illustrations and details to describe key ideas; **SL.1.2** ask and answer questions about details in a text read aloud, information presented orally, or through other media

# *What Do You Do with a Tail Like This?*

by Steve Jenkins and Robin Page

**SUMMARY** In this guessing book, readers learn about the different ways that animals use their noses, ears, tails, eyes, mouths, and feet.

**ABOUT THE AUTHOR** **Steve Jenkins** has always been interested in science and art. Reading to his children inspired him to combine these interests into children's books. He has written four children's books with his wife, **Robin Page**.

## Discuss Genre and Set Purpose

**INFORMATIONAL TEXT** Read the title with children and show them some of the illustrations. Discuss how an informational book gives facts, or true information, about a topic. Use the title to help children predict what they think the book might be about.

**SET PURPOSE** Help children set a purpose for listening, such as to find information about the ways that some animals use their body parts.

**TEXT COMPLEXITY RUBRIC**

| Overall Text Complexity | | *What Do You Do with a Tail Like This?* INFORMATIONAL TEXT |
|---|---|---|
| | | ACCESSIBLE |
| Quantitative Measures | Lexile | N/A |
| | Guided Reading Level | N/A |
| Qualitative Measures | Text Structure | less conventional compare/contrast structure |
| | Language Conventionality and Clarity | some unfamiliar language |
| | Knowledge Demands | some specialized knowledge required |
| | Purpose/Levels of Meaning | implied, but easy to identify |

**SEGMENT 1** pp. 2–15

### Academic Vocabulary

Read each word with children and discuss its meaning.

**pesky** (p. 14) • annoying; bothersome

**warn** (p. 14) • to tell or show someone that something is about to happen

**capture** (p. 27) • to catch and hold in one place

**opposable** (p. 30) • able to move towards and touch the other fingers or toes on a hand or foot

## FIRST READ Think Through the Text

Have children use text evidence to answer these questions.

**p. 2** • *What are some of the body parts that animals use in different ways?* *noses, ears, tails, eyes, mouth, and feet* **SL.K.2, SL.1.2**

**pp. 4–7** • *How does an elephant use its nose?* *to give itself a bath* *How do you know?* *The text says that if you're an elephant, you use your nose to give yourself a bath. The picture shows an elephant spraying itself with water.* **RI.K.7, RI.1.7**

**pp. 8–11** • *How are crickets' ears different from the ears of many other animals?* *Crickets have ears on their knees instead of on their heads.* **RI.K.3, RI.1.3**

**pp. 12–15** *What are some different ways that animals use their tails?* *They use them to hang, keep away flies, and protect themselves.* **SL.K.2, SL.1.2**

## SECOND READ Analyze the Text

- Point out each animal on pages 6–7. Encourage children to ask questions to clarify the names of the animals. Then have children answer questions to confirm their understanding. Ask: *Which animal has a good sense of smell?* *a hyena* *How do you know?* *The text says that if you're a hyena, you find your next meal with your nose.* **RI.K.4, RI.1.4**
- Reread pages 10 and 11. Ask: *Which animal probably lives in a hot place?* *the jackrabbit* *How do you know?* *The text says that jackrabbits use their ears to keep them cool. If they need to stay cool, they probably live some place where it is hot.* **SL.K.2, SL.1.2**
- Reread and display page 15. Ask: *What does the monkey's tail look like?* *It looks like a hook.* **RI.K.7, RI.1.7**

### ENGLISH LANGUAGE LEARNERS

**Use Visuals**

Point to and say the name of each animal on pages 6 and 7. Have children repeat each name and point to the corresponding animal. Have children take turns asking and answering questions about the animals.

### RESPOND TO SEGMENT 1

**Classroom Collaboration**

Have partners summarize what they have learned about animals so far. Tell them to ask questions about anything they don't understand.

## ENGLISH LANGUAGE LEARNERS

**Use Gestures**

Point to and name body parts, such as eyes, feet, mouth, nose, and ears. Have children point to each body part as you say it and repeat the name. Have them point to and name the corresponding body part on one of the animals in the book.

**RESPOND TO SEGMENT 2**

**Classroom Collaboration**

Have small groups work together to summarize what they have read so far. Have them ask questions about what they don't understand.

**Common Core Connection**

**RI.K.7** describe relationships between illustrations and the text; **W.K.2** use drawing, dictating, and writing to compose informative/explanatory texts; **W.K.5** respond to questions/suggestions from peers and add details to strengthen writing; **SL.K.2** confirm understanding of a text read aloud, information presented orally, or through other media by asking/answering questions and requesting clarification; **SL.K.3** ask and answer questions to seek help, get information, or clarify something not understood; **SL.K.6** speak audibly and express thoughts, feelings, and ideas clearly

**RI.1.5** know and use text features to locate facts or information; **RI.1.7** use illustrations and details to describe key ideas; **RI.1.10** read informational texts; **W.1.2** write informative/explanatory texts; **W.1.5** focus on a topic, respond to questions/suggestions from peers, and add details to strengthen writing; **SL.1.2** ask and answer questions about details in a text read aloud, information presented orally, or through other media; **SL.1.6** produce complete sentences when appropriate to task and situation

## FIRST READ Think Through the Text

Have children use text evidence to answer these questions.

**pp. 16–19** • *How does a four-eyed fish use its eyes? A four-eyed fish uses its eyes to look above and below the water at the same time.* **SL.K.2, SL.1.2**

**pp. 20–23** • *Why does the gecko have sticky feet? It walks on ceilings. What might happen if the gecko did not have sticky feet? It would fall off the ceiling.* **SL.K.2, SL.1.2**

**pp. 24–27** • *How do all the animals use their mouths? All the animals use their mouths to eat.* **RI.K.3, RI.1.3**

## SECOND READ Analyze the Text

- Guide children to look at the pictures on pages 22–23. Ask: *Which foot looks like a hand? the chimpanzee's Why do you think the chimpanzee's foot might look like a hand? The chimpanzee uses its feet to feed itself, just like we use our hands to feed ourselves.* **RI.K.7, RI.1.7**
- Reread the description of the mosquito on page 26 and have children look at the picture. Ask: *What does the mosquito's mouth look like?* Sample answer: *a straw or a needle Why do you think the mosquito's mouth looks like this?* Sample answer: *The mosquito sucks blood, so it uses its mouth like a straw or a needle.* **RI.K.7, RI.1.7**
- Reread the description of the anteater on page 27. Ask: *How does the illustration go with the text? The text says that anteaters have long tongues, and the illustration shows an anteater with its long tongue.* **RI.K.7, RI.1.7**
- Have children look through the text and ask and answer questions about the different animals. Guide them to refer to the animals by name as they ask and answer the questions. For example: *How are a chameleon's eyes different than a bush baby's eyes? A chameleon's eyes are on either side of its head so it can see in two different directions at the same time; a bush baby has two big eyes in front so it can only see in one direction, but it can see really well at night.* **RI.K.4, RI.1.4**

## FIRST READ Think Through the Text

Have children use text evidence to answer these questions.

**p. 28** • *Earlier in the book, we saw a picture of a mole. It had an unusual star-shaped nose. Now I just read more about the mole's nose. Why does the mole have a star-shaped nose?* Its nose is like fingers that help it find its way underground. **SL.K.2, SL.1.2**

**p. 29** • *Earlier in the book, we read about the jackrabbit and decided that it must live in hot places. Now I just read more about the jackrabbit. Where does the antelope jackrabbit live?* in the deserts of the American Southwest **SL.K.2, SL.1.2**

**p. 30** • *Earlier in the book, we read about how the chimpanzee's feet look like our hands. Now I just read more about the chimpanzee. What is one way chimpanzees are like people?* They have opposable thumbs. *What does it mean to have opposable thumbs?* They can use the thumb on each hand to touch each of their other fingers. *What is one way they are different?* They have opposable big toes. **SL.K.2, SL.1.2**

## SECOND READ Analyze the Text

- Show children pages 28–31. Ask: *If you were reading this book on your own, how would you use this part of the book? Think about how we just used it together.* Sample answer: *I would use it to find more information about each kind of animal.* **SL.K.2, RI.1.5**
- Guide children to look at pages 28–31, pointing out text features such as the headings, the illustrations, and the bold-faced type. Ask: *If you wanted to find more information about the yellow-winged bat, how could you look for it in this section?* I would look in the Ears section. I would look for the word bat in dark type and for the picture of the bat. **SL.K.2, RI.1.5**
- Have children share additional questions they have about the different animals. Model reading aloud about one of the animals to find the answer. **SL.K.3, SL.1.2**

# Independent/Self-Selected Reading

If children have already demonstrated listening comprehension of *What Do You Do with a Tail Like This?*, have them practice reading comprehension skills using an independent reading book. Model selecting a book from the classroom library. Help them read the title of the book, the author's name, and any information about the book on the back or inside cover. Suggested titles:

- *Animals Grow and Change* by Bobbie Kalman
- *Big Beasts* by Katharine Kenah **RI.1.10**

### WRITE & PRESENT

1. Have small groups work together to ask and answer questions about the animals, including the illustrations and text details. **SL.K.2, SL.1.2**
2. Ask children to choose an animal from the selection and write a question about how it uses a certain body part, such as its eyes or tail. Then have them write an answer to their question, including at least one detail. Guide children to use pages 28–31 to find additional details. Tell them to draw a picture that shows the animal using its special body part. **W.K.2, W.1.2**
3. Have children share their drawings and writing with their small group. Ask them to add details to their writing based on their group's suggestions. **W.K.5, W.1.5**
4. Ask children to present their work to classmates. Encourage classmates to ask and answer questions about the presentation. **SL.K.6, SL.1.6**

*See Copying Masters, pp. 242–245.*

### STUDENT CHECKLIST

**Writing**

- ✔ Write a question about how an animal uses a body part.
- ✔ Write an answer to the question that includes at least one detail.
- ✔ Use correct language conventions.

**Speaking & Listening**

- ✔ Participate effectively in a collaborative discussion.
- ✔ Ask and answer questions about text details.
- ✔ Describe details in their writing and drawing.

## OBJECTIVES

- Describe relationships between illustrations and the text
- Understand the life cycle of a pumpkin
- Analyze text using text evidence

***From Seed to Pumpkin* is broken into three instructional segments.**

SEGMENTS



### Options for Read-Aloud

*Be sure to display the book's pictures and read with expression to model fluent reading.*

**Uninterrupted** Focus on the flow of the story by reading aloud without stopping for comments or questions.

**Interactive** Stop at appropriate places while reading to make comments and ask children questions. Also, invite children to share their own comments and questions.

### Common Core Connection

**RI.K.3** describe the connections between individuals, events, ideas, or information in a text; **RI.K.7** describe relationships between illustrations and the text; **SL.K.2** confirm understanding of a text read aloud, information presented orally, or through other media by asking/answering questions and requesting clarification

**RI.1.3** describe the connection between individuals, events, ideas, or information in a text; **RI.1.7** use illustrations and details to describe key ideas; **SL.1.2** ask and answer questions about details in a text read aloud, information presented orally, or through other media

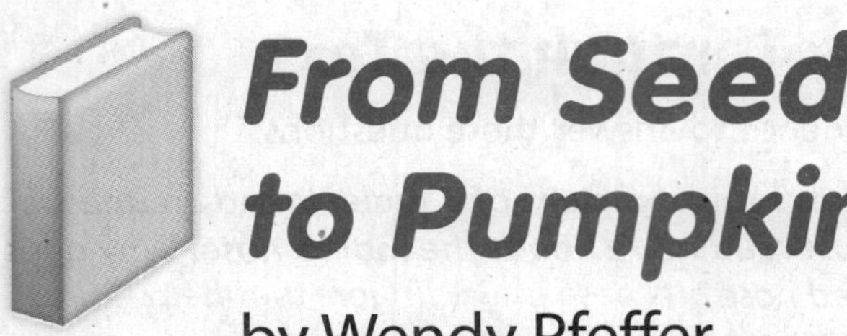

# *From Seed to Pumpkin*

by Wendy Pfeffer

**SUMMARY** This book tells about the life cycle of the pumpkin plant. Detailed illustrations and helpful graphic features supplement the informational text.

**ABOUT THE AUTHOR** **Wendy Pfeffer** has written many books for children about science and nature. Many of her ideas come from observing the world around her. Pfeffer also visits schools to conduct writing workshops with children.

## Discuss Genre and Set Purpose

**INFORMATIONAL TEXT** Display the book and read the title together. Discuss with children that an informational book gives facts, or true information, about a topic. Guide children to point out the graphic features, such as the cut-away diagram on pages 6–7, that provide additional information.

**SET PURPOSE** Help children set a purpose for listening, such as to find out information about how pumpkin seeds grow into pumpkins.

### TEXT COMPLEXITY RUBRIC

| Overall Text Complexity | | *From Seed to Pumpkin* INFORMATIONAL TEXT<br>ACCESSIBLE |
|---|---|---|
| Quantitative Measures | Lexile | N/A |
| | Guided Reading Level | N/A |
| Qualitative Measures | Text Structure | largely simple graphics, supplementary to understanding text |
| | Language Conventionality and Clarity | some unfamiliar or academic words |
| | Knowledge Demands | some specialized knowledge required |
| | Purpose/Levels of Meaning | explicitly stated |

## SEGMENT 1 pp. 4–13

**Academic Vocabulary**

Read each word with children and discuss its meaning.

**moist** (p. 6) • damp; a little bit wet

**energy** (p. 10) • power; strength to do something

**attract** (p. 19) • to cause something to come near

**wither** (p. 20) • to shrink or dry up

**bare** (p. 29) • uncovered

**remain** (p. 29) • stay in the same place

## FIRST READ Think Through the Text

Have children use text evidence to answer these questions.

**pp. 4–5** • *What season is it?* spring *What is the farmer doing?* planting pumpkin seeds SL.K.2, SL.1.2

**p. 8** • Have children look at the illustration. Ask: *What are green shoots? Green shoots are little stems poking up from the earth. Where do they come from? They grow from the seeds and are now long enough to show above the ground.* RI.K.7, RI.1.7

**p. 11** *How do plants make food? The leaves use energy from the sun, air, and water from the soil to make sugar that feeds the plant.* SL.K.2, SL.1.2

**pp. 12–13** *How are new leaves and seed leaves different? The new leaves are rough and prickly. The seed leaves are smooth and rounded.* RI.K.3, RI.1.3

## SECOND READ Analyze the Text

- Have children look at the illustrations on the first several pages. Ask: *How can you tell from the pictures that it is springtime? The trees have green leaves on them; the farmer and children are wearing short-sleeved shirts and hats; the sun is shining.* RI.K.7, RI.1.7
- Reread pages 6–7. Point out how the text and the pictures go together to give information. Say: *The text says that roots dig down and that there are tubes inside them. It also says that water from the soil goes up the tubes, just like juice goes up a straw.* Ask: *How does the picture support this information? The illustrator circled some of the roots and pointed an arrow to a picture of a girl drinking from a straw. Those pictures match the text.* RI.K.7, RI.1.7
- Ask children to summarize what they have learned so far about the life cycle of a pumpkin. Remind them that a summary includes only the most important details. Sample answer: *Pumpkin seeds grow in soil; shoots come through the earth and become seedlings. The seedlings grow new leaves.* SL.K.2, SL.1.2

### ENGLISH LANGUAGE LEARNERS

**Use Visuals**

Use the illustrations to explain words such as *seeds, roots, tubes,* and *shoots*. Point to each word, and have children repeat after you. Then reinforce word meanings by having children complete sentence frames such as:

*The farmer plants _____.* seeds

*The _____ grow down in the ground.* roots

### RESPOND TO SEGMENT 1

**Classroom Collaboration**

Have partners summarize what they have learned so far about the life cycle of a pumpkin. Encourage them to ask questions about anything they don't understand.

**ENGLISH LANGUAGE LEARNERS**

**Use Gestures**

Use gestures or demonstration to clarify words and phrases such as *up, down, stand tall, open, close,* and *grow larger and larger*. Have children repeat after you and then use the words and phrases in oral sentences.

**RESPOND TO SEGMENT 2**

**Classroom Collaboration**

Have small groups work together to create a short summary, as well as raise questions that might be answered in the next segment.

COMMON CORE **Common Core Connection**

**RI.K.3** describe the connections between individuals, events, ideas, or information in a text; **RI.K.7** describe relationships between illustrations and the text; **W.K.2** use drawing, dictating, and writing to compose informative/explanatory texts; **W.K.5** respond to questions/suggestions from peers and add details to strengthen writing; **SL.K.2** confirm understanding of a text read aloud, information presented orally, or through other media by asking/answering questions and requesting clarification ; **SL.K.3** ask and answer questions to seek help, get information, or clarify something not understood; **SL.K.6** speak audibly and express thoughts, feelings, and ideas clearly

**RI.1.3** describe the connection between individuals, events, ideas, or information in a text; **RI.1.7** use illustrations and details to describe key ideas; **RI.1.10** read informational texts; **W.1.2** write informative/explanatory texts; **W.1.5** focus on a topic, respond to questions/suggestions from peers, and add details to strengthen writing; **SL.1.2** ask and answer questions about details in a text read aloud, information presented orally, or through other media; **SL.1.6** produce complete sentences when appropriate to task and situation

## FIRST READ Think Through the Text

Have children use text evidence to answer these questions.

**pp. 14–15 •** *What do the tubes in a pumpkin stem do?* *In each set of tubes, one tube takes water to the leaves. The other tube sends food back down to the roots.* **SL.K.2, SL.1.2**

**pp. 16–17 •** *How do pumpkin plants grow?* *They spread out over the ground.* **SL.K.2, SL.1.2**

**pp. 18–19 •** *How do the flowers look different during the day than they do at night?* *During the day, the flowers are closed. At night, the flowers open and bees buzz around them.* **RI.K.3, RI.1.3**

**pp. 20–21 •** *What happens to the pumpkins during the summer?* *The flowers wither and hard fruits grow on the vines. These fruits grow larger and larger.* **SL.K.2, SL.1.2**

## SECOND READ Analyze the Text

- Show children page 14. Say: *The text tells us that one tube takes water from the soil up to the leaves. The other tube takes food back down so the pumpkin can grow. How does the illustration show this?* *The illustration includes one arrow pointing up to show that one tube takes water up to the leaves. It also has a down arrow to show that one tube sends food down so the plant can grow.* **RI.K.7, RI.1.7**
- Reread page 19. Ask: *Can pumpkins grow without bees?* no *Why do you think that?* *Bees take the pollen from the male flowers to the female flowers so that pumpkins can grow.* **SL.K.2, SL.1.2**
- Show children page 21. Say: *How can you use the picture to understand the text better?* Sample answer: *The text says that the fruits grow larger. The picture shows how large the fruits grow.* **RI.K.7, RI.1.7**
- Have children review what they learned about the life cycle of a pumpkin in the first segment. Then ask them to explain what happens next. Sample answer: *The stems grow into vines; flowers bud; hard fruits begin to grow and then get bigger and bigger.* **RI.K.3, RI.1.3**

SEGMENT 3 pp. 22–31

## FIRST READ Think Through the Text

Have children use text evidence to answer these questions.

**pp. 22–23** • *What is happening outside that shows that summer is over?* *The corn stalks are turning brown; the leaves are turning red, orange, and yellow; and the pumpkins are changing color.* **SL.K.2, SL.1.2**

**pp. 26–27** • *What will happen to the pumpkins?* *Some will be made into jack-o'-lanterns; others will be turned into pumpkin pies.* **RI.K.3, RI.1.3**

**pp. 28–31** • *How does the pumpkin patch look different in the winter than it looks in the spring?* *In winter, only a few dead vines remain. In spring, there are green shoots after the farmer plants the new pumpkin seeds.* **RI.K.3, RI.1.3**

## SECOND READ Analyze the Text

- Reread page 22. Point to the picture and ask: *How does the illustration help show what season it is?* *The leaves have changed color and are falling off the tree. The children are wearing long-sleeved shirts and pants.* **RI.K.7, RI.1.7**
- Guide children to look back through the illustrations on pages 22–25. Review what they have learned about vines and pumpkins. Ask: *What do you think would happen if pumpkin vines grew straight up?* Model using the text and illustrations to respond. Sample answer: *The text says that pumpkins grow big and fat. The illustration shows that the vines are thin. If the vines grew straight up, the pumpkins might be too heavy for them. Since the vines sprawl across the ground, the pumpkins can rest on the ground, too.* **RI.K.7, RI.1.7**
- Reread pages 28–31. Ask: *Why do farmers plant pumpkin seeds in spring instead of winter?* *It is cold in the winter. The text tells us that the pumpkin vines are dead in the winter. The pumpkin seeds need warm sun to help them grow, so the farmer waits for spring to plant them.* **RI.K.3, RI.1.3**

# Independent/Self-Selected Reading

If children have already demonstrated listening comprehension of *From Seed to Pumpkin,* have them practice comprehension skills using another book. Model selecting a book from the classroom library. Help them read the title of the book, the author's name, and any information about the book on the back or inside cover. Suggested titles:

- *Seeds* by Ken Robbins
- *How Flowers Grow* by Emma Helbrough **RI.1.10**

### WRITE & PRESENT

1. Have small groups discuss how text details and illustrations in the selection helped them understand how a pumpkin grows. Encourage children to ask and answer questions about the illustrations and text details. **SL.K.2, SL.1.2**
2. Individual children write a description of the key idea of how a pumpkin grows by using illustrations and textual details from the selection. Suggest that children add drawings to their descriptions. **W.K.2, W.1.2**
3. Have children share their drawings and writing with a partner. Ask them to add details to their writing based on their partner's suggestions. **W.K.5, W.1.5**
4. Individual children speak in audible, complete sentences to present their work. **SL.K.6, SL.1.6**

*See Copying Masters, pp. 242–245.*

### STUDENT CHECKLIST

#### Writing

- ✔ Write sentences that explain how a pumpkin grows.
- ✔ Draw pictures of a pumpkin to show the steps in this process.
- ✔ Use correct language conventions.

#### Speaking & Listening

- ✔ Participate effectively in a collaborative discussion.
- ✔ Ask and answer questions about text details.
- ✔ Describe details in their writing and drawing.

## OBJECTIVES

- Ask and answer questions to clarify understanding
- Use illustrations to comprehend text
- Identify facts about whales
- Analyze text using text evidence

**_Amazing Whales!_ is broken into three instructional segments.**

### SEGMENTS

**SEGMENT 1**. . . . . . . . .pp. 4–11
**SEGMENT 2**. . . . . . . .pp. 12–21
**SEGMENT 3**. . . . . . . .pp. 22–31

### Options for Reading

*Be sure to display the book's pictures and read with expression to model fluent reading.*

**Uninterrupted** Focus on the flow of the text by reading aloud without stopping for questions.

**Interactive** Stop at appropriate places while reading to make comments and ask questions. Also, invite children to share their own comments and questions.

### Common Core Connection

**RI.K.3** describe the connection between individuals, events, ideas or information in a text; **RI.K.4** ask and answer questions about unknown words; **RI.K.7** describe relationships between illustrations and the text; **SL.K.2** confirm understanding of a text read aloud, information presented orally, or through other media by asking/answering questions and requesting clarification

**RI.1.3** describe the connection between individuals, events, ideas or information in a text; **RI.1.4** ask and answer questions to determine or clarify the meaning of words and phrases; **RI.1.7** use illustrations and details to describe key ideas; **SL.1.2** ask and answer questions about details in a text read aloud, information presented orally, or through other media

# *Amazing Whales!*

by Sarah L. Thomson

**SUMMARY** This photo essay tells about the physical characteristics and habitats of humpbacks, killer, blue, and other kinds of whales (including dolphins and porpoises) and how scientists are trying to save them from extinction after many years of overhunting and environmental pollution.

**ABOUT THE AUTHOR** **Sarah L. Thomson** has written all the books in the Wildlife Conservation Society series. Along with *Amazing Whales!*, the series includes books on tigers, sharks, gorillas, and snakes. Of her clear, vivid style, the American Library Association says that Ms. Thomson writes with "admirable simplicity." A former children's book editor in New York, Thomson now writes full time in Maine.

## Discuss Genre and Set Purpose

**INFORMATIONAL TEXT** Display the cover of the book and read the title aloud. Page through the book with children, and point out the photographs. Discuss how the photos let them know that this book provides facts, or true information about real things.

**SET PURPOSE** Help children set a purpose for listening, such as to learn facts and details about whales.

### TEXT COMPLEXITY RUBRIC

| Overall Text Complexity | | *Amazing Whales!* INFORMATIONAL TEXT<br>ACCESSIBLE |
|---|---|---|
| Quantitative Measures | Lexile | N/A |
| | Guided Reading Level | N/A |
| Qualitative Measures | Text Structure | simple science |
| | Language Conventionality and Clarity | some unfamiliar or academic words |
| | Knowledge Demands | some specialized knowledge required |
| | Purpose/Levels of Meaning | single topic |

## SEGMENT 1 pp. 4–11

### Academic Vocabulary

Read each word with children and discuss its meaning.

**mammals** (p. 6) • animals that give birth to live babies

**temperature** (p. 6) • degree of warmth or coldness

**calf** (p. 9) • a baby cow or whale

**drown** (p. 9) • to die by sinking into water

## FIRST READ Think Through the Text

Have children use text evidence to answer these questions.

**pp. 2–3** • *What's special about the blue whale? It is the biggest animal that has ever lived on Earth. What comparisons does the author make to show how big it is? It is as long as a basketball court, its eyes are as big as softballs, and its tongue weighs as much as an elephant.* **SL.K.2, SL.1.2**

**pp. 4–5** • *How are dolphins and porpoises different from blue whales? They aren't as big. The smallest dolphin is only five feet long. Look at the photograph. What do they have on their backs? a fin* **RI.K.7, RI.1.7**

**pp. 6–7** • *What are mammals? Mammals are animals that do not lay eggs. They are warm-blooded.* **RI.K.4, RI.1.4**

**pp. 8–11** • *How does a whale mother lift its baby up to the surface of the ocean? The mother swims under the baby so that the baby is on her back. Then the mother swims up to the surface.* **RI.K.7, RI.1.7**

## SECOND READ Analyze the Text

- *On page 6, the text says that there are 80 kinds of whales. How are they all alike? They are all warm-blooded mammals that live in the ocean. They breathe air and have baby calves.* **RI.K.3, RI.1.3**
- *Pages 6–9 tell about mammals. What kinds of animals aren't mammals? Animals that lay eggs are not mammals. What are some examples of mammals given in the text? dogs, monkeys, and people* **RI.K.3, RI.1.3**
- Have children summarize what they have learned so far. Ask: *What are some important facts about whales? There are many different kinds of whales; they are different sizes; they are all mammals.* **SL.K.2, SL.1.2**

### Domain Specific Vocabulary

**warm-blooded** (p. 6) • having a body temperature that is steady and warm

**blowhole** (p. 10) • the opening on the top of a whale's head

**blow** (p. 10) • a column of mist that is formed when a whale blows through its blowhole

### ELL ENGLISH LANGUAGE LEARNERS

**Use Gestures**

Have children use gestures to demonstrate key concepts. To show that mammals breathe air, have children hold their breath and pretend to duck under water for a short period of time. Then ask them to resurface to breathe. Then ask them to use simple language to explain what they did.

### RESPOND TO SEGMENT 1

**Classroom Collaboration**

Have partners or small groups work together to create a chart to record questions and answers they have about whales.

### Domain Specific Vocabulary

**squid** (p. 13) • an animal with a soft body and ten arms

**krill** (p. 16) • tiny shrimp-like creatures

**pod** (p. 18) • a group of whales, dolphins, or porpoises

**breach** (p. 22) • jump out of the water and come splashing down

### ENGLISH LANGUAGE LEARNERS

**Model Pronunciation**

Model the pronunciation of challenging words, such as *toothed* and *baleen*. Say each of these words, and have children repeat after you. Have them use the words in oral sentences about whales.

### RESPOND TO SEGMENT 2

**Classroom Collaboration**

Have children work in small groups to summarize what they have learned and ask questions about anything they don't understand.

**Common Core Connection**

**W.K.5** respond to questions/suggestions from peers and add details to strengthen writing; **W.K.8** recall information from experiences or gather information from sources to answer a question; **SL.K.6** speak audibly and express thoughts, feelings, and ideas clearly

**RI.1.10** read informational texts; **W.1.5** focus on a topic, respond to questions/suggestions from peers, and add details to strengthen writing; **W.1.8** recall information from experience or gather information from sources to answer a question; **SL.1.6** speak audibly and express thoughts, feelings, and ideas clearly

## FIRST READ Think Through the Text

Have children use text evidence to answer these questions.

**pp. 12–15** • *What are the two kinds of whales? toothed whales and baleen whales* *How are they different? Toothed whales have hard, sharp teeth in their mouths. Baleen whales have baleen, which is made of the same material as fingernails. It's strong, but can bend.* **SL.K.2, SL.1.2**

**pp. 16–19** • *How do killer whales get their food? They hunt in pods. How do baleen whales get their food? They open and then shut their mouths. Krill and other small creatures are trapped inside. The whale then squeezes out the water and keeps the krill as food.* **SL.K.2, SL.1.2**

**pp. 20–21** • *What is one thing that killer whales and humpback whales have in common? They make sounds. What are some of the sounds they make? squeaks, whistles, groans, chirps, creaks How are male humpback whale sounds different? They make sounds over and over again for hours.* **SL.K.2, SL.1.2**

## SECOND READ Analyze the Text

- Review pages 15–17. Have children compare the way toothed whales get food with the way baleen whales get food. Ask: *Why do baleen whales need to trap fish or krill in their mouths? They don't have teeth to catch fish so they have to trap them.* **RI.K.3, RI.1.3**
- *Why do killer whales hunt in pods? It's easier to kill a big whale when they hunt in a group. How can you tell from the text how many whales might be in a pod? The text says a whale mother, and her children and even her grandchildren sometimes live in one pod, so that is at least five whales.* **RI.K.3, RI.1.3**
- Have children look through the photographs on pages 12–21. Ask: *What did you learn about whales from the photographs that you did not learn from the text?* Sample answer: *what different whales actually look like, including their shape and color* **RI.K.7, RI.1.7**

**Academic Vocabulary**

Read each word with children and discuss its meaning.

**signal** (p. 22) • send a sign or message

**survive** (p. 30) • stay alive

## FIRST READD Think Through the Text

Have children use text evidence to answer these questions.

**pp. 22–23** • *What is breaching? Breaching is when whales jump out of the water and splash back down. What do some people think breaching is? a way of communicating, or talking, with other whales* **SL.K.2, SL.1.2**

**pp. 24–25** • *Why are whales in danger? They are hunted by killer whales, sharks, and people.* **SL.K.2, SL.1.2**

**pp. 26–27** • *What are some things people do to harm whales? People dump trash or spill oil in the ocean where the whales live.* **SL.K.2, SL.1.2**

**pp. 30–31** • *What are some things people can do to help whales? People can keep the ocean clean and make safe places for whales to live.* **SL.K.2, SL.1.2**

## SECOND READ Analyze the Text

- Have children look at the photograph on pages 26–27. Ask: *How can you use the text to understand what is happening in the photograph? The text says whales get caught in fishing nets, and if they are not freed, they cannot swim to the surface. This makes me think that the person must be helping the whale get free.* **RI.K.7, RI.1.7**
- *What do scientists do when they go out in boats? They count whales. They follow them and learn more about them. Why do they do this? to try and figure out new ways to keep whales safe* **RL.K.3, RL.1.3**
- Read page 32 about The Wildlife Conservation Society and Whales. Ask: *Why did the author include this information? for people who want to know more about whales How do you know? The last paragraph names a website to go to if you want to find out more about whales and other endangered animals.* **SL.K.2, SL.1.2**

## Independent/Self-Selected Reading

If children have demonstrated listening comprehension of *Amazing Whales!*, have them practice comprehension skills using another book. Model selecting a book from the classroom library. Suggested titles:

- *DK Eyewitness Book: Whale* by Vassili Papasatavrou
- *Amazing Tigers!* by Sarah L. Thomson **RI.1.10**

### WRITE & PRESENT

1. Have children work in groups to ask and answer questions about details from the text. Have them use a KWL chart to organize their ideas. **SL.K.2, SL.1.2**
2. Children write a question from the KWL chart at the top of a page and respond to it with a written paragraph. Have them draw a picture to go with their information. **W.K.8, W.1.8**
3. Children work with partners to share their writings and drawings with each other and edit their work. **W.K.5, W.1.5**
4. Individual children present their final work to classmates. **SL.K.6, SL.1.6**

*See Copying Masters, pp. 242–245.*

### STUDENT CHECKLIST

**Writing**

- ✔ Include questions and answers.
- ✔ Give important facts.
- ✔ Use correct language conventions.

**Speaking & Listening**

- ✔ Communicate with group members.
- ✔ Listen while others speak.
- ✔ Speak clearly when giving a presentation.

## OBJECTIVES

- Identify important ideas and supporting details
- Describe the relationship between illustrations and text
- Describe the connection between drag and flying

*How People Learned to Fly* is broken into three instructional segments.

**SEGMENTS**

| | |
|---|---|
| SEGMENT 1 | pp. 4–13 |
| SEGMENT 2 | pp. 14–21 |
| SEGMENT 3 | pp. 22–31 |

### Options for Reading

*Be sure to display the book's pictures and read with expression to model fluent reading.*

**Uninterrupted** Focus on the flow of the text by reading aloud without stopping for comments or questions.

**Interactive** Stop at appropriate places while reading to make comments and ask children questions. Invite children to share their own comments and questions.

### Common Core Connection

**RI.K.3** describe the connection between individuals, events, ideas or information in a text; **RI.K.4** ask and answer questions about unknown words; **RI.K.7** describe relationships between illustrations and the text; **SL.K.2** confirm understanding of a text read aloud, information presented orally, or through other media by asking/answering questions and requesting clarification

**RI.1.3** describe the connection between individuals, events, ideas or information in a text; **RI.1.4** ask and answer questions to determine or clarify the meaning of words and phrases; **RI.1.7** use illustrations and details to describe key ideas; **SL.1.2** ask and answer questions about details in a text read aloud, information presented orally, or through other media

# How People Learned to Fly

by Fran Hodgkins

**SUMMARY** This informational text describes the progress from dreaming of flight to modern airplane travel. For ages, people watched birds, studied the laws of gravity, and made experimental aircraft. In 1903, the dream became a reality when the Wright brothers launched the first powered flight. Today, thousands of people travel in airplanes every day.

**ABOUT THE AUTHOR** **Fran Hodgkins** considers New England her home. She was born in Massachusetts and worked at a publishing house in Boston before moving to Maine to write nonfiction for children. In all, she has written over 18 books on a variety of topics.

## Discuss Genre and Set Purpose

**INFORMATIONAL TEXT** Display the cover and read the title aloud. Then page through the book with children, inviting them to comment on the pictures. Ask them whether they think the book tells a story or gives facts. Confirm that it is an informational text with facts about flying.

**SET PURPOSE** Help children set a purpose for listening, such as to learn information about flying.

**TEXT COMPLEXITY RUBRIC**

| Overall Text Complexity | | *How People Learned to Fly* INFORMATIONAL TEXT<br>ACCESSIBLE |
|---|---|---|
| Quantitative Measures | Lexile | N/A |
| | Guided Reading Level | N/A |
| Qualitative Measures | Text Structure | organization of main idea and details may be complex, but is clearly stated and generally sequential |
| | Language Conventionality and Clarity | some unfamiliar or academic words |
| | Knowledge Demands | some specialized knowledge required |
| | Purpose/Levels of Meaning | implied, but easy to identify from context |

**Academic Vocabulary**

Read each word with children and discuss its meaning.

**soaring** (p. 7) • flying high in the sky
**designed** (p. 11) • drew the plans and created
**gravity** (p. 12) • a force that pulls things toward Earth

## FIRST READ Think Through the Text

Have children use text evidence to answer these questions.

**pp. 4–7** • *How are birds, kites, and paper airplanes alike? They all fly through the air.* SL.K.2, SL.1.2

**pp. 8–9** • *What do the pictures on these two pages show? They show people around a fire telling stories. One story is about a horse with wings. The other story is about a young boy with wings who is falling into the ocean.* RI.K.7, RI.1.7

**pp. 10–11** • *What do the text and the pictures help you learn on these pages? People tried to build different kinds of flying machines and they learned a lot when the machines didn't work.* RI.K.7, RI.1.7

**pp. 12–13** • *What is gravity? Gravity is a force that keeps everything on earth.* RI.K.4, RI.1.4

## SECOND READ Analyze the Text

- *On pages 8–9, the text says that people told stories about people and animals that could fly. How do the pictures help you better understand the text?* Sample answer: *They show examples of two of these old stories.* RI.K.3, RI.1.3
- Point out that pages 10–11 show people trying out different kinds of flying machines. Remind children that the text says that people learned a lot as they tried out these ideas. Ask: *What do you think the people in these pictures learned?* Sample answer: *They learned how different kinds of wings work and that flying machines need power in order to lift people off the ground.* RI.K.3, RI.1.3
- *Pages 12–13 tell about gravity. Why is gravity important if you want to learn how to fly?* Sample answer: *Gravity pulls things down to earth. If you want to fly, you need to design a machine that is stronger than gravity and can move you away from earth.* RI.K.4, RI.1.4

**Use Visuals**

Show children pages 6–7 and name the things that can fly. Have children repeat the words after you. Ask children to use each word and the word *fly* in a complete sentence. Then ask them to name other things that can fly and use the words in sentences.

**RESPOND TO SEGMENT 1**

**Classroom Collaboration**

Have partners work together to share knowledge and ask questions about anything they don't understand.

### Domain Specific Vocabulary

**molecules** (p. 14) • smallest unit of a kind of matter with the properties of that substance

**gliders** (p. 22) • simple aircraft with wings and some moving parts but no engine

**currents** (p. 25) • masses of flowing air

**thrust** (p. 27) • a force that moves things forward

**aviation** (p. 32) • having to do with flight

### ENGLISH LANGUAGE LEARNERS

**Use Visuals**

To help children understand key words, refer to the visuals and ask questions that can be answered using the words. For example: *What does the picture on page 24 show?* a glider *How would you describe it?* It has long, thin wings.

### RESPOND TO SEGMENT 2

**Classroom Collaboration**

Have partners summarize key terms and related concepts. Have children refer to the illustrations to support ideas.

**Common Core Connection**

**W.K.2** use drawing, dictating, and writing to compose informative/explanatory texts; **W.K.5** respond to questions/suggestions from peers and add details to strengthen writing

**RI.1.10** read informational texts; **W.1.2** write informative/explanatory texts; **W.1.5** focus on a topic, respond to questions/suggestions from peers, and add details to strengthen writing

### Academic Vocabulary

Read each word with children and discuss its meaning.

**angle** (p. 15) • the place, position, and direction from which two surfaces meet

**useful** (p. 18) • easy or good to use

**flight** (p. 20) • a trip through the air

## FIRST READ Think Through the Text

Have children use text evidence to answer these questions.

**pp. 14–17** • *What is drag? Drag is when the wind pushes against something and slows it down. What else can the wind do to kites and other flying objects? It can lift them up into the air.* RI.K.3, RI.1.3

**pp. 18–19** • *What idea did people get by watching birds? that they would need wings to fly* SL.K.2, SL.1.2

**pp. 20–21** • *What are gliders? Look at the picture on page 21 if you're not sure. A glider is a simple flying machine. It is very light and has wings, but it doesn't have an engine.* RI.K.7, RI.1.7

## SECOND READ Analyze the Text

- Show children page 15. Ask: *How does the kite tail and string help keep the kite in the sky? They keep the kite at an angle to the wind that lets the wind lift it up.* RI.K.3, RI.1.3
- *How are gliders like kites? Gliders are like kites because they just use wind power. How are they different? They are bigger and more complicated than most kites. Plus, people can fly in gliders. Kites aren't big enough to carry people.* RI.K.3, RI.1.3
- Guide children to understand that the invention of early aircraft followed the same steps as a lot of other inventions. Help children summarize the important steps in the invention process, referring specifically to the invention of flying machines. Ask: *How do you know people wanted to learn to fly? They told stories about flying and studied animals and things that could fly. How did people learn more about flying? They experimented and made simple models. Why were people eventually successful? They tried a lot of different ideas until they found ones that worked.* RI.K.3, RI.1.3

**Academic Vocabulary**

Read each word with children and discuss its meaning.

**arched** (p. 22) • having an upward curve
**engine** (p. 26) • a machine that turns energy into movement
**cargo** (p. 27) • suitcases and other things carried on an airplane

## FIRST READ Think Through the Text

Have children use text evidence to answer these questions.

**pp. 25–27** • *Why were engines added to airplanes? An engine helps an airplane move forward faster and creates more lift. What can an airplane with an engine do that a glider cannot do? It can carry extra weight.* SL.K.2, SL.1.2

**pp. 28–31** • *Who built the first successful powered airplane? When was it built? The Wright brothers built the first successful powered aircraft in 1903. In what ways has air travel changed since then? Airplanes can now fly faster than sound. They can fly around the world without landing.* SL.K.2, SL.1.2

## SECOND READ Analyze the Text

- Review the content and illustrations on pages 22–23. Ask: *What would happen if a wing only had an arch on the bottom, not on the top? It wouldn't fly very well. The air would push the wing on the bottom, but it wouldn't pull the wing on top.* RI.K.7, RI.1.7
- Review pages 22–23 and pages 26–27. Then ask: *What's the difference between lift and thrust? Lift is the force that carries an aircraft higher into the air. Thrust is a force that makes an aircraft go forward.* RI.K.3, RI.1.3
- Reread pages 32–33. Point out that these pages have special features. Ask: *What do they tell about? One page gives facts about the history of flying. The other page gives directions for making a paper airplane. Why do you think these features were included?* Sample answer: *They were included to give more information about flying.* SL.K.2, SL.1.2

## Independent/Self-Selected Reading

If children have demonstrated comprehension of *How People Learned to Fly*, have them practice and apply skills using another book. Model selecting a book from the classroom library. Help children read the title of the book, the author's name, and any information about the book on the back or inside cover. Suggested titles:

- *Forces Make Things Move* by Kimberly Brubaker Bradley
- *Kids' Paper Airplane Book* by Ken Blackburn RI.1.10

### WRITE & PRESENT

1. Have children perform the "arm spinning" experiment described on pages 16–17. Have them talk about what they feel against their arms as they spin. Remind children that the push of air they feel is called drag. Have children talk about the connection between drag and flying. RI.K.3, RI.1.3
2. Ask partners to work together to write a paragraph about how performing the arm-spinning experiment helped them understand the connection between drag and flying. Suggest they draw a picture to accompany their paragraph. W.K.2, W.1.2
3. Have partners share their writings and drawings in small groups and edit their work. W.K.5, W.1.5
4. Individual children turn in their final drafts to the teacher.

*See Copying Masters, pp. 242–245.*

### STUDENT CHECKLIST

**Writing**

- ✔ Write about and illustrate how the arm-spinning experiment helped show the connection between drag and flying.
- ✔ Include details.
- ✔ Use correct language conventions.

**Speaking & Listening**

- ✔ Engage effectively in collaborative conversations.
- ✔ Ask and answer questions about the experiment.
- ✔ Describe the experiment in their own writing and drawing.

# "Mix a Pancake"

by Christina Rossetti (1893)

Illustrated by Arthur Hughes (from the 1893 edition)

Mix a pancake,
Stir a pancake,
　Pop it in the pan;
Fry the pancake,
Toss the pancake,—
　Catch it if you can.

# "Singing-Time"

by Rose Fyleman (1919)

I wake in the morning early
And always, the very first thing,
I poke out my head and I sit up in bed
And I sing and I sing and I sing.

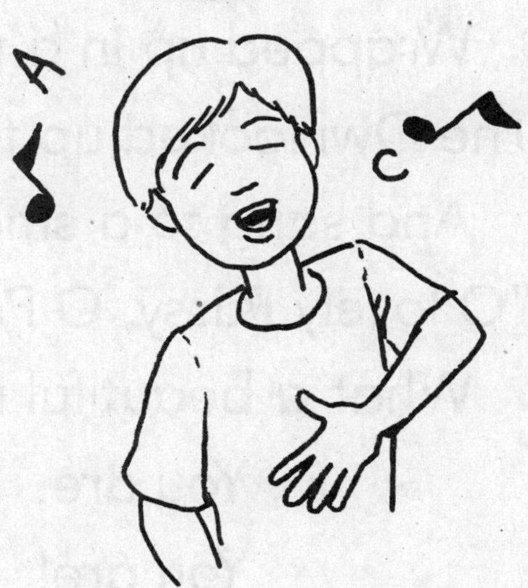

# "The Owl and the Pussy-Cat"

Written and illustrated by Edward Lear (1871)

I

The Owl and the Pussy-Cat went to sea
    In a beautiful pea-green boat:
They took some honey, and plenty of money
    Wrapped up in a five-pound note.
The Owl looked up to the stars above,
    And sang to a small guitar,
"O lovely Pussy, O Pussy, my love,
    What a beautiful Pussy you are,
            You are,
            You are!
    What a beautiful Pussy you are!"

II

Pussy said to the Owl, "You elegant fowl,
How charmingly sweet you sing!
Oh! let us be married; too long we have tarried:
But what shall we do for a ring?"
They sailed away, for a year and a day,
To the land where the bong-tree grows;
And there in a wood a Piggy-wig stood,
With a ring at the end of his nose,
His nose,
His nose,
With a ring at the end of his nose.

III

"Dear Pig, are you willing to sell for one shilling
   Your ring?" Said the Piggy, "I will."
So they took it away, and were married next day
   By the Turkey who lives on the hill.
They dined on mince, and slices of quince,
   Which they ate with a runcible spoon;
And hand in hand, on the edge of the sand,
   They danced by the light of the moon,
         The moon,
         The moon,
   They danced by the light of the moon.

# Academic Vocabulary

**Little Bear**
beautiful
birthday
friends
snow

***Are You My Mother?***
could
where

***Green Eggs and Ham***
anywhere
ham
try
would

***Put Me in the Zoo***
violet

***Frog and Toad Together***
afraid
brave
dream
list
seed

***Owl at Home***
guest
pleasant
whirled
whooshed

***Pancakes for Breakfast***
batter
ingredients
sift

***Hi! Fly Guy***
amazing
pest
rescue
surprised

**"As I Was Going to St. Ives"**
kits
wife

**"Mix a Pancake"**
pancake
stir
toss

**"Singing Time"**
early
poke
wake

**"Halfway Down"**
halfway
instead
nursery

**"Drinking Fountain"**
fountain

**"Poem"**
soft

**"Wouldn't You?"**
blow

**"Laughing Boy"**
palms

**"By Myself"**
dimple
gong
gospel

**"Covers"**
asleep
cover
creep
nighttime

**"It Fell in the City"**
hydrants

**"Celebration"**
dusk
feasting
leaps
stomps

**"Two Tree Toads"**
alas
sighed

***The Wonderful Wizard of Oz***
astonished
bounded
broad
dazzled
fierce
grateful
gravely
meek
misfortune
ordinary
rejoicing
scramble
shriek
wept

***Little House in the Big Woods***
chores
harvest
mend
muzzle
primly
savage
scampering
sleek
solemn
spacious
stoop
stump
swift

***Mr. Popper's Penguins***
curious
decision
famous
flippers
pecking
plunge
stroll
strut
sulking
trained
untidy
voyage
waddling

***Finn Family Moomintroll***
clambered
departure
lure
pandemonium
suspicious

***A Story, A Story***
captives
chuckled
command
crept
flamboyant
frond
furious
proclaimed
related
royal
spun
tatter
terrible

***The Paper Crane***
company
gentle
guests
overjoyed
perform
travelers

***Lon Po Po: A Red-Riding Hood Story from China***
cunning
disguised
embraced
furious

***Family Pictures***
border
future
scene
shelter

***Tomás and the Library Lady***
cot
chattered
dump
eager
thorny

***Kitten's First Full Moon***
full moon
porch
tumbled

**"The Fox's Foray"**
declared
foray
married
shrill
strife

**"April Rain Song"**
gutter
lullaby

***Zin! Zin! Zin! a Violin***
bleating
coiled
descends
galore
mellow
mournful
silken
sleek
slender
sliver

***A Tree Is a Plant***
bare
bark
blossoms
ripe
soil
stem

***My Five Senses***
aware
senses
sight
touch

***Starfish***
float
glide
prickly
underside

***A Weed Is a Flower: The Life of George Washington Carver***
advice
agriculture
college
crops
slaves

***Truck***
diner
limit
speed
tunnel

***I Read Signs***
beware
caution
detour
express
lane

***Let's Find Out About Ice Cream***
blends
factory
pumps
spiral
tanks
warehouse

**"Garden Helpers"**
pests
soil
web

**"Wind Power"**
electricity
energy
whip up
windmill
rises

***The Year at Maple Hill Farm***
conveyor
divided
eaves
harvest
marshy
migrant
molt
shorn
suspicious
temperamental
windfall

***Fire! Fire!***
aerial
attach
blares
equipment
report

***Follow the Water from Brook to Ocean***
erosion
gush
journey
polluted

***Water, Water Everywhere***
cycle
planet
pollute
surface

***Earthworms***
crawl
segment
soil
surface
tube
tunnel

***What Do You Do With a Tail Like This?***
capture
opposable
pesky
warn

***From Seed to Pumpkin***
attract
bare
energy
moist
remain
wither

***Amazing Whales!***
calf
drown
mammals
signal
survive
temperature

***How People Learned to Fly***
angle
arched
cargo
designed
engine
flight
gravity
soaring
useful

Name ____________________

# *Little Bear*

**Teacher:** Have children choose one key event from a story in *Little Bear*. Ask them to write sentences to tell the beginning, middle, and end of the story they chose. Remind children to use correct punctuation and capitalization. Then suggest that they draw three pictures on the back of this sheet to illustrate the three parts of the story. Encourage children to share their work with the class and tell how their writing relates to the parts of the story.

Name ______________________________

# *Are You My Mother?*

**Teacher**: Have children write sentences that give information about their favorite part of the book *Are You My Mother?* They may wish to continue their writing and illustrate their sentences on the back of this sheet. When children are finished, ask them to share their work with the class.

Name

# *Green Eggs and Ham*

**Teacher:** Have children write sentences about one prediction they made while reading *Green Eggs and Ham*. Ask them to describe their predictions and tell whether the predictions were correct. Remind children to use correct punctuation and capitalization. Then have them draw a picture in the space above to show their prediction. Finally invite children to share their work with the class.

Name ______________________________

# Put Me in the Zoo

**Teacher:** Have children write sentences to give their opinion about whether the zoo would be a good place for Spot. Encourage them to use details to support their opinion. Tell children to use the back of this sheet to continue their writing or to draw a picture. Remind them to use correct punctuation and capitalization in their sentences. Then invite children to share their work with the class.

Name ___________________________________________

# Frog and Toad Together

**Teacher:** Have children choose an important lesson about friendship that they learned from reading about Toad and Frog's adventures. Have them write sentences to describe the big idea and use details to explain the lesson. Children may wish to use the back of this sheet to continue their writing or to draw a picture. Remind them to use correct punctuation and capitalization. Then ask children to share their work with the class.

Name ______________________________

# *Owl at Home*

**Teacher:** Have children write sentences to tell what is the same and what is different between the characters and events in *Owl at Home* and those in "The Owl and the Pussy-Cat." Remind children to use correct punctuation and capitalization. Then have children draw a scene or a character from each text to illustrate their sentences. Finally ask children to share their work with the class.

Name ______________________________

# *Pancakes for Breakfast*

**Teacher:** Have children write sentences to explain how they know that *Pancakes for Breakfast* is a story and "Mix a Pancake" is a poem. They may wish to use the back of this sheet to continue their writing. Remind children to use correct punctuation and capitalization. Children may also wish to draw pictures of images from both texts. Then invite children to share their work with the class.

Name ______________________________

# *Hi! Fly Guy*

**Teacher:** Have children write sentences about the story events that include details that tell the beginning, middle, and end of the story. Remind them to use correct punctuation and capitalization in their writing. Then ask children to draw a picture to illustrate each part of the story. Finally ask volunteers to share their work with the class.

Name ___________________________

# "As I Was Going to St. Ives"

**Teacher:** Have children write sentences that describe the ways that repetition is used in the nursery rhyme "As I Was Going to St. Ives." Remind children to use correct punctuation and capitalization. Then ask them to draw a picture to illustrate the nursery rhyme. Finally encourage children to share their work with the class.

Name ______________________________

# "Mix a Pancake"

**Teacher**: Help children write sentences to explain how they know that "Mix a Pancake" is a poem and *Pancakes for Breakfast* is a story. They may wish to use the back of this sheet to continue their writing. Remind children to use correct punctuation and capitalization. Children may also wish to draw pictures of images from both texts. Then invite children to share their work with the class.

Name ______________________________

# "Singing-Time"

**Teacher:** Have children write sentences to explain how rhythm and repetition help create the mood in "Singing-Time." Remind them to use correct punctuation and capitalization. Children may wish to continue their writing and draw a picture about the poem on the back of this sheet. Finally ask volunteers to share their work with the class.

Name ______________________________

# "Halfway Down"

**Teacher**: Have children write sentences to tell how rhyme and visual presentation make the poem "Halfway Down" fun to read. Remind children to use correct punctuation and capitalization. They may choose to draw a picture about the poem on the back of this sheet. Then invite children to share their work with the class.

Name ____________________

# "Drinking Fountain"

**Teacher:** Have children choose one scene from the poem "Drinking Fountain." Ask them to write sentences about the visual imagery in the scene they chose. Remind children to use correct punctuation and capitalization. Then encourage children to illustrate their sentences on the back of this sheet. Finally have volunteers share their work with the class.

Name ___

# "Poem"

**Teacher**: Help children write sentences to describe how tone and repetition help create the mood in the poem. They may wish to continue their writing and illustrate their sentences on the back of this sheet. Remind children to use correct punctuation and capitalization. Then invite them to share their work with the class.

Name ______________________________

# "Wouldn't You?"

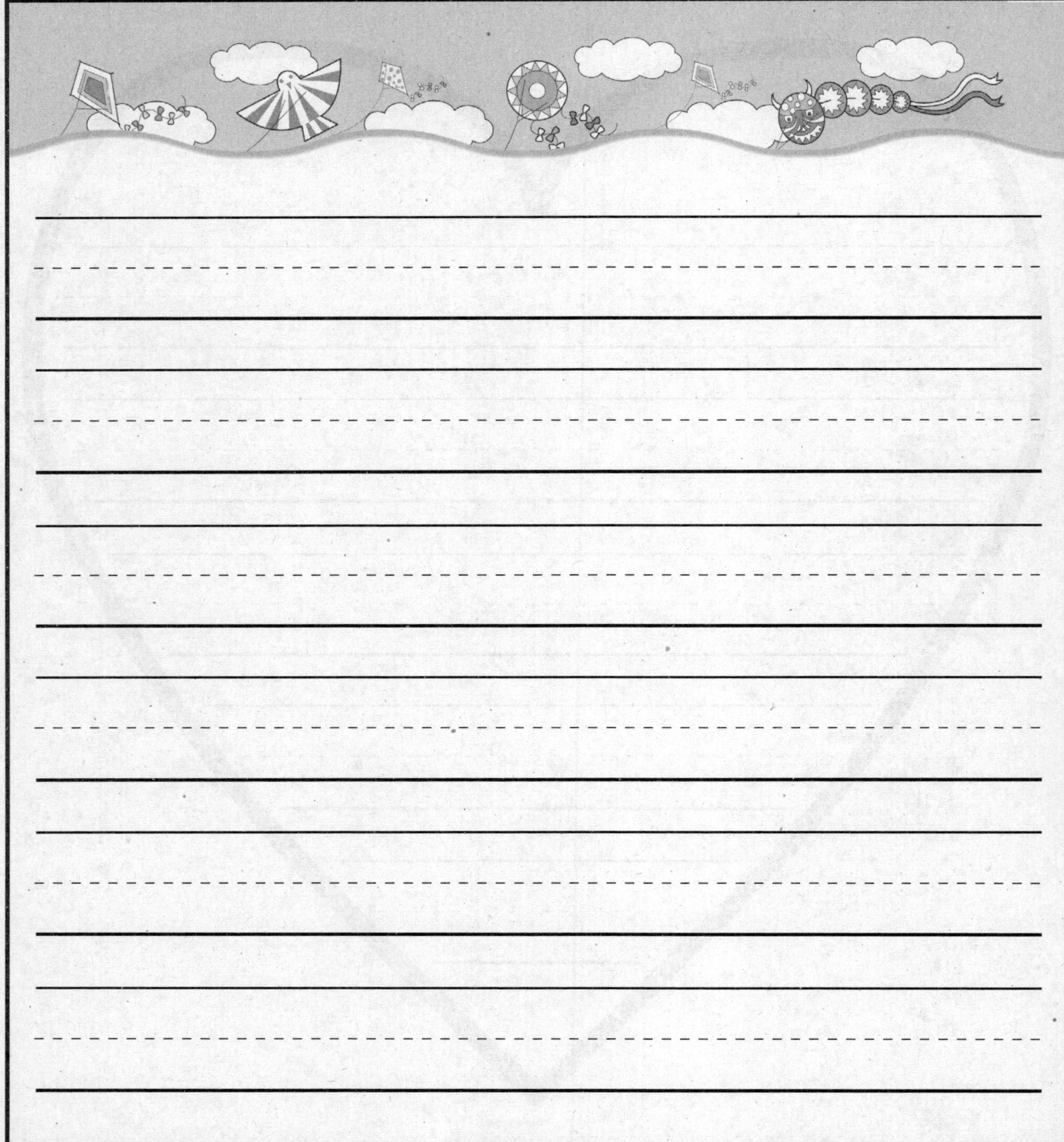

**Teacher:** Help children write sentences to explain how rhyme and repetition make the poem "Wouldn't You?" fun to read. They may wish to continue their sentences and draw a picture on the back of this sheet. Remind children to use correct punctuation and capitalization. Finally encourage children to share their work with the class.

COMMON CORE

Name ______________________________

# "Laughing Boy"

**Teacher**: Have children give their opinion of whether they like haikus. Then guide them to write sentences about their opinion and to include details from the poem "Laughing Boy" to support it. Remind children to use correct punctuation and capitalization. Then tell children to use the back of this sheet to draw a picture about the poem. Finally invite volunteers to share their work with the class.

Name ______________________________

# "By Myself"

**Teacher:** Have children write sentences to tell why they like themselves. Then invite children to illustrate their sentences. Finally ask volunteers to share their work with the class.

Name ______________________________

# "Covers"

Teacher: Have children choose one or more scenes from the poem "Covers." Ask them to write sentences to describe the scene or scenes they chose. Remind children to use correct punctuation and capitalization. Then invite children to illustrate their writing. Finally have volunteers share their work with the class.

Name ________________________________________________

# "It Fell in the City"

**Teacher:** Have children write sentences about what they liked in the poem. Ask them to include two reasons with details from the poem to support their opinions. Remind children to use correct punctuation and capitalization. Then suggest that they draw an image from the poem that they especially liked on the back of this sheet. Finally have children share their work with the class.

COMMON CORE

Name ______________________________

# "Celebration"

**Teacher**: Help partners use a computer to research an American Indian celebration. Have children use vivid verbs from the poem "Celebration" and other verbs to write sentences about the celebration they researched. Remind children to use correct punctuation and capitalization. Then ask children to illustrate the American Indian celebration. Finally have them share their work by speaking clearly in a voice that can be understood by others.

Name ______________________________

# "Two Tree Toads"

**Teacher:** Have children choose one animal and help them write sentences that use alliteration with the initial sound of that animal's name. Tell children to include details about what the animal looks like and how it acts. Then invite children to use the back of this sheet to continue their writing and to draw a picture of the animal. Remind children to use correct punctuation and capitalization. Finally have volunteers share their work with the class.

Name ______________________________

# *The Wonderful Wizard of Oz*



**Teacher**: Have children draw a picture that shows one major event in *The Wonderful Wizard of Oz*. Then help them write about the event in their picture. Tell children to be sure to include details about the setting and the characters involved. Remind them to use correct punctuation and capitalization. Then invite volunteers to share their work with the class.

Name ____________________

# *Little House in the Big Woods*

**Teacher:** Have children write sentences about one key event from *Little House in the Big Woods*. Tell them to include details from the text to tell more about the event. Then suggest that they use the back of this sheet to illustrate the key event. Finally encourage children to share their work with the class and tell how their writing relates to the story.

Name ____________________

# *Mr. Popper's Penguins*

**Teacher**: Have children write sentences about one key event in *Mr. Popper's Penguins*. Help them include at least two details from the story in their sentences. Remind children to use correct punctuation and capitalization. They may want to continue their writing and draw a picture of the key event on the back of this sheet. Then have volunteers share their work with the class.

Name ______________________________________________

# *Finn Family Moomintroll*

**Teacher:** Have children choose one character from *Finn Family Moomintroll* and draw a picture of a story event in which that character has a main part. Then help them write sentences to describe the character and the story event in their drawing. Remind children to use correct punctuation and capitalization. Finally have volunteers share their work with the class.

Name ______________________________

# *A Story, a Story*

**Teacher**: Have children choose a character, a setting, or one particular story event to write about. Tell them to include at least one thing they learned from the text and one thing they learned from a picture in *A Story, a Story*. Ask children to draw a picture and continue their writing on the back of this sheet. Remind them to use correct punctuation and capitalization. Then have children share their work with the class.

Name ________________________________

# *The Paper Crane*

**Teacher:** Have children write sentences to describe the restaurant owner in *The Paper Crane*. Help them use one or more of the sensory words from the text in their sentences. Remind children to use correct punctuation and capitalization. Then ask them to draw a picture of the restaurant owner. Finally have children share their work with the class.

Name ______________________________

# Lon Po Po: A Red-Riding Hood Story from China

**Teacher**: Have children use the back of this sheet to draw three pictures that show what happens in the beginning, middle, and end of the story. Then help them write sentences that describe each pictured event. Remind children to use correct punctuation and capitalization. Finally ask them to share their work with the class and tell how their writing relates to the parts of the story.

Name ____________________

# Family Pictures

Teacher: Have children choose the family event that they liked best and draw a picture of it in the picture frame above. Then help them write sentences to describe the characters and event in their picture. Ask them to write a title for their picture in the space in the frame. Finally ask them to use audible, complete sentences to share their work with the class.

COMMON CORE

Name ______________________________

# Tomás and the Library Lady

**Teacher**: Help children write a summary of the story that includes the story's characters, setting, and major events. They may want to use the back of this sheet to continue their writing and illustrate their sentences. Remind children to use correct punctuation and capitalization. Finally invite children to share their summaries with the class.

Name ________________________________

# Kitten's First Full Moon

**Teacher:** Have children write sentences to describe what Kitten is like. Ask them to include text details from the story that helped them understand Kitten's character. They may want to continue their writing and illustrate their sentences on the back of this sheet. Remind children to use correct punctuation and capitalization. Finally have volunteers share their descriptions of Kitten with the class.

Name ______________________________

# "The Fox's Foray"

**Teacher**: Have children write sentences that explain why a poet repeats words in a poem. Tell them to include examples from "The Fox's Foray" in their writing. Remind children to use correct punctuation and capitalization. Then ask them to draw a picture of their favorite image from the poem. Finally encourage volunteers to share their work with the class.

Name ______________________________

# *Over in the Meadow*

**Teacher:** Have children write sentences to explain how repetition is used in *Over in the Meadow*. Ask them to include at least one example of repetition from the poem. Remind them to use correct punctuation and capitalization. Children may wish to draw a picture about the poem on the back of this sheet. Finally have children share their work with the class.

Name ______________________________

# "The Owl and the Pussy-Cat"

**Teacher**: Help children write sentences to tell what is the same and what is different between the characters and events in "The Owl and the Pussy-Cat" and those in *Owl at Home*. Remind them to use correct punctuation and capitalization. Then ask children to draw a picture that shows the differences between the two texts. Finally encourage volunteers to share their work with the class.

Name

# "April Rain Song"

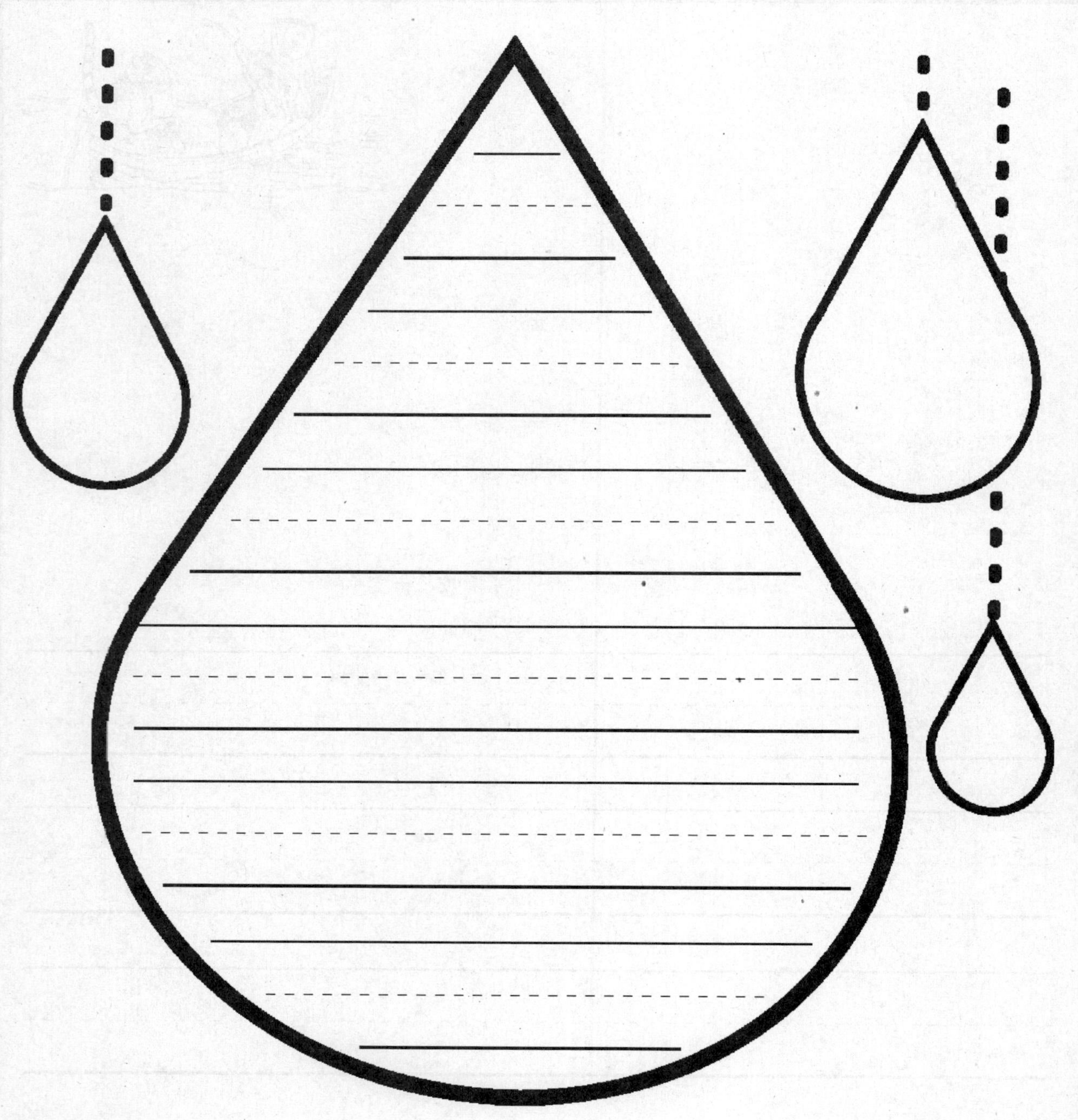

**Teacher:** Have children write sentences to describe rain using sensory language. Encourage them to describe what rain looks, feels, sounds, tastes, and smells like. Children may wish to continue their writing and illustrate their sentences on the back of this sheet. Remind children to use correct punctuation and capitalization. Finally have children share their sentences and drawings with the class.

Name ____________________

# Zin! Zin! Zin! A Violin

**Teacher**: Have children draw a picture of their favorite musical instrument. Then help them write a short paragraph or poem about the instrument. Have them include at least one sensory image in their writing. They may wish to continue writing on the back of this sheet. Then have children share their work with the class.

Name ______________________________

# A Tree Is a Plant

**Teacher:** Have children give their opinion of which is the best season for the apple tree. Help children write or dictate sentences that provide reasons for their opinion. Remind them to use correct punctuation and capitalization. Then ask them to draw a picture on the back of this sheet of the apple tree in the season they wrote about. Finally have children share their opinions with the class.

Name ______________________________

# *My Five Senses*

**Teacher**: Have children draw a real or imagined scene where one or more senses are used. Then help them write sentences to describe the scene. Ask them to include details about the five senses from the text. Remind children to use correct punctuation and capitalization. Finally have volunteers share their ideas and examples with the class.

Name ___________________________________________

# *Starfish*

**Teacher:** Guide children to write about one of the following topics: the different kinds of starfish, the life cycle of a starfish, or how starfish eat and move. Have them tell whether they learned the information from the book's text or illustrations. Children may wish to continue their writing on the back of this sheet. Then have children illustrate their writing. Finally ask children to share their work with the class.

Name ______________________________

# A Weed Is a Flower

**Teacher**: Help children write about the most important events in George Washington Carver's life. Tell them to give the events in the correct sequence. Remind them to use correct punctuation and capitalization. Then children may draw a picture of George Washington Carver or an important event in his life. Finally have volunteers share their work with the class.

Name ______________________________

# *Truck*

**Teacher:** Have children write sentences to explain what happens first, next, and last in *Truck*. Guide them to use time-order words to describe the sequence of events. Children may wish to illustrate their sentences. Then have volunteers share their work with the class.

Name ___________________________________

# I Read Signs

**Teacher**: Have children draw a sign that is included in *I Read Signs*. Then tell children to write sentences to explain what the sign says, its graphic features, and the reason for the sign. Remind children to use correct punctuation and capitalization. Finally encourage children to show their drawings and share their sentences with the class.

Name ______________________________

# *Let's Find Out About Ice Cream*

**Teacher:** Have children write sentences to explain how ice cream is made. Guide them to use information from the text to describe the correct sequence of events. Remind children to use correct punctuation and capitalization. Then have children draw a picture to show one part of how ice cream is made. Finally encourage children to share their work with the class.

Name ______________________________

# "Garden Helpers"

**Teacher**: Have children draw a picture of a garden helper and then write sentences that tell how that worm or bug helps in the garden. Tell them to use the information and illustrations in the text. Remind children to use correct punctuation and capitalization. Finally have volunteers share their work with the class.

Name ______________________________

# "Wind Power"

**Teacher:** Have children choose two examples from the text that show the power that wind has. Tell children to draw a picture of each example in the boxes above. Then guide them to write a caption for each example. Finally have volunteers share their illustrations and captions with the class.

Name ______________________________

# The Year at Maple Hill Farm

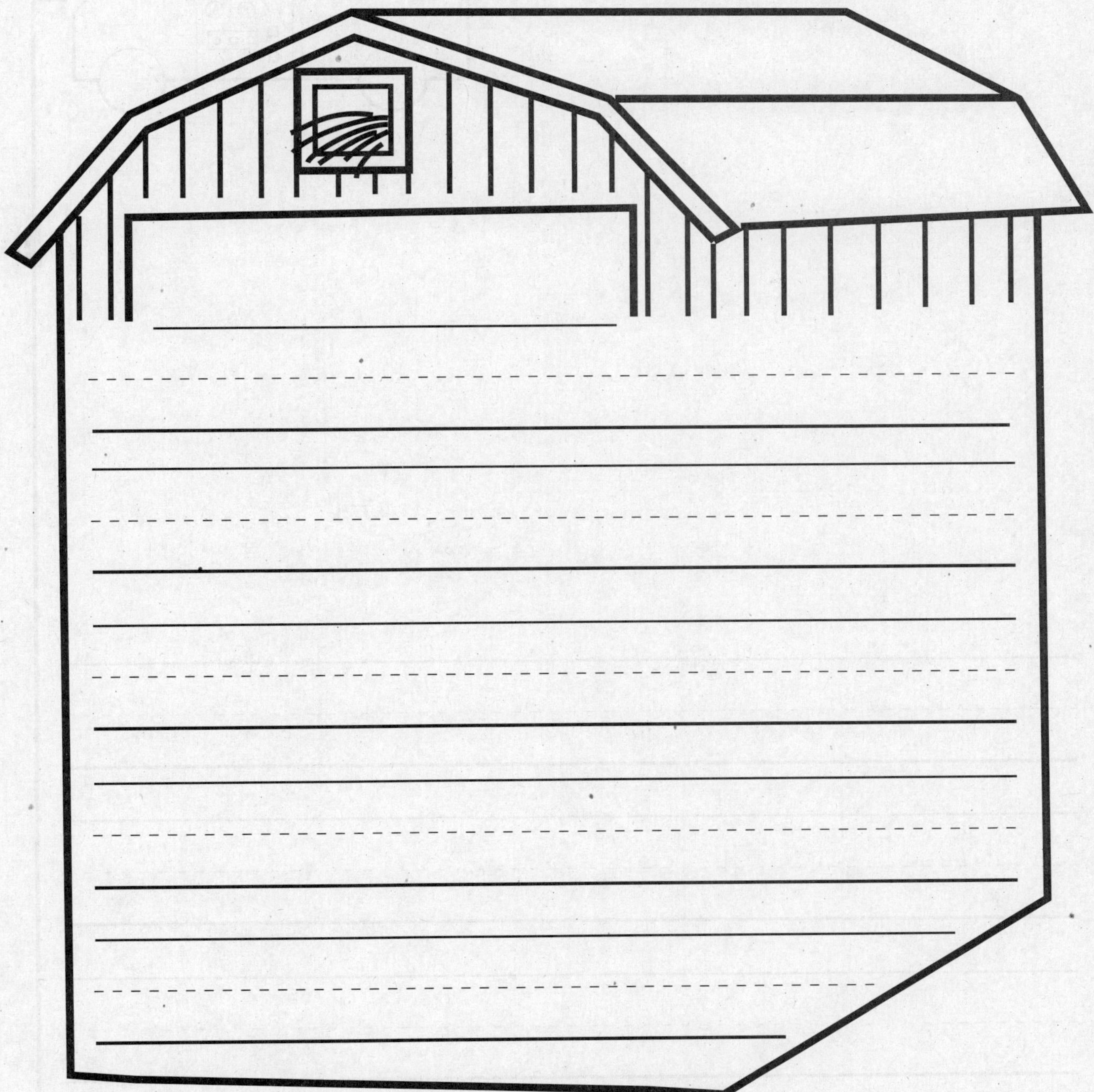



**Teacher**: Have children write sentences about one month or one season at Maple Hill Farm. Tell them to include a main topic and supporting details from the text. Children may wish to continue writing and illustrate their sentences on the back of this sheet. Remind them to use correct punctuation and capitalization. Then ask children to share their work with the class.

Name ____________________

# Fire! Fire!

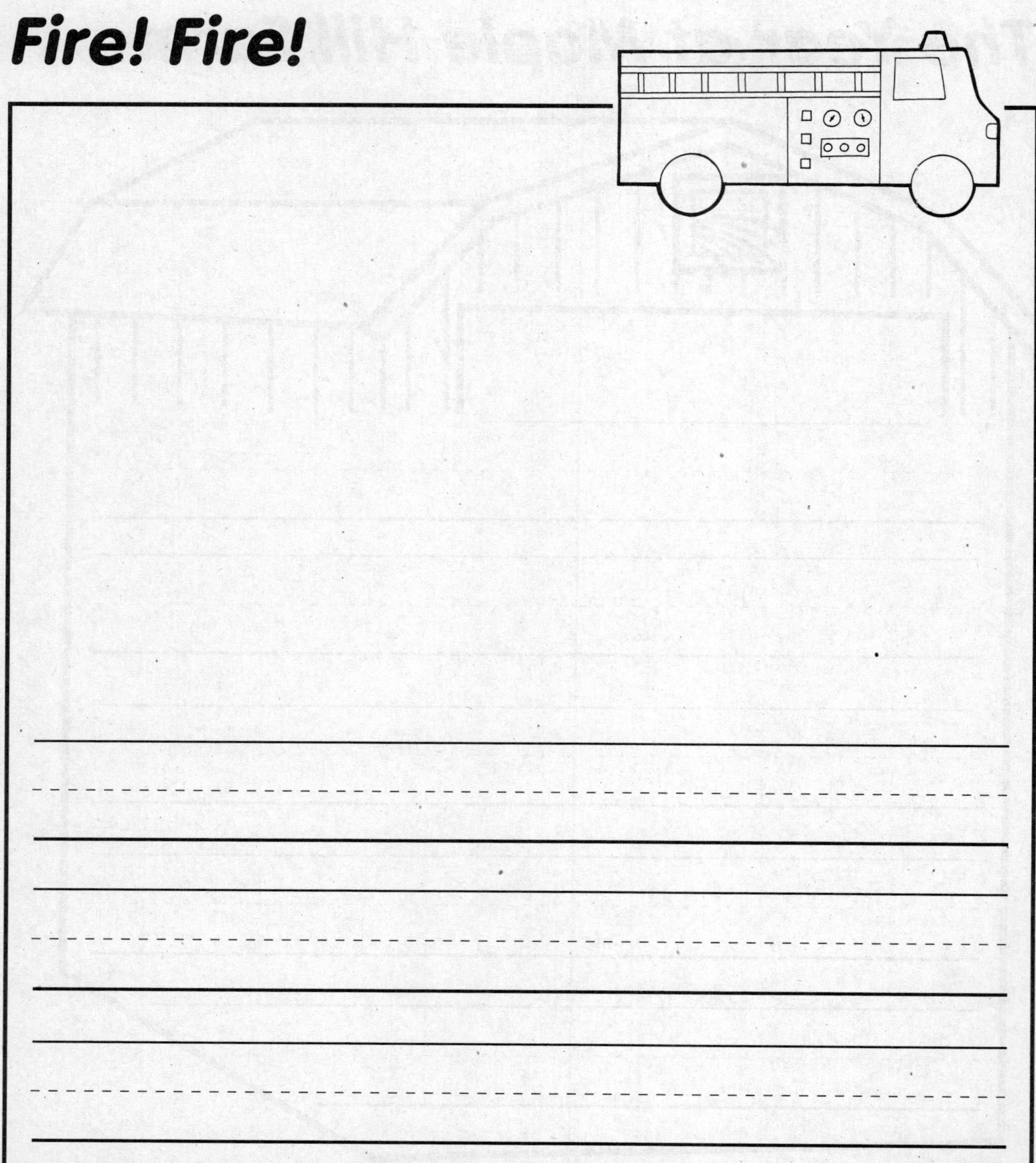

**Teacher:** Have children write sentences to describe how firefighters would respond to a fire in a city, on a farm, in the forest, or on the waterfront. Encourage them to use key details from the text. Children may wish to continue their writing on the back of this sheet. Then ask children to draw a picture. Finally ask children to share their work with the class.

Name ______________________________

# Follow the Water from Brook to Ocean

**Teacher**: Help children write a sentence that tells the main topic of *Follow the Water from Brook to Ocean*. Then ask them to use key details from the text to write sentences that tell what happens to water. Children may wish to continue writing and draw a picture on the back of this sheet. Remind them to use correct punctuation and capitalization. Finally have volunteers share their work with the class.

Name ______________________________

# Water, Water Everywhere

**Teacher:** Have children write sentences to explain the uses and importance of water. Guide them to use information from the text in their writing. Children may wish to continue their writing and illustrate their sentences on the back of this sheet. Finally encourage children to share their sentences and illustrations with the class.

Name ______________________________

# *Earthworms*

**Teacher**: Help children choose one of the topics from *Earthworms* and write a summary of it. Tell them to include a topic sentence and one or two supporting details from the text. Have children continue their writing on the back of this sheet. Then have children draw a picture to illustrate their writing. Finally encourage children to share their sentences and illustrations with the class.

Name ______________________________

# What Do You Do with a Tail Like This?

**Teacher:** Have children choose an animal from the text and write a question about how that animal uses a certain body part, such as its eyes or its tail. Then help them use at least one detail from the text to write an answer to their question. Have children draw a picture to illustrate their work. Tell them to continue their writing on the back of this sheet as necessary. Remind them to use correct punctuation and capitalization. Finally have volunteers share their work with the class.

Name

# *From Seed to Pumpkin*



**Teacher**: Have children write sentences to describe how a pumpkin grows. Encourage them to include information from the text and illustrations in their writing. Remind children to use correct punctuation and capitalization. They may wish to draw a picture on the back of this sheet to add to their descriptions. Then have volunteers share their work with the class.

Name ___________________________________________

# Amazing Whales!

**Teacher:** Have children write a question about something they wanted to know from the text. Then help them use information from the text to answer the question in complete sentences. Children may wish to continue their writing and create a drawing on the back of this sheet. Remind children to use correct punctuation and capitalization. Finally encourage children to share their work with the class.

Name ______________________________

# How People Learned to Fly

**Teacher**: Help children write sentences about how performing the arm-spinning experiment helped them understand the connection between drag and flying. Tell them to include information about drag and flying from the text. Remind children to use correct punctuation and capitalization. Have them continue their writing on the back of this sheet as necessary. Then have them illustrate their sentences. Finally ask volunteers to share their work with the class.

Name ____________________________________

# Kindergarten Writing Checklist

Did I . . .

| | |
|---|---|
| ☐ capitalize my sentences? | ☺ 😐 ☹ |
| ☐ use end marks? | ☺ 😐 ☹ |

## Opinion

| | |
|---|---|
| ☐ name my topic or book? | ☺ 😐 ☹ |
| ☐ give my opinion? | ☺ 😐 ☹ |

## Informative

| | |
|---|---|
| ☐ name what I am writing about? | ☺ 😐 ☹ |
| ☐ give some information? | ☺ 😐 ☹ |

## Narrative

| | |
|---|---|
| ☐ tell a story? | ☺ 😐 ☹ |
| ☐ give the events in order? | ☺ 😐 ☹ |
| ☐ tell how the characters acted because of story events? | ☺ 😐 ☹ |

Name ______________________________

# Kindergarten Speaking and Listening Checklist

Did I . . .

## Speaking

| | |
|---|---|
| ☐ tell about people, places, things, and events? | ☺ 😐 ☹ |
| ☐ give details? | ☺ 😐 ☹ |
| ☐ add drawings? | ☺ 😐 ☹ |
| ☐ take turns speaking? | ☺ 😐 ☹ |
| ☐ speak so others can hear me? | ☺ 😐 ☹ |
| ☐ clearly tell about thoughts, feelings, and ideas? | ☺ 😐 ☹ |

## Listening

| | |
|---|---|
| ☐ follow rules for discussions? | ☺ 😐 ☹ |
| ☐ listen to others? | ☺ 😐 ☹ |
| ☐ ask and answer questions? | ☺ 😐 ☹ |
| ☐ ask for more information? | ☺ 😐 ☹ |

Name ______________________________

# Grade 1 Writing Checklist

Did I . . .

| | |
|---|---|
| ☐ capitalize my sentences? | ☺ 😐 ☹ |
| ☐ check my punctuation and spelling? | ☺ 😐 ☹ |

## Opinion

| | |
|---|---|
| ☐ name my topic or book? | ☺ 😐 ☹ |
| ☐ tell my opinion and give a reason? | ☺ 😐 ☹ |
| ☐ write an ending? | ☺ 😐 ☹ |

## Informative

| | |
|---|---|
| ☐ name my topic and give facts? | ☺ 😐 ☹ |
| ☐ write an ending? | ☺ 😐 ☹ |

## Narrative

| | |
|---|---|
| ☐ tell a story with events and details? | ☺ 😐 ☹ |
| ☐ use time-order words? | ☺ 😐 ☹ |
| ☐ write an ending? | ☺ 😐 ☹ |

Name ______________________________

# Grade 1 Speaking and Listening Checklist

Did I . . .

## Speaking

| | |
|---|---|
| ☐ tell about people, places, things, and events? | ☺ 😐 ☹ |
| ☐ give details? | ☺ 😐 ☹ |
| ☐ add drawings? | ☺ 😐 ☹ |
| ☐ take turns speaking? | ☺ 😐 ☹ |
| ☐ clearly tell about ideas and feelings? | ☺ 😐 ☹ |
| ☐ use complete sentences? | ☺ 😐 ☹ |

## Listening

| | |
|---|---|
| ☐ follow rules for discussions? | ☺ 😐 ☹ |
| ☐ listen to others? | ☺ 😐 ☹ |
| ☐ ask and answer questions? | ☺ 😐 ☹ |
| ☐ respond to what others say? | ☺ 😐 ☹ |
| ☐ ask for more information? | ☺ 😐 ☹ |

# Performance Rubric

Use this rubric to evaluate writing and performance tasks.

| | Focus and Support | Organization and Structure |
|---|---|---|
| Score 6 | 6<br>The writing is focused and supported by facts or details. | 6<br>The writing has a clear introduction and conclusion (or beginning and ending). Ideas are clearly organized. |
| Score 5 | 5<br>The writing is mostly focused and supported by facts or details. | 5<br>The writing has an introduction and a conclusion. Ideas are mostly organized. |
| Score 4 | 4<br>The writing is mostly focused and supported by some facts or details. | 4<br>The writing has an introduction and a conclusion. Most ideas are organized. |
| Score 3 | 3<br>Some of the writing is focused and supported by some facts or details. | 3<br>The writing has an introduction or a conclusion but might be missing one. Some ideas are organized. |
| Score 2 | 2<br>The writing is not focused and is supported by few facts or details. | 2<br>The writing might not have an introduction or a conclusion. Few ideas are organized. |
| Score 1 | 1<br>The writing is not focused or supported by facts or details. | 1<br>The writing is missing an introduction and a conclusion. Few or no ideas are organized. |

| Word Choice and Voice | Language Conventions |
|---|---|
| **6**<br>Ideas are linked with words, phrases, and clauses. Words are specific. The voice connects with the reader in a unique way. | **6**<br>The writing has no errors in spelling, grammar, capitalization, or punctuation. There are a variety of sentences. |
| **5**<br>Most ideas are linked with words, phrases, and clauses. Words are specific. The voice connects with the reader. | **5**<br>The writing has few errors in spelling, grammar, capitalization, or punctuation. There is some variety of sentences. |
| **4**<br>Some ideas are linked with words, phrases, and clauses. Some words are specific. The voice connects with the reader. | **4**<br>The writing has some errors in spelling, grammar, capitalization, or punctuation. There is some variety of sentences. |
| **3**<br>Some ideas are linked with words, phrases, or clauses. Few words are specific. The voice may connect with the reader. | **3**<br>The writing has some errors in spelling, grammar, capitalization, or punctuation. There is little variety of sentences. |
| **2**<br>Some ideas are linked with words, phrases, or clauses. Few words are specific. The voice may connect with the reader. | **2**<br>The writing has many errors in spelling, grammar, capitalization, or punctuation. There is little variety of sentences. Some sentences are incomplete. |
| **1**<br>Ideas may not be linked with words, phrases, or clauses. No words are specific. The voice does not connect with the reader. | **1**<br>The writing has many errors in spelling, grammar, capitalization, or punctuation. There is no variety of sentences. Sentences are incomplete. |

# Bibliography

**Agee, Jon.** "Two Tree Toads." *Orangutan Tongs: Poems to Tangle Your Tongue.* Jon Agee. New York: Hyperion, 2009

**Aliki.** *A Weed Is a Flower: The Life of George Washington Carver.* New York: Simon and Schuster, 1988 (1965)

**Aliki.** *My Five Senses.* New York: HarperCollins, 1989 (1962)

**Anonymous.** "As I Was Going to St. Ives." *The Oxford Dictionary of Nursery Rhymes.* Edited by Iona and Peter Opie. Oxford: Oxford University Press, 1997 (1951)

**Anonymous.** "The Fox's Foray." *The Oxford Dictionary of Nursery Rhymes.* Edited by Iona and Peter Opie. Oxford: Oxford University Press, 1997 (1951)

**Arnold, Tedd.** *Hi! Fly Guy.* New York: Scholastic, 2005

**Atwater, Richard and Florence.** *Mr. Popper's Penguins.* Illustrated by Robert Lawson. New York: Dell, 1966 (1938)

**Bang, Molly.** *The Paper Crane.* New York: Greenwillow, 1985

**Baum, L. Frank.** *The Wonderful Wizard of Oz.* Illustrated by W. W. Denslow. Boston: Houghton Mifflin, 1993 (1899)

**Bulla, Clyde Robert.** *A Tree Is a Plant.* Illustrated by Stacey Schuett. New York: HarperCollins, 1960

**Chute, Marchette.** "Drinking Fountain." *Read-Aloud Rhymes for the Very Young.* Selected by Jack Prelutsky. Illustrated by Marc Brown. New York: Knopf, 1986

**Ciardi, John.** "Wouldn't You?" *Read-Aloud Rhymes for the Very Young.* Selected by Jack Prelutsky. Illustrated by Marc Brown. New York: Knopf, 1986

**Crews, Donald.** *Truck.* New York: Mulberry, 1980

**DePaola, Tomie.** *Pancakes for Breakfast.* San Diego: Harcourt Brace, 1978

**Dorros, Arthur.** *Follow the Water from Brook to Ocean.* New York: HarperCollins, 1991

**Eastman, P. D.** *Are You My Mother?* New York: Random House, 1988 (1960)

**Fyleman, Rose.** "Singing-Time." *Julie Andrews' Collection of Poems, Songs, and Lullabies.* Selected by Julie Andrews and Emma Walton Hamilton. Paintings by James McMullan. New York: Little, Brown, 2009

**Garza, Carmen Lomas.** *Family Pictures.* San Francisco: Children's Book Press, 1990

**Gibbons, Gail.** *Fire! Fire!* New York: HarperCollins, 1984

**Giovanni, Nikki.** "Covers." *Vacation Time: Poems for Children.* Illustrated by Marisabina Russo. New York: William Morrow, 1980

**Greenfield, Eloise.** "By Myself." *Honey, I Love and Other Love Poems.* Pictures by Diane and Leo Dillon. New York: HarperCollins, 1978

**Haley, Gail E.** *A Story, A Story.* New York: Aladdin, 1970

**Henkes, Kevin.** *Kitten's First Full Moon.* New York: Greenwillow, 2004

**Hoban, Tana.** *I Read Signs.* New York: Greenwillow, 1983

**Hodgkins, Fran.** *How People Learned to Fly.* Illustrated by True Kelley. New York: Collins, 2007

**Hughes, Langston.** "April Rain Song." *Favorite Poems: Old and New.* Selected by Helen Ferris. Illustrated by Leonard Weisgard. New York: Doubleday, 1957

**Hughes, Langston.** "Poem." *Make a Joyful Noise: Poems for Children by African-American Poets.* Edited by Deborah Slier. Illustrated by Cornelius Van Wright and Ying-Hwa Hu. New York: Scholastic, 1991

**Hurd, Edith Thacher.** *Starfish.* Illustrated by Robin Brickman. New York: HarperCollins, 1990 (1962)

**Jansson, Tove.** *Finn Family Moomintroll.* Translated by Elizabeth Portch. London: Puffin, 1961 (1948)

**Jenkins, Steve, and Robin Page.** *What Do You Do With a Tail Like This?* Boston: Houghton Mifflin, 2003

**Langstaff, John.** *Over in the Meadow.* Illustrated by Feodor Rojankovsky. San Diego: Harcourt Brace, 1985 (1957)

**Lear, Edward.** "The Owl and the Pussy-Cat." *Oxford Book of Poetry for Children.* Compiled by Edward Blishen. Illustrated by Brian Wildsmith. New York: Peter Bedrick, 1963

**Llewellyn, Claire.** *Earthworms.* Photographs by Barrie Watts. London: Franklin Watts, 2000

**Lobel, Arnold.** *Frog and Toad Together.* New York: HarperCollins, 1972 (1971)

**Lobel, Arnold.** *Owl at Home.* New York: HarperCollins, 1975

**Lopez, Alonzo.** "Celebration." *Song and Dance.* Selected by Lee Bennett Hopkins. Illustrated by Cheryl Munro Taylor. New York: Simon & Schuster, 1997

**Lopshire, Robert.** *Put Me in the Zoo.* New York: Random House, 1988 (1960)

**Merriam, Eve.** "It Fell in the City." *Read-Aloud Rhymes for the Very Young.* Selected by Jack Prelutsky. Illustrated by Marc Brown. New York: Knopf, 1986

**Milne, A. A.** "Halfway Down." *Favorite Poems: Old and New.* Selected by Helen Ferris. Illustrated by Leonard Weisgard. New York: Doubleday, 1957

**Minarik, Else Holmelund.** *Little Bear.* Pictures by Maurice Sendak. New York: HarperCollins, 1985 (1957)

**Mora, Pat.** *Tomás and the Library Lady.* Illustrated by Raul Colón. New York: Knopf, 1997

**Moss, Lloyd.** *Zin! Zin! Zin! a Violin.* Illustrated by Marjorie Priceman. New York: Simon & Schuster, 1995

**National Geographic Young Explorers.** "Garden Helpers." *National Geographic Society.* September 2009. http://www.nationalgeographic.com/ngyoungexplorer/0909/readstory.html

**National Geographic Young Explorers.** "Wind Power." *National Geographic Society.* September 2011. http://www.nationalgeographic.com/ngyoungexplorer/0911/readstory.html

**Pfeffer, Wendy.** *From Seed to Pumpkin.* Illustrated by James Graham Hale. New York: HarperCollins, 2004

**Provensen, Alice and Martin.** *The Year at Maple Hill Farm.* New York: Aladdin, 2001 (1978)

**Rauzon, Mark J., and Cynthia Overbeck Bix.** *Water, Water Everywhere.* San Francisco: Sierra Club Books, 1994

**Reid, Mary Ebeltoft.** *Let's Find Out About Ice Cream.* Photographs by John Williams. New York: Scholastic, 1996

**Rossetti, Christina.** "Mix a Pancake." *Read-Aloud Rhymes for the Very Young.* Selected by Jack Prelutsky. Illustrated by Marc Brown. New York: Knopf, 1986

**Seuss, Dr.** *Green Eggs and Ham.* New York: Random House, 1988 (1960)

**Thomson, Sarah L.** *Amazing Whales!* Photographs by the Wildlife Conservation Society. New York: HarperCollins, 2005

**Wilder, Laura Ingalls.** *Little House in the Big Woods.* New York: HarperCollins, 1960 (1932)

**Wright, Richard.** "Laughing Boy." *Winter Poems.* Selected by Barbara Rogasky. Illustrated by Trina Schart Hyman. New York: Scholastic, 1994

**Young, Ed.** *Lon Po Po: A Red-Riding Hood Story from China.* New York: PaperStar, 1989

# Internet Resources

***Use the following websites to locate additional resources for teaching the exemplar texts. Check the website for your state's department of education for specific information on the implementation of the Common Core State Standards.***

*http://aasl.jesandco.org/*

*http://www.achieve.org/achieving-common-core*

*http://www.achievethecore.org/*

*http://www.ascd.org/common-core-state-standards/common-core.aspx*

*http://www.ccsso.org/documents/2012/common_core_resources.pdf*

*http://www.corestandards.org/*

*http://www.engagingeducators.com/*

*http://www.ncte.org/standards/commoncore*

*http://www.ode.state.or.us/wma/teachlearn/commoncore/ela-publishers-criteria.pdf*

*http://www.parcconline.org/*

*http://www.reading.org/Resources/ResourcesByTopic/CommonCore-resourcetype/CommonCore-rt-resources.aspx*

*http://www.smarterbalanced.org/*

*https://www.teachingchannel.org/videos?categories=topics_common-core*